D0942447

GOTHIC
(RE)VISIONS

SUNY Series in Feminist Criticism and Theory
Michelle A. Massé, Editor

GOTHIC (RE)VISIONS

Writing Women as Readers

SUSAN WOLSTENHOLME

State University
of New York
Press

PR
830
.T3
W6
1993

Published by
State University of New York Press, Albany

© 1993   State University of New York

All rights reserved

Printed in the United States of America

No part of this book may be used or reproduced
in any manner whatsoever without written permission
except in the case of brief quotations embodied in
critical articles and reviews.

For information, address State University of New York
Press, State University Plaza, Albany, NY 12246

Production by Susan Geraghty
Marketing by Bernadette LaManna

Library of Congress Cataloging-in-Publication Data

Wolstenholme, Susan, 1949–
    Gothic (re)visions : writing women as readers / Susan
Wolstenholme.
        p.   cm. — (SUNY series in feminist criticism and theory)
    Includes bibliographical references and index.
    ISBN 0–7914–1219–9 (alk. paper) : $44.50. — ISBN 0–7914–1220–2
(alk. paper : pbk.) : $14.95
    1. Horror tales, English—History and criticism. 2. English
fiction—Women authors—History and criticism. 3. American fiction-
-Women authors—History and criticism. 4. Horror tales, American-
-History and criticism. 5. Gothic revival (Literature)—Great
Britain. 6. Gothic revival (Literature)—United States. 7. Women
and literature—Great Britain. 8. Women and literature—United
States. 9. Women—Books and reading. 10. Feminism and literature.
I. Title. II. Series.
PR830.T3W6   1993
823'.08729099287—dc20
                                                                91–42254
                                                                CIP

10 9 8 7 6 5 4 3 2 1

For my parents
Edith Wolstenholme
and
John L. Wolstenholme

CONCORDIA COLLEGE LIBRARY
PORTLAND. OREGON 97211

CONTENTS

LIST OF ILLUSTRATIONS

PREFACE

Literary criticism of the last twenty years or so has suggested a special relationship between "female" and "Gothic."[1] But why? To discuss Gothic fiction's preoccupation with "women's themes" (such as marriage or childbirth), or to point out that women have frequently written such novels (as well as read them), does not really account for such interest. How and why do Gothic conventions insert themselves into such writers' textual practices in the first place?[2] Is there anything specific to Gothic narrative that makes it particularly appropriate for dealing with gender issues, especially issues related to women's relationship to representation?

I contend that Gothic narrative has special potential to deal with the issues of writing and reading as a woman for formal reasons. Critics have often noted that Gothic-marked fiction particularly relies for its effect on the textual representation of a deliberately composed stage scene, which assumes an implied spectator, and also that these novels often allude to the theater and to individual plays.[3] I believe that both this structure and these allusions participate in establishing "woman" as a textual position—or, to frame the issue in terms of a different discourse, that they suggest a meditation on the issue of writing as a woman—and that, recurring from text to text, they establish a pattern that becomes a recognizable symbolic code.

A book which takes for its field of study a group of texts signed by women (as does this one) might seem inevitably to fall under the rubric of "Anglo-American" feminist criticism, which has often taken as its project the delineation of a "women's tradition"[4]—and to be subject to the charge of implicitly making some assumptions that recent theory has disputed (such as the "essential" nature of "woman"). While any feminist critic today must take account of such charges, and carefully examine the hold which discourses of masculinist humanism continue to exert, the previous generation of feminist critics—in this country, at any rate—has been one enabling condition (among others) for other, more theoretically conscious "post-structuralist" feminist work.[5] Here and now it makes political sense (even if nothing else) for feminist critics to direct attention to woman-signed texts, though that need not be the only project of a gender-conscious criticism. Such a choice of itself underscores gender as one issue in reading and writing (among others) in a way that a choice of all male-signed texts still need not, though it could.

Certainly Anglo-American concern with a canon of texts by women is one of the conditions which has fostered my study, though it is not my intention to suggest a counter-tradition or a canon of women's Gothic fiction. Nor is my point to establish the (related) point of influence from one such writer to the next. Such issues as "influence" and "inheritance" (a word that connotes the system of the passing down of male privilege) obviously work according to masculinist models. To take one example, Gilbert and Gubar's *The Madwoman in the Attic*, certainly one of the most influential of Anglo-American studies concerned with the issues of literary tradition and generation, employed Harold Bloom's masculinist account—which worked from another male-authored account of men's relationships, that of Freud. That of course does not make it "wrong" or even invalid for women. It simply suggests one way of looking at the issue of writing as a woman; there may be others.

Alternatively, one might ask how to square any woman writer's "anxiety of authorship," her tentative assumption of the masculine-defined, masculine-identified textual voice, with that same writer's reinscription in her own texts of the texts of other women writers? What could one mean by a "woman's voice" in a text—either the writer's own or that of other women whose textual voices she might evoke? Since both her own writing and that of other women writers must inevitably fall under the sign of the father, her use of these writers is especially problematic. I wish to suggest how these writers reread one another's texts, almost as a special code which conveyed a message about writing.

What has been called "French Feminism" (that is, influenced by mainly psychoanalytic French theory, wherever practiced), with its emphasis on textuality, has had the merit of forcing the critic to acknowledge a break with the tenets of the masculinist bias of traditional humanism. Although deconstructive modes of inquiry (and not only those claiming to be "feminist") have been criticized on the grounds of paying too little attention to history, and thus being insufficiently grounded in political and economic realities, such study directs attention to the text itself; for any literary text—like any political or social structure—is also an institution for reinforcing power relationships within a culture. Thus in asserting a textual position for "women" as readers and writers, one which simultaneously challenges masculinist discourse (by allowing a place for women in a field where masculine privilege excludes us) and nonetheless holds it in place (by necessarily representing the status quo, by suggesting how "women's place" must be continually renegotiated), these texts provide a site for examining such power relationships. Recently, gender studies have moved in the direction of becoming more historically based; and while my own study is not explicitly historicist, I would hope that it is neither ahistorical nor antihistorical.

I wish to sidestep such notions as "influence" and "inheritance" among women writers, to describe more usefully the relationship among these particular texts, and readers textually coded as "women."[6] I intend the term "women writers" to mean a symbolic community characterized not by a position of marginality nor by terms of an opposing "dominant" position nor by a common bond of directly accessible experience, but rather by symbolic exchange among the group itself.[7] Accordingly, the "relationships" I am talking about are intertextual.

Discussing mentoring relationships among women of unequal status in Italian feminism, Teresa De Lauretis has stressed that understanding women's communities as cultural constructs suggests an approach which may transform any reductive "essentializing" of women. De Lauretis focuses on a group of women in Italy who, from a cultural perspective which drew on ideas from both the United States and continental Europe, began a project of reading literary works by women. The group self-consciously examined the different roles which they themselves assumed within the community they formed, and came to identify a figure of female authorization, inscribed in the writing and employed in their practices, named "the symbolic mother," a metaphor that "permits the exchange between women across generations and the sharing of knowledge and desire across differences"; they also perceived the mother-daughter relationship as symbolic.[8] This structure of relationships redefines the terms for interaction from what they are within masculinist social-symbolic structures. Such an approach as De Lauretis suggests, with its emphasis on the cultural construction of women, who act autonomously but remain related to masculine dominance, may well be useful to feminist considerations of "women writers" and women as readers, who together constitute a women's reading community. For my discussion, I will assume that to study "women writers" is itself a self-consciously political decision, that "woman" is a textual position, and also that such terms as "mother" and "daughter" might be usefully employed as metaphors in a feminist discusssion.

I focus on moments where women writers write their writing acts into their texts, sometimes explicitly, sometimes in passages that suggest metaphors for the act of writing as a woman. The writing act presents itself as performance, where the action and the audience (and hence the reader) are written into the text as "scene." Such an emphasis on "scene" stresses the text's discontinuity and presents the text as composed of separate, individual moments—something like what Wordsworth calls "spots of time."

The scene of (a woman) writing, rewritten into another woman-signed text in similar terms, doubly acts as a model for the transaction between reader and text, because by evoking another text it again calls attention to the act of writing it describes. These texts inscribe the issue of women's writing, first, by evoking prior texts by women, an act that calls attention to its own repetition, its evocation of the performance of writing by a woman in another text that reenacts the same performance; and second, by rewriting a particular scene that recurs in these novels: the scene where performance itself is at issue. Accordingly, such scenes also suggest how we as readers of these novels reenact that relationship in our readings. In that sense they create within and for themselves not only textualized women in the position of "writer," but also textualized "women readers" as part of the same symbolic community. In one sense, this book is a critique of critiscism by and of "women writers," where some possible meanings of that term are explored. My focus is on reflexive gestures in texts, coded moments that suggest the texts' preoccupation with their own production, instances where these texts teach us to read them as re-writings that are re-readings.

ACKNOWLEDGMENTS

A friend and colleague mentioned to me that he found himself reevaluating the acknowledgments section of a text, which he as a reader often skipped right over, as he was finishing a book of his own: he found himself with a deep sense of the debt of appreciation that he owed many people, and wanted to thank them all personally. I feel the same way. I profited from the suggestions of many people. For their scholarly support and advice, I am grateful to Mary Jacobus and Harry Shaw, both of whom helped this project grow from its initial stages; also, to Dorothy Mermin, Mark Seltzer, and Joel Porte, all of whom read earlier drafts and offered advice. I want to thank Toni Cade Bambara, who urged me to write about *Frankenstein*. Thanks also to my copyeditor, Lisa Metzger.

For grant support, I am grateful to the Cayuga Community College Foundation and the Faculty Development Committee. Thanks also to the Mary McEwen Schimke Scholarship Foundation, administered by Wellesley College, whose enlightened policy provides funding specifically for aid on the "home front" during the completion of scholarly projects, and to Cornell University for fellowship aid.

For courtesy and help, as well as permission to reprint Fuseli's *The Nightmare*, I wish to thank the Detroit Institute of Arts.

Special thanks goes to Cayuga Community College, which has been most supportive in providing me with the time necessary to work on scholarly projects. Although community colleges are not research institutions, Cayuga has employed some administrators who recognize that research and teaching are not mutually exclusive, and that instructors with the opportunity to keep their minds alive may sometimes be all the better as teachers for that opportunity. To Tom Steenburgh goes my special thanks; but many others have helped me. I am extremely grateful to the entire library staff, without whose help in securing materials I could not have completed this project. I'd like especially to thank Martha Lollis, Margaret Devereaux, and Judy Campanella, whose help was above and beyond the call of duty, including at one point the personal delivery of an interlibrary loan book to my house after working hours. Thanks also to Tom Casella, David Harbaugh, and others in the computer lab. For their personal support over the years this book has come into being, I'd like to thank Howard Nelson and Ron Snead; my gratitude also goes to Helena Howe, David Richards, and Dan Labeille, as well as to the professional community of women that is beginning to form itself anew there, and that is bound to lead to much more fruitful work in both teaching and writing.

Thanks also go to Mary Zamniak for helping to make it possible for me to work. To Mary Crowley goes my thanks for teaching me much about mother/daughter relationships; and a special thanks goes to Raphael Crowley, for clerical assistance; to both of them goes my thanks for their patience in sharing their life with this book, as with another sibling.

Finally, my thanks goes to John Crowley, who helped me in many ways, as a scholar and colleague, friend and helpmeet.

PART I

What's Female About Gothic?

CHAPTER 1

Dreams and Visions

Here is Mary Shelley's account of the genesis of *Frankenstein*:

> I saw—with shut eyes, but acute mental vision—I saw the pale student of unhallowed arts kneeling beside the thing he had put together. I saw the hideous phantasm of a man stretched out, and then, on the working of some powerful engine, show signs of life and stir with an uneasy, half vital motion. Frightful must it be.... His success would terrify the artist; he would rush away from his odious handiwork, horror-stricken.... He sleeps; but he is awakened; he opens his eyes; behold the horrid thing stands at his bedside, opening his curtains, and looking on him with yellow, watery, but speculative eyes.[1]

Strikingly similar in its recounting of the originary vision of a work of fiction is Harriet Beecher Stowe's account of the genesis of *Uncle Tom's Cabin*, written in the third person:

> The first part of the book ever committed to writing was the death of Uncle Tom. This scene presented itself almost as a tangible vision to her mind while sitting at the communion-table in the little church in Brunswick. She was perfectly overcome by it, and could scarcely restrain the convulsion of tears and sobbings that shook her frame. She hastened home and wrote it, and her husband being away she read it to her two sons of ten and twelve years of age.... From that time the story can less be said to have been composed by her than imposed upon her. Scenes, incidents, conversations rushed upon her with a vividness and importunity that would not be denied. The book insisted upon getting itself into being, and would take no denial.[2]

Both these accounts, written some years after the births of the texts they describe, depict writing women who write themselves into these anecdotes. Both are passive recipients, even victims, of their visions. In each case, the narrating woman doubles

3

herself in the text: as narrator of what has occurred in the past, she "sees" herself as spectator of a dream vision. Both writers represent the origins of their work by, first of all, objectifying their own earlier "selves"; that is, by deliberately "envisioning" a prior self as a young woman whose status as a writer is uncertain. Both passages, in effect, mime their subject matter, the transcription of a "vision" into language; they re-present the vision of a vision. And both, finally, find it necessary to hide behind the convention of a third person narrative: Stowe, directly; Shelley, beginning in the first person, then creating her male protagonist, who comes to double this younger fictive self. While she lies on her bed with closed eyes, the first vision of Victor Frankenstein looms over her; she imagines him ("the artist") taking refuge in his bed, doubling her position, where the Monster, doubling her nightmarish vision, looms over him.

The idea of describing the origin of a verbal text as a dream is not new with these writers or unique to women writers. The convention of the dream narrative can be traced back to the Middle Ages, and Horace Walpole began its reestablishment as a convention for describing the origin of a Gothic novel:

> Shall I even confess to you, what was the origin of this romance! I waked one morning, in the beginning of last June, from a dream, of which, all I could recover, was, that I had thought myself in an ancient castle (a very natural dream for a head like mine filled with Gothic story), and that on the uppermost banister of a great staircase I saw a gigantic hand in armour. In the evening I sat down, and began to write, without knowing in the least what I intended to say or relate. The work grew on my hands and I grew fond of it.[3]

By locating the origin of a Gothic story in a dream, Walpole establishes a convention of accounting for a text that women writers could usefully adapt in instructive ways. While his account resembles Shelley's and Stowe's in some particulars, it differs from theirs in others. Walpole creates neither a third person "cover" for his earlier self nor a double within the text. And while he imagines himself to have been asleep, within the dream he locates himself in an ancient castle, rather than lying home in wait for his vision; by contrast, Shelley and Stowe imagine themselves nowhere but where they are. Also, his emphasis is on what he saw. He attributes no emotional reaction to himself in his vision, no terror like Shelley's, no "tears and sobbings" like Stowe's, but an immediate need to begin to write. For Shelley and Stowe, these imagined images are freighted with implications about their positions as women who write. Like the medieval dream convention, but this time with a feminine emphasis, the dream offers an excuse, an explanation, for the production of texts by women writers. How is it that Mary Shelley came to think of and to dilate upon so hideous an idea? As the text of *Frankenstein* itself as well as this dream account suggest, the "hideous idea" was both the monster as a fictional character *in* the text and the monster as figure *for* the text. This double "monster," as if by its own accord, came to her in a dreamlike vision; she was hardly responsible for it herself. How did the little lady Harriet Beecher Stowe come to create a text that, at least plausibly if not accurately, could be called the cause of the Civil War? It came to her in a vision, and at church, too. If the devil had sent one vision, God sent the other; in any case, neither was the making of the woman, who merely accepted and transcribed what was sent to her.

These accounts literalize "vision" as a metaphor for authorial perspective, as an excuse for literary production. Shelley and Stowe need to justify their authorial voices because, as much recent literary theory and criticism has suggested, the position of "artist" is one that has been proscribed for women.[4] Women more suitably fill the culturally assigned role of the object of a man's gaze, which a man as artist may elevate to the role of the art object. "You *are* a poem," says Will Ladislaw to Dorothea, in one instance of a woman artist's (evidently approving) perception of a man's appropriation of her authorial role, while he assigns to a woman the role of text.[5] Like Shelley and Stowe, any woman who wishes to write must negotiate ways of circumventing such proscriptions. While Stowe's third person account and Shelley's doubling herself as a character may undermine their own positions as gazing artists, nonetheless, both women must usurp the positions of the gazing male artist if they are to write. They frame and project their apparitions of themselves within the boundaries of a mental space within which they watch and which the reader is also invited to watch.

Such framing of accounts specifically as spectacles is an artistic gesture recurrent within the works whose geneses they recount, as it is in Gothic novels generally. Gothic fiction is frequently described as having a particularly "visual" quality. In these novels, the reader is frequently called upon to witness scenes specifically framed *as* scenes, sometimes through the perspective of a character, at other times through a narrator. Often a character becomes a "scene" in offering herself (usually but not always it is a female character) for the reader's gaze. The reader may be doubled by a character who acts as spectator, who presents a perspective through which actions or objects become legible, perhaps through what a character says and does, perhaps through a physical imprint of an emotional or psychical state. And while the author assumes the perspective of gazing artist, the image of a woman is often written into the text as object but one which, through its disruption of the course of the narrative, may threaten the authority of that gaze.

Coral Ann Howells has argued that in Gothic novels,

> as readers we are consistently placed in the position of literary voyeurs, always gazing at emotional excess without understanding the why of it.... The springs of these emotions elude us, so that we can only look on with appalled fascination as floods of feeling rush through the characters distorting their physical features with alarming rapidity.[6]

In her account, such terms as "sensational, theatrical and melodramatic" to characterize these texts are intended not as pejorative but as descriptive, of a particular style of suggesting emotions and actions, a style expressly visual in its reliance on gestures and pictorial effects. The reader/voyeur of "Gothic" novels (historically defined as having been written between 1790 and 1820 in England) holds a position nearly equivalent to that of the audience of a play, in part (as she argues) because these novels tended to textualize eighteenth-century notions of Shakespeare.[7]

I think that the terminology here is absolutely right especially because of the eroticism implicit in the notion of "voyeurism." I wish to stress these sexually charged implications, for this structure of seeing and looking, with its erotic implications, is gender coded. Because of the conventional gendering of the relationship between a spectacle and spectator (that is, the conventional masculine coding of the position of the spectator), Gothic use of visions is centrally implicated in the preoccupation with gender issues that these novels typically evince. The gendering of Gothic representation is related to its special visual quality and not only to imagery that allows for a thematics of such issues as female sexuality and maternity. This set of images assumes a position in a formal structure where the dynamics suggest a special relationship with the thematic "content."

But if the gaze is male, what happens when the writer is female?[8] If she can speak only from a masculine-coded perspective, where (if anywhere) is there room for subversion, for alterity? Is it even possible for a woman to speak "as a woman"? My answer is, yes, that the shadow games played within the visual structuring of this mode makes this absence, as it were, visible.

I wish to examine how such visual structuring suggests the gendering of these texts, to look at such issues as who or what becomes a spectacle, who sees it, where the narrator and reader are situated in relation to both spectacle and spectator, and what these relationships imply about gender. Howells's description of the reader as a "literary voyeur" is particularly apt in view of the sexual thematics of these novels. I wish to investigate what it means to be a "literary voyeur," in terms of the gender coding of the literary and the voyeuristic. I want to suggest, first of all, that the Gothic novel's relationship to drama is part of a pattern of tropes written into the text and related to a fiction of presence and visibility that all novels employ but that carries a special significance here. Second, this pattern plays on notions of spectacle and erotic ways of looking which foregrounds sexual difference as an issue in these novels, an issue complicated further by the female signatures that these texts bear.

The idea that the gaze is male has been elaborated in art and film criticism, much of this discussion in response to an article by Laura Mulvey, "Visual Pleasure and Narrative Cinema."[9] An assumption which I am making here is that, while (as recent art criticism has acknowledged) art must be translated to verbal discourse in order to be accessible to criticism, so too does a reciprocal process take place: fictional discourse deliberately attempts to create "pictures," especially "Gothic" and Gothic-marked narrative, which repeatedly attempts to defy the boundaries of its own genre both by summoning visual texts and by structuring itself as scene. The translation from one medium to another is neither automatic nor complete; and as Mulvey warns, her own argument is specific to film. Even so, narrative film and novels both tell stories; both aspire to suggest a continuity which must necessarily patch its own inevitable gaps.

Working from the Freudian notion that the image of woman speaks castration, Mulvey discusses the male gaze of the camera.[10] In film, she argues, Woman is the bearer of meaning, not the maker of meaning, while Man bears the look which interprets her image. Film offers the male-coded spectator two opposed structures of looking: one, scopophilic, produces pleasure by offering a person as an object of vision which will induce sexual pleasure. This structure demands that the object of sight be recognized as "other," the bearer of an erotic identity different from that of the spectator. The second is narcissistic and offers identification with the image—thus the male spectator is generally offered a male protagonist with whom to identify. But as Mulvey notes, these two structures are contradictory, the first being a function of sexual instinct and the second of libidinal cathexis of the self (that is, a [mis]recognition whereby the reflection becomes introjected). Spectacle and narrative tend to split because the first of these is associated with stasis; the second, with action. And in fact, in Mulvey's account the woman's image freezes narrative action in moments of erotic contemplation; it suggests a gap in the narrative that must be patched over.

But, always speaking castration, this image threatens to evoke the anxiety it originally signified. As escape from the threat that the sight of the woman always conveys, the (male) spectator has two choices. The first reiterates and intensifies the scopophilia which described one half of the original structure of looking; the object is isolated, glamorized, overvalued, and fetishized—and thus made reassuring. The object is detached from the linear time of the narrative and appears in stopped action. The second alternative, like the narcissism in the originally described structure of seeing, takes place in linear time and demands a narrative. Mulvey suggests how the fetishized image of the woman threatens precisely what film and novels have in common, their narrational quality. A woman's image often, typically, threatens film with exposure of its incoherence.

Like films, novels are often haunted by the fetishized presence of a woman; and Mulvey suggests a way of reading this presence as a pressure on narrative, acting to disrupt or advance it. But while Mulvey works from the premise that the films she discusses were usually made by men, what about novels, which are often written by women? If we take seriously the notion that the law of language is under the sign of the father, as well as the much-documented historical, sociological reality that writing was the province of men, even a woman writing is implicitly coded masculine. But do the male-defined structures of representation which women must adapt leave any room for expressing their own desires? Essays by Freud, some of which lie behind Mulvey's observations, offer some suggestions as to where a woman might locate herself within the structure of looking and seeing. Three in particular—"The 'Uncanny,'" "A Child is Being Beaten," and the fragment "Medusa's Head"—locate women at different points in this structure.

In "The 'Uncanny,'" Freud assigns no gender to the gaze itself; it suggests certain consequences of gazing for men and for women.[11] In Freud's reading of E. T. A. Hoffmann's story "The Sandman," while the eyes of the castrating father are of central importance, Freud also characterizes women to be not only the object of a gaze but gazing subjects; and the gaze of women and girls evidently threatens him. Evidently the female gaze, as well as the woman's body that forms the object of the man's gaze, is frightening, something to be avoided, perhaps disallowed or repressed. To relieve the anxiety it creates in men, the woman's gaze must be sacrificed to the woman's role as object and to the man's gaze.

According to Freud's account, however, it is not the women themselves but the repressive process that produces the uncanny (it's also not the uncanny that produces repression); and what inscribes the repression is its return.[12] The painted women that frighten Freud in the red-light district are uncanny because of their repeated appearance; but female sexuality itself—a woman's genitals—is, Freud suggests, by its nature so *heimlich* as to be *unheimlich*. Like a woman's genitals, the prostitutes are reminders of female sexuality, though they suggest not women's desire but women's availability to men. Freud suggests that a woman's sexuality, as the object of a *man's* gaze, is by its nature always a "return," always a reminder of his "homely" origins. A woman's gaze and a woman's sex are both uncanny, terrifying; implicitly, they are also near equivalents, both suggesting terrible power over men.

Toward the end of "The 'Uncanny,'" Freud differentiates between two stories in which appear a severed hand. While one (by Hauff) produces an uncanny effect, a story by Herodotus does not. Freud accounts for this dissimilarity in affect in terms of the reader's identification. But the issue of identification is decidedly marginal in this essay, where Freud assumes the (masculine) perspective of the reader to be close to his own—in opposition to that of the gazing women he describes. However, in the essay "A Child Is Being Beaten," this issue of identification, with its relationship to otherness and sexual desire, becomes central.

In "A Child Is Being Beaten," Freud begins by taking up again instances of gazing young girls; but here he suggests how this gaze ceases to be female and how masochistic identification works. Here, Freud at first notes that his study is based on six cases, only four of which are female; but later the male patients drop out of his account. In the course of his account, he establishes that the character in the fantasy with whom the subject identifies changes gender identity as the subject clarifies her own point of entry into the fantasy and simultaneously removes herself from sexuality.[13] In a wonderfully efficient instance of psychic economy, what happens as the child moves from Stage 1 to Stage 2 of her neurosis is that the girl who constructs the "beaten child" fantasy establishes for herself what seems to be an ungendered position as spectator, from which she can retain sexual gratification through identifying with a boy and simultaneously can punish herself for constructing such fantasies. One effect of the process is that masochistic fantasy comes to replace sexual identity.[14] But it also offers a model for a girl to assume the role of spectator, one that operates by a different process than the operation for spectatorship through the eyes of a man that Mulvey describes.[15] The girl looks, but in assuming the role of spectator she ceases to be a girl and identifies with the imaginary boy at whom she looks. This essay is especially significant because it suggests that while a girl might be the spectator, she cannot hold both that position and also that of object of vision, nor can she retain her own gender identity while looking. A girl can look, but there is still no "female gaze" here; and what she sees is a boy as object, with whom she nonetheless identifies.

If "A Child Is Being Beaten" conveys the complexity of a girl's assumption of the spectator role, "Medusa's Head" makes apparent its inverse: the implications of the woman in the role of object. Here, the gaze is clearly that of a man. As in "The 'Uncanny,'" where Freud persistently averts his eyes from the women whose presence he reports,[16] in "Medusa's Head," Freud here also diverts his gaze, this time from the Medusa. Like Perseus in the myth, Freud looks at the Medusa only as reflected; Freud sees the Medusa only in the reaction of the man who gazes at her. Here, in contrast with "The 'Uncanny'" and "A Child Is Being Beaten," the woman is entirely an object, terrible and threatening. Paradoxically, she both embodies the threat of castration and evokes its defense both in the "petrifying" effect she has upon the spectator as well as in her snaky tresses, a "multiplication of penis symbols."

All Gothic fiction might be said to employ a kind of sado-masochism. Both film and literary criticism have recognized this dynamic in suggesting some degree of continuity between Gothic novels and contemporary narratives of violence to women, particularly slasher films.[17] But an important difference stems from the media themselves: novels really have no equivalent to that insistent eye of the camera, which imposes a more or less consistent point of view. In Gothic novels, perspective is vaguer, diffused through different "eyes"—the narrator's own and those of various characters—and thus offers various vantage points to the narrating voice, diffuse, de-centered, moving. Although many of the films that have been the object of feminist inquiry achieve a kind of coherence through the presence of a seeing eye (a coherence that patches over the incoherence suggested by the disruptive female body the same film may fetishize), these novels are more obviously incoherent. I mean this incoherence less as a negative aesthetic trait than as a distinctive feature that reveals the double, even duplicitous, position of the author, and that offers that position to the reader. Like the girl watching her whipping-boy stand-in, the reader of these novels must sometimes occupy a double position. This double stance must be problematic—in the girl's fantasy, she identifies with a boy and holds an ungendered role as spectator—at the same time that it offers the liberating possibility of undermining the conventional spectator's role. Sometimes, of course, a woman writer may clearly assume a masculine perspective which she invites the reader to share—as, for example, in George Eliot's early fiction, in much of the fiction of Willa Cather, or, as I will demonstrate, in Ann Radcliffe's *The Italian*. But the writer's role read in terms suggested by "A Child Is Being Beaten" need not be read simply as a man's role.

The Gothic structure of looking and being-looked-at offers certain "covers" for the coding of women within the text, because its plot often revolves around the issue of seeing and hiding. The main attraction and raison d'être of Gothic cathedrals resembles that of the Gothic structures of their literary counterparts: both contain secrets and mysteries within their innermost parts, with which they entice the spectator/reader. The Gothic architectural spectacle hides its theological mysteries under the cover of opulent display. Playing upon the notion of spectacle with which the cathedral issues its invitation to people, churches make use of literal veils and enclosures—for example, the veil that hides the tabernacle, or the tabernacle itself—as well as of sacramental symbols which both hide and make available the theological mysteries they represent. The sacramental outward sign becomes not only a cover; it also provides access to what it covers. Gothic novels also make extensive use of visual patterns of veiling and hiding, both on a verbally explicit level and structurally, also as a way of simultaneously hiding and giving form.[18]

Like the uncanny, a "Gothic moment" is a moment of (mis)recognition, where hiding from sight and revealing become indistinguishable from one another. Reflexively, it meditates on the problem of representation in terms especially appropriate for suggesting the double role of a woman writer. Its Gothic vision doubles the artist's vision of the text, at the same time suggesting what representation lacks. Sometimes a Gothic vision (in the sense of dream or hallucination) and artistic "vision" (in the sense of the author's idea of what she is about) completely merge.

And the absence at the center of such texts may be discerned as maternal, in part because it conjures those mother texts which it re-sees.[19]

CHAPTER 2

Woman as Gothic Vision
(The Italian)

Echoes of Elizabethan theater, specifically Shakespeare, resound through the dark vaults of Ann Radcliffe's *The Italian*. The forbidden love between Ellena di Rosalba and Vincentio di Vivaldi resembles the love of Romeo and Juliet; like Juliet's sighs, Ellena's draw her lover to her balcony; later Vivaldi enlists a monk to perform a secret marriage ceremony like that of those other, less fortunate star-crossed lovers. *Macbeth*-style ghosts beckon assassins to their tasks, crimes which are instigated by the wicked Marchesa, Vivaldi's "unmothered" mother, who acts with "a man's courage" (p. 168).[1] Like Lady Macbeth, the Marchesa is haunted by her crimes to her death.[2] Lest such references elude the reader, Radcliffe calls additional attention to her Shakespearean models in many of her chapter epigraphs.[3]

Such detail suggests that Shakespeare acted as one of Radcliffe's literary fathers; but any father-daughter relationships among writers is bound to be fraught with as much peril as promise for any literary daughter. The point of claiming such a relationship, as Radcliffe does, is to establish her own legitimacy—in something very much like a legal as well as a literary sense. Shakespearean characters, situations, and epigraphs pointedly claim validity for the text here, just as they had for Walpole, who deliberately employed them to that effect. At the same time, they underscore the fragility of such status when measured against the "parent" genre and claimed by an upstart subgenre. For a woman who wrote Gothic fiction, the paternal relationship becomes additionally complicated by questions of gender; for the woman writer shared an anomalous status with the Gothic text she produced.

As recent criticism has so frequently implied, to speak of relationships between writers as father-daughter relationships suggests a number of questions.[4] Relationships between literary "fathers" and "daughters," like those between actual fathers and daughters, are fraught with special problems; for women writers are supposed to be anxious not only about Influence but also about Authorship itself. Modeling their literary identity on male predecessors, women who write are bound to be caught in a conflict between their identities as women and as writers, which must appear to be mutually exclusive.

But if "woman" is a position from which to speak, what is this "woman's identity" that conflicts with a "writer's identity"? What might be meant by such terms as "woman" and "writer"? Is there such a thing as a "woman's voice" in a literary text?

As part of a literary conversation with men who wrote Gothic novels, in particular with Horace Walpole and "Monk" Lewis, Radcliffe succeeded in claiming Gothic as "female" in terms of what might be called "maternal presence," a textual space which challenges the representation even though confined by it. In *The Italian*, Radcliffe relies not only on the power of her artistic gaze, legitimized through its association with Shakespeare and theater, but also on its subversion through a duplicity that the text characterizes as "feminine." Although the term "female Gothic" was not originated specifically in connection with Radcliffe,[5] it has since been assumed to include her, with some justification. For Radcliffe was reinventing Gothic as female not only by rewriting "Monk" Lewis a little more tastefully, and by focusing on women as characters, but also by reclaiming a certain textual space for a woman as reader and writer. Certain key Gothic scenes in Radcliffe subvert the social and literary conditions which put them in place (the "authority" of the masculine-coded position of authorship, for example) by allowing a space for a woman-coded position.

The text of *The Italian* provides an instance that suggests the complex relationship between "female Gothic" novels and Shakespearean theater. When Ellena leaves Spalatro's seaside house with the villains Schedoni and Spalatro, she goes under the protection of a father, whose identity as such is based on a misreading; but she also presumably leaves behind the bones of her real father, who is buried in that very house. Similarly, *The Italian* seeks the protection of its father genre, drama, at the same time it seeks escape and leaves behind the "bones" of the genre, physical visual representation itself. And like the protection of Schedoni, or for that matter any father, even a "true" one, the protection the parent genre offers is fictive by its nature in that it depends on the reconstruction of a certain history and on a certain amount of faith. Like Ellena but more deliberately, Radcliffe employs the illusion of the father-daughter relationship to her advantage.

The special ways that Radcliffe employs Shakespeare suggest a different sort of model for generational relationships than the Oedipal pattern which critics often invoke (with its variations). In some ways Shakespeare is not so evidently suited to the role of father to literary daughters as, for example, Milton,[6] the rewriter of the great patriarchal founding myth of Judeo-Christian culture. The well-known image of the blind Milton being read to by daughters creates a picture almost allegorical in its significance, suggestive of both the dominance of patriarchal culture and its reliance on women's work. By contrast, Shakespeare is a far less suitable father figure. His own historical identity sometimes a matter of pseudo-scholarly amusement and speculation, the enigmatic and multi-identified Shakespeare has been perceived as androgynous. Shakespeare is certainly not a "father" to *The Italian* in the same sense that Milton is father, for example, to *Frankenstein*: that is, as a predecessor who must be struggled against, rewritten, and annihilated through the text. The presence of Shakespeare is that of a guide. His "spirit" is deliberately summoned; the writer's interest is not in *revising* him but in conjuring him, to use his invoked presence to confirm the validity of what she is doing. And while *Paradise Lost* is the rewritten text for Milton's literary daughters, and while what gets rewritten is mainly the Creation-myth plot, the presence of Shakespeare in *The Italian* is diffuse and not limited to the overbearing presence of a single plot or text. Authority lies in Radcliffe's adaptation of not only plot but also scenes and characters, and not from one work but several: *Macbeth, Romeo and Juliet, Hamlet*. Finally, Shakespeare's presence is apparent as a kind of absence: *The Italian* is obviously different from anything by Shakespeare because it is a narrative text to be read in solitude, not a play. It signals distance, not only from the invoked Shakespeare but also from the Renaissance world where drama, a literature "read" socially by an audience that sat together in a theater, was the dominant literary mode, a genre unlike written narrative, which is read privately and "staged" mentally.[7]

In Radcliffe's textual theater, not only is the public space of the theater "interiorized" to a mental space. Within the text, interior spaces are described to serve as stages for enacting dramas; and characters come to serve the function of audience, viewing other characters who perform. Interiors establish privileged spaces for restaging scenes which (re)appear outside these spaces. Doubling these spaces are textualized "interior spaces": against the dramatized story plays a textual space set within another text; and inset tales redouble the "dream spaces" suggested by interiors.[8] The relationship between the actors and spectators within the text doubles the relationship between the narrator of a tale and its listener, who are implictly doubled by the novel and its reader. What can be said about tales framed within the narrative appears to be true of narrative generally, particularly of the text of *The Italian* itself. The narrative presents situations figuring its structure where viewers (or listeners or readers) are associated with what is explicit, English, and masculine, and pictures or performers become associated with darkness, foreignness, and femininity. The mental "world of nervous breakdown"[9] with which this novel concerns itself additionally figures, reconstitutes, and makes explicit this relationship. Characters stage their own fears within their own mental space; and the reader assumes the position of voyeur from a safe perspective.[10]

GENDERING THE SPECTATOR

In its concern with reading, *The Italian* suggests motifs from Freud's "The 'Uncanny.'" Like Freud in "The 'Uncanny,'" we find ourselves in *The Italian* to be repeatedly walking down the same street, in obsessive repetitions of scenes, though the text seemed to have directed our steps elsewhere. Like "The 'Uncanny,'" *The Italian* concerns woman and the theme of seeing and being seen; as in Freud's essay, "veiling" becomes a double movement, synonymous with its opposite.[11]

But unlike Freud, Radcliffe does not avert her gaze from the veiled woman. She places her on center stage in the opening scene after the prologue. Radcliffe herself is not a "veilmaker"; she is an observer of veils that have already been made.[12] And ironically—ironic because Radcliffe's medium is "literature," though of the popular sort, and Freud's is "science"—Freud is the writer who places greater faith in representation. Unlike Freud, Radcliffe suggests a radical mistrust of representation, particularly of the stage representation of which she makes such free use. And unlike her protagonist Ellena, Radcliffe can both make use of her father-protector and distrust him. Radcliffe enjoys the fiction of "fatherhood" by simultaneously making use of it and implicitly exposing the fiction.

In these pages, drama as father-form appears only as a decrepit version of its former grand self. The text recounts a literal staging at only one point, a peculiarly debased theatrical performance. Framed by the main narrative and intertwined with a crucial inset narrative, a crudely produced version of a classic play commands the attention of Schedoni, Ellena, and their guide as they make their way from the house which was to be the site of Ellena's murder, back to Naples. Even though the play is poorly done, it retains power over its audience. For the reader, though, the "uncanny" in this scene becomes legible in the reaction of Schedoni. The antics at the fair through which the company pass act as a brief interlude that recapitulates the themes of the previous section—the monk turned to a devil, the daughter murdered by her father—and the parallel has meaning only through the perspective of Schedoni, through which the reader comprehends it.

The function of staged scenes in *The Italian*, both this one on the literal stage and others staged in interior spaces, resembles that of inset stories, in that both recount and reflect in distorted form events in the outer narrative. This particular scene, for instance, works toward motivating the telling of the novel's key inset narrative, the story about Spalatro's disposal of the corpse that is evidently, it later appears, the body of Schedoni's brother and Ellena's true father, murdered by commission of Schedoni. Begun just before the scene at the fair and interrupted by Schedoni, this story twists around the story of the evil Barone di Cambrusca, who resembles Schedoni, the evil Count di Bruno. The destruction of the Barone's house by earthquake foreshadows the destruction of the house of Di Bruno; in both cases, a daughter is set free. As Schedoni remarks, the peasant guide's narrative "resembles a delirious dream more than a reality" (p. 284), particularly in recapitulating, in displaced form, events that belong to Schedoni's life. Schedoni makes a felicitous comparison; for the narrative is "dreamlike" not only in an eighteenth-century sense but also in a post-Freudian sense—not in its symbology, but in its reuse of content from outside its own space. Like dreams in Freud, narratives in *The Italian* are characterized by gaps, alterations of chronology, and ambiguous figures. Though the Barone di Cambrusca resembles Schedoni, the distinction between the two does not entirely collapse, even though their separate narratives merge at one point in the peasant's recitation of the tales. Like the opening scene and the scene at the fair, the story the peasant spins is an uncanny re-presentation of the novel's plot. And like the play Schedoni witnesses, this mysterious story begins to be legible through Schedoni's reaction to it.

The first three scenes of *The Italian* also play with notions of the theater as spectacle and suggest how in this text relationships between spectacle and audience are gendered. The first "interior space" in *The Italian*, the vault of the church of the Santa Maria del Pianto, recalls the earliest English theater. This opening scene serves a function analogous to that of an Elizabethan prologue. It stages a dumb show, where the main characters and action of the novel itself—the criminal, the confession, the church hierarchy—are acted in brief, to be witnessed by the visiting Englishman, who substitutes for the reader. Like the theater, this "interior space" is a dream world. Set off from the laws of the world outside, the church is governed by another set of laws nonetheless dependent on that world. Exiled from the external world as a repressed desire is exiled from the conscious mind, the assassin who haunts the church is at liberty only within the confines of the church. The Englishman/reader acts as a waking consciousness, a questioner of what occurs in the dream space, at the same time that he represents (by invoking it) the law that keeps the troublesome figure of the assassin hidden.

The structure of the second scene of the novel is similar: again, a character acts as audience for the action in a church.

Here, Vivaldi acts as spectator, viewing Ellena. In the opening scene, the customs and cultural practices of Italy both hide the meaning of what transpires there and act as a spur to the Englishman's curiosity, and therefore come to highlight and elucidate this meaning. Ellena's veil serves a similar function here. Although they act as dividing lines and as signifiers of difference, these veils, one physical and literal and the other cultural and figurative, at the same time link the spectator with the object he views.

That the viewing spectator in both cases is coded male is neither a coincidence nor a surprise, though perhaps curious in view of the many women who read Gothic novels. Vivaldi, like the visiting Englishman, offers the vantage point from which a story can be discovered. Like the Englishman, Vivaldi becomes the reader's eyes, the presence that inquires and interprets. The fictional frame story implicitly confirms Vivaldi, the Englishman, and the reader to hold identical positions. The reader becomes inscribed in the text as the Englishman, who receives the text of *The Italian* as a response to his questions about what he sees in the church; he in turn is reinscribed in *that* text as Vivaldi. To be a reader means to see, to interpret, and to assign meaning from a masculine subject position; and any woman who reads the novel, any real-life version of Jane Austen's Catherine Morland, must become a man to enter the text. The novel teaches the woman who reads it to identify against her own sex.[13]

If, however, she identifies as "woman," she is inscribed in the text as Ellena, the object of Vivaldi's gaze. "Woman" holds the structural position of the criminal in the opening scene. Women and criminals are alike, not only in acting as the unruly elements of a culture, its disruptive forces; they are its scapegoats and the bearers of its collective guilt; and here they are also similar in being the embodiments of stories to be unfolded, the walking representations of tales about to be told. And both, finally, effect a sort of escape from the gazing man: for Ellena, literally as she evades Vivaldi's gaze, even though she is subjected to it momentarily, under cover of the very veil that revealed her to him; and for the criminal in the church, not just figuratively but actually aided by figuration; that is, by a reminder of the inner narrative, which distracts the inquiring Englishman.

But if the text of *The Italian* is a response to the questions of the Englishman, it is a peculiarly ambiguous one. Like a dream, this text answers his questions only by suggestion, analogy, and substitution: the church which constitutes the theater in the frame story becomes the scene where action in the inner narrative takes place; both stories concern murder. But the assassin in the opening scene does not actually appear in the tale which the Englishman reads, nor does the text finally explain what he has witnessed. What the Englishman has acquired is not necessarily a "meaning" but a physical object, the text of a story, given to him as a gift.

The revelation of a confession initially unlocks the story. The confessional in the opening scene is a sign of the story to be told and the link between this scene and the inner narrative. One function of the confessional is to obviate the necessity of the (male) gaze that has allowed both narratives, inner and outer, to begin. Authorities need not watch what will certainly be confessed.[14] And a narrative confession provides a voyeuristic experience that allows a story to substitute for the gaze. But in reducing the necessity for surveillance, the confessional changes only the terms, not the gendering. The recipient of the narrative, the confessor, is mandated to be masculine, and by a powerful order, that of canon law.

The confessional also acts as a sign of how a *scene* changes specifically to a *narrative*. While the opening scene of the novel evokes the theater, the confessional is a setting where a narrative is told but where nothing and no one, not even the narrating penitent himself (the narrative's "author"), is seen. Unlike the stage but like a novel, the confessional frames an intimate narration. And the confessional suggests the mechanism by which the object of the gaze might watch herself as a mental image—thereby internalizing that masculine-coded authoritative gaze which defines, controls, and punishes. The confessional, made into a mental image that signifies guilt, can act to forestall and prevent the sin that might otherwise have to be confessed; it acts as an internalized method of surveillance. Within the confessional, of course, power relationships are gendered: while both men and women go to confession, only a man can hold the powerful position of priest and confessor. The confessional as sign in the frame story contests whatever is disruptive about the inner narrative itself because it acts as a means of containment. But at the same time, the confessional itself breaks the frame of the narrative by appearing in both the inner and outer stories; the appearance of the same confessional *within* this inner narrative reminds the reader of its internalized presence. As something which both escapes confinement and reminds the reader of authority, narrative both undermines and reinforces prevailing power arrangements.

These opening scenes establish another convention of Gothic-marked texts: an analogy between physical darkness and femininity. Ellena and the monk who haunts the church are also alike in being enigmatic because physically "different" from the men who gaze at them—Ellena, by being a woman, and the monk, by being Italian and dark.[15] In later novels marked with Gothic conventions, such "darkness" becomes stressed in terms of a difference described as "racial." And the analogy between Ellena and this monk set up in these opening scenes counters the later antagonistic relationship between Ellena and Schedoni, whom this first "assassin" monk clearly prefigures. Like other Gothic narratives, *The Italian* suggests an ambivalent relationship between villain and heroine. Schedoni's quick conversion from predator-murderer to father-protector can be read as a confusion between, on the one hand, his alliance and identification with the woman who is his victim, and—on the other hand—his suspicion of her and their enmity. This complex relationship of affinity and hostility between fair maiden and dark villain, apparent in Radcliffe, becomes a convention of later Gothic-marked fiction.[16] Here I wish simply to stress the similar structural positions (as object) that the dark monk and the fair heroine hold in the opening sections of the novel, a similarity that finds an echo later, when Schedoni comes to believe Ellena is his daughter and works on her behalf because he perceives her as emblem of his paternal interests.

Shortly after this double opening, the set of scenes that evoke the *Romeo and Juliet* balcony scene reinforce this novel's link with the theater. Revising drama, it stages a theater of the mind. In the first of these, Vivaldi, haunting the precincts of his lady's villa (as Radcliffe's young lovers tend to do), hears a choir chanting a requiem, which reminds him of the hymn sung by Ellena in the church. Then

Overcome by the recollection, he started away, and...reached another side of the villa, where he soon heard the voice of

Ellena herself, performing the midnight hymn to the Virgin, and accompanied by a lute, which she touched with most affecting and delicate expression. He stood for a moment entranced...a light issuing from among the bowery foliage of a clematis led him to a lattice, and shewed him Ellena.... Her fine hair was negligently bound up in a silk net, and some tresses that had escaped it, played on her neck, and round her beautiful countenance, which now was not even partially concealed by a veil. (pp. 11–12)

Even when she presumes herself to be alone, Ellena "performs." But Ellena, who is no artist and exerts no control over her performance, is both literally and figuratively "artless," and can claim the innocence that that description suggests. (Does the implied praise of her lack of self-consciousness suggest that an "artful" woman is "guilty"?) She is not concealed by a veil because she does not need to be now; she is veiled by the art through which she performs. Like the audience of a play, Vivaldi is barred from contact with the performer, at least at first. But the proscenium on the eighteenth-century stage really was a thin boundary,[17] as is the barrier between Vivaldi and Ellena here; when Vivaldi transgresses this limit, the performance ends for him. The power established by the position the gazing spectator holds remains in force only as long as he remains the audience.

But while the performance ends for Vivaldi, it has only begun for the novel's reader, who continues in the position that Vivaldi has vacated. During Vivaldi's second visit, he becomes a "performer" for Ellena, by serenading her; and while Ellena evidently hears him (the text later makes clear), she declines the position of audience, to remain instead the desired spectacle that now is withheld. Finally, during Vivaldi's third visit, the balcony scene proceeds.

At this point the lovers are not on a balcony but in a "small pavilion" (p. 26). But the scene resembles its counterpart in Shakespeare's play not only because it is a scene between lovers at night on the grounds of the lady's house; as in *Romeo and Juliet* and the first scene of this sequence in *The Italian*, this scene is initiated by the lady's self-betrayal. More accurately, she, like Juliet, is betrayed by language, as her words, uttered as a monologue, are overheard by her lover, who then reveals himself and enters the scene rather than remaining an anonymous audience. Once again her performance—her art—appears not to be under her own control, a lack which once again appears to be to her credit. Later in the same scene, an "involuntary smile" contradicts the meaning of her words "I cannot be detained Signor, or forgive myself for having permitted such a conversation" (p. 27). Like the nun's veil Ellena will wear, both verbal and physical language betray. What Vivaldi sees, her smile, suggests its own language, one that escapes representation in a written narrative. Later that same smile will be specifically termed "ineffable," a word whose etymology literally denotes *unspeakable* (from Latin *effari*, to speak out). What is "ineffable" here is associated with a language of unmediated presence which sometimes (as here) contradicts verbal language, but which also (as here) may be unstable, as is verbal language.

These scenes suggest a *gendered* relationship between audience and spectacle, at least in terms of this text. Within the text, the gaze of a spectator is gendered male, and a similar relationship is implied between the text of this novel and its reader. By way of contrast with these scenes where men watch women (which install this relationship for the reader's imitation while reading this text), when a man is the object of a gaze, the dynamics function differently. For example, another interior space as the site of performance is the hall of the Inquisition. Here, the Inquisitors and Vivaldi rotate the roles of audience and actor. If Vivaldi is, on the one hand, the spectator of the impressive drama that the Inquisition stages, he also holds, like Ellena, the position of appropriable object, carefully watched, literally carried off, and physically confined. His words acquire meaning only as interpreted by his questioners, so that what he says gets twisted and used against him. But unlike Ellena, Vivaldi, assuming the role of audience, sometimes becomes the questioner himself, the presence that controls the performance. Even when in a relatively powerless position, a man assumes the powerful position of spectator more easily than does a woman.

REPETITIONS AND DOUBLINGS

The plot, characters, and circumstances in *The Italian*'s first two scenes are so often repeated that the scene acquires the quality of a ritual, or a novelistic analogue to a repeated chorus: a relationship is set up between audience and performer, the performer always on the verge of escape, or wishing to escape, and always veiled or heavily cloaked. Usually an interior space similarly determines the theater where the performance takes place. The hall at the convent of San Stefano, for example, where Ellena is confined, divides into two parts on the night of the abbess' feast and Ellena's escape; and the pilgrims and monks, including Vivaldi, become the audience (the word is specifically used) viewing veiled women, the "lady Abbess," the nuns, and Ellena. The veils these women wear both hide and also reveal them; they code them as the actors on the stage. For example, Ellena's veil allows her position on this "stage," as it disguises her as a nun and protects her. Later, on the stage of another interior, the Benedictine chapel where she is to be married, the same veil will betray Ellena. In the climax of the scene at San Stefano, Vivaldi not metaphorically but literally carries off Ellena, the object of his gaze.

In its obsessive, uncanny repetitions, *The Italian* invites some final determinate meaning. But such repetitions resist being read typologically because the text provides no reference point for its reader. Typological narrative refers its reader to a text that "explains" everything; *The Italian* does not. One hallmark of Radcliffean Gothic is that explanations never really explain much, even those explanations of such ghosts and mysterious voices as make nightmarish the world that is postulated as "real." While *The Italian* tends to rely on this sort of machinery less than, for example, *Udolpho* (because it relies on its tighter plot and more complex characters; that is, the conventions of realistic narrative), the text is similarly invested with the nightmare it depicts as opposed to its own analysis of how that nightmare came to be. Something always finally escapes the analysis. Inset stories (and plays) here, like dreams, double events in the narrative. While these stories and plays may *refer* to the outer narrative, and while they may appear to be "staged" like dreams in similarly relying on gaps and alterations of chronology, they are like dreams in this narrative but unlike dreams as explained by Freud in that they are not really *explained* by the outer narrative.[18] To understand the function of these doublings, we must read them not as coded texts which point to "meanings" in the outer narrative but, as "The 'Uncanny'" suggests, as obsessive repetitions which act as signposts of repression; their content is less important than the repetition itself. While interpretation and meaning are central concerns of this text, it is less concerned with producing a meaning than with meditating on how meanings are produced. Doublings serve the function of distancing which allows a degree of mastery. Inner narratives here resemble the dark enclosed spaces where characters lie concealed. The text plays a game with its reader, inviting us to discover which interior narratives match; that is, where do similarities become identities? Floating signifiers interpretable only in context, characters themselves float from one narrative to another. Near the beginning of the novel, Vivaldi confronts Schedoni to accuse "the secret adviser, who steals into the bosom of a family only to poison its repose" (p. 51). When Schedoni begins to defend himself, Vivaldi disingenuously responds that his insults belong not necessarily to Schedoni, but to "the author of my injuries...; you, father, can best inform me whether they apply to you." A similar verbal move is repeated often throughout the novel. Are Schedoni and the author of Vivaldi's injuries the same person? Is the monk of Paluzzi the same person as the mysterious visitor in Vivaldi's cell? Was the sinner who confessed to Father Ambroso the one in Paulo's story? Like dreams, narratives simultaneously disguise characters and identify them.

Characters also double for one another. Schedoni, acting as her agent, doubles for the Marchesa; Spalatro doubles for him. Conspiracy between Schedoni and Spalatro replaces the conspiracy between the Marchesa and Schedoni; what is a seductive struggle for power and assertion of will between Schedoni and the Marchesa becomes recast between Schedoni and Spalatro as an attempt at murder; and Schedoni's murder of Nicola di Zampari and his simultaneous suicide become the final stage of the struggle. The Marchesa, Spalatro, and Nicola all replace one another in struggle with Schedoni. Each character represents the others; and their deaths, therefore, also nearly coincide. Who a character actually *is* depends on the chain of substitutions in which that character appears; and when the chain of substitutions changes, a character's function changes. Substituting for Ellena's "good" father, Schedoni's role as agent for disruption reverses; he attempts to join together what he had previously tried to put asunder. "Good" characters also substitute for one another. Just after the funeral of Bianchi, Ellena reflects: "The more tenderly she lamented her deceased relative, the more tenderly she thought of Vivaldi; and her love for the one was so intimately connected with her affection for the other that each seemed strengthened and exalted by the union" (p. 57). Vivaldi, that is, substitutes for Bianchi; both substitute for Ellena's mother.

What is at stake in such obsessive doublings is clarified in one key scene, where Ellena sees her real mother, Olivia, for the first time. This scene doubles the opening scene of chapter 1 (after the prologue), where Vivaldi first sees Ellena. In the opening scene in the church of San Lorenzo, Vivaldi, drawn by Ellena's voice raised in song, tries to penetrate her veil. Later in the San Stefano convent chapel, attracted by Olivia's singing, Ellena attempts to do the same (p. 86).

The parallel between these two scenes is particularly suggestive because it emphasizes the degree to which the relationship between reader and text, modeled on that between spectator and object, has become eroticized. It also further complicates the relationship by establishing the desired object as a maternal body. All the seductiveness of the earlier scene is implicit in the later homo-erotically incestuous courtship, where Ellena, substituting for Vivaldi, becomes the timid lover wooing another woman. Or to turn the scenes around, in light of the second scene, Ellena in the first acts as substitute for her mother. Vivaldi's desire for Ellena (Vivaldi as Ellena's substitute from the later scene) can be read as desire for the "good" mother; and by consummating this desire, Vivaldi would escape the clutches of the "bad" mother, the Marchesa, just as Ellena's attraction to her own mother helps her to elude the Abbess, another "bad mother."

But as the text has suggested, a woman cannot unproblematically maintain the position of the spectator. Here, Ellena is the circulating "middle term" of the equations: she is both object (of Vivaldi's gaze) and subject (gazing at Olivia). Her position finally differentiates itself from Vivaldi's in the earlier scene: unlike Ellena at the beginning of the novel, Olivia throws back her veil. Ellena's response is to identify herself with Olivia; she reads

Olivia's face in light of her own situation. Sexual desire, which for Vivaldi becomes domesticated as desire for marriage, becomes identification for Ellena. One effect of the unstable relationships between the woman-as-spectator and woman-as-object is to neutralize desire, which transforms itself at the moment when Ellena identifies with the mother for whom she longs. When identification replaces desire, the daughter is (narcissistically) left in the double position of herself and the desired Other. But it's also true that the relationship between the women here, and between desire and identification, works like desire between men,[19] except that here there is no need for a "middle term" as mediator. The relationship between mother and daughter is evidently so direct that it nearly collapses personal boundaries. And like Ellena, Olivia speaks a silent language, as she bids Ellena farewell at the end of this scene "by a smile of ineffable pity" (p. 87).

HER BODY/HER VOICE

The veiled woman, then, would seem to embody that repression which doubling indicates here, a repression which is revealed to be associated with woman's maternity and sexuality. But not only that; she also links the issue of repression with storytelling.

One point of resemblance between Schedoni and the mute criminal in the opening dumb show is that like that criminal, Schedoni never tells his own story. The position of the criminal (or the woman) is the position assigned to Schedoni: disruptive but marginalized, controlled by the presence that sees and interprets, representative of a story to be unfolded, though mute. He represses his story to hide his past crimes, and on the mystery of that repression turns the plot of the novel. "Gothic suspense" results from the tension between the uncovering of the story and the repression that resists this uncovering—a process that resembles psychoanalytic narrative. The story unfolds a guilty secret. Each time Schedoni's story is retold, we come closer to a kind of "truth," the secret sin that "explains" the dysfunction of the social mechanisms in the "present" of the primary narrative. And the story unravels as does a psychoanalytic narrative: little by little in successive inset tales intertwined with what appears to be irrelevant material, marked by holes in the narrative and confusing chronology.

"Veiling" acts as metaphor for such resistance to the telling of stories. Schedoni casts metaphorical "impenetrable veils" at two key points. At his first entrance he is described as "an Italian...whose family was unknown, and from some circumstances, it appeared, that he wished to throw an impenetrable veil over his origin" (p. 34). Much later he contrives to throw "an impenetrable veil over the face of Ellena" (p. 245) with her forged arrest by the Inquisition. Both "veils" conceal crimes against women, mother and daughter, who here once again substitute for one another. Schedoni's campaign against Ellena reenacts his rape of her mother, and his attempt to kill Ellena resumes his attempt on her mother's life. If homoeroticism is the "unspeakable" presence in the novel *Melmoth the Wanderer*,[20] incestuous rape certainly is one of the unspeakable presences here. For Radcliffe, writing *The Italian* as corrective to Lewis's *The Monk*, a text not just less squeamish about rape and incest but actually relishing its own sordid details, decorum veils predatory sex. Although the rape of Ellena's mother is clearly referred to but supposedly neutralized and partially redeemed by subsequent marriage (and has occurred tastefully offstage, before the novel's "present"), Schedoni's attacks on Ellena, which hold their terror partly because they suggest a sexual threat, are disguised and given other pretexts. The text ends up by subjecting Schedoni's "impenetrable veils" to the family, which implicates itself in the mystification[21]: Schedoni's "origin" becomes represented in terms of his own family and personal history and the future as the "*giorno felice*" that unites Vivaldi and Ellena. But the two veils finally conceal whatever lies behind them.

Early on, Schedoni's story is told in only its broadest outlines (p. 34); later it becomes clear that some of the cryptic narratives that have been told are associated with his history (though it is not clear how); still later, more of his story is told (pp. 225–26); and two veiled monks, Nicola and Father Ansaldo, fill in the story further (pp. 337–49; 359–65). But it is Olivia, the veiled woman who, in substituting for the veiling that language suggests, finally unveils the conclusion and provides its final details, aided by another woman, the servant Beatrice. Like the terminal narrative of a psychoanalytic explanation, the "explained" story makes sense as a way of imposing coherence on threatened incoherence; it acts retrospectively. It explains the chaos which is otherwise incomprehensible. This typically Gothic plot—the discovery of a family's secret, originary crime—really explains little more than the Radcliffean machinery which explains such mysterious events as ghosts and voices, since the text is charged more with the bizarre present than with the explanatory fiction. Finally, even the story for which the veiled woman stands creates only a narrow, precarious bridge over a gap in the text.

In general, storytelling within the *The Italian* presents itself as a mode of comedy. Characters such as Schedoni, who aspire to the status of "tragic," tend to have their stories unfolded by others. Stories within the narrative tend to be told by servants who play the part of fools. Narratives, like plays in these pages, are tales told by idiots. Though lives and inheritances hinge on stories, for the most part stories are the property of those who only half-understand them, and are repeated to audiences who are often unappreciative and wish either to hurry the story along or not to hear it at all. In this way, the authorial voice (Radcliffe, we might say) seems deliberately to undermine its own position, the "authority" of authorship. But two institutions create frames to elicit stories, which these frames invest with solemnity and distance: the Inquisition and the confessional. However, the stories they elicit are themselves just barely speakable and get told only after much resistance, sometimes because the speaker does not wish to tell the story, sometimes because of a psychological block such as guilt.

Schedoni's story comes to the reader both doubly framed and doubly interrupted: we hear it through both the Confession *and* the Inquisition; and, partially related by Paulo chapters earlier, told finally by Schedoni anonymously as "a penitent" through his confessor, and marked by groans, pauses, and hesitations.

The story that cannot be told becomes associated in the text with things that cannot be seen. One characteristic of both the confessional and the Inquisition is that both institutions urge stories to be revealed by *telling*—while their own power is affirmed through visual hiding. In the confessional, confessor and penitent hear but never see one another; in *The Italian*, part of the mystery depends on Schedoni and Father Ansaldo remaining anonymous to one another. The Inquisition cloaks its agents in heavy robes and masks, and does not even trust these: at one point, Vivaldi is blindfolded so that he cannot see. The Inquisition scene is marked by a continual teasing of "visible" against "invisible" and of both against what can be heard: the mysterious monk (Zampari) appears to Vivaldi; but he will be invisible (though present) at the Inquisition's questioning (p. 321). He will *appear* (p. 322; emphasis in the text). His voice is heard.

On the one hand, that is, the veiled figure is finally always opaque: the story resists being told and, when told, appears only through a tunnel of frames; the veiled woman discloses nothing but more veiled figures, which themselves, at the very moment when narrative promises to reveal all, are hidden by a literal blindfold. On the other hand, the story seduces with the promise of the revelation of what has been hidden.

In *The Italian*, "meaning" sometimes seems to lie beyond representation—in, for example, sights and sounds that narrative can only suggest but not represent: the sound of a voice or of music, a special kind of smile. In this way, as with the use of comic characters to tell stories, the text appears to undermine its own authority. The revelation of the plot hinges on what is not only unreadable but also unrepresentable in a written text, the voice. Ellena's voice attracts Vivaldi to her even before he sees her veil; Olivia's voice attracts Ellena; and the final strands of mystery are unwound when Olivia recognizes the voice of Beatrice. The voice can be neither read nor opposed. Unlike veils, words, and images, it does not deceive. The language of the voice is the language that preceded inscription in verbal language. It is a language of presence only, a sign of a preverbal, mother-dominated state of existence. A signal that marks recognition among the "good" characters, voice moves everyone, even villains, to pity: the Marchesa is touched by the sound of a sung requiem (p. 177) just after she has concluded her plot to kill Ellena; the Benedictine priest who hears the kidnapped Ellena calling Vivaldi wipes away his tears though his heart has been "cold" (p. 191). While voice cannot be represented in a written text, it manifests itself here as presiding spirit, associated with the feminine and the maternal.

Just as the "ineffable" manifests itself. Like the voice, the "ineffable" smile of Ellena (p. 39) and of Olivia can neither be represented nor hidden, read nor misread; but it is visible in its effects. It speaks its own language: "Ellena's ineffable smile appealed more eloquently to his [heart] than the most energetic language could have done" (p. 39). This smile, of "ineffable sweetness" (p. 151) has rhetorical effect: it persuades Vivaldi of Ellena's affection ("I believe it is your smile, rather than the accuracy of your explanation, that persuades me to a confidence in your affection," pp. 152–53). While in Gothic fiction horrors are often termed "unspeakable," the "ineffable" will turn out to be not far from that, in that both suggest versions of the uncanny.[22] Like the "unspeakable," the ineffable evidently functions with a sexual dimension. And what is "ineffable" not only cannot be spoken, it need not be spoken because it speaks itself. Like the voice, unlike ordinary representation and unlike what can be spoken or represented, its appeal is direct and unmistakable.

That this unrepresentable, "ineffable" presence allied with voice is a maternal presence is confirmed by another uncannily recurrent image of a veiled mother whose face and body express what cannot otherwise be expressed. The patron of the church in the prologue, the Church of the Santa Maria del Pianto (Our Lady of Pity or Tears) is the same Sorrowful Mother, another veiled woman, who is patron of the convent where Ellena finally finds protection and refuge, the Santa della Pieta. That convent stands in opposition to the earlier, horrific Convent of San Stefano, whose patron, the first Christian martyr, testifies to human brutality and the legal logic that condemns to death. The "pity" she conveys, expresses, and spreads to the gazing spectator lies beyond a writable language governed by laws. It resembles that mercy that the presence of another person makes possible in the opening scene, where someone provides food to the criminal only because the poor wretch must not starve. The Mother of Pity, of the Pietà, represents what Schedoni had attempted to veil: as mother she suggests birth, while her tears remind one of the death she mourns. As Christ-bearer, she herself is a veil, hiding the Divine Light. Her language is her own image, with which the viewer is invited to identify as mourner over the dead body of Christ. But her quasi-divine status imposes a reverential distance between her and the spectator.

A text that similarly relies on "pity" to supplement the language it employs would of course be termed "sentimental," a rubric under which Radcliffean Gothic clearly falls. "Sentimental" fiction deliberately (not naively) relies on a language "beyond language," which subverts verbal language. That vacillation between desire and identification similar to that between Ellena and Olivia when Ellena first sees her mother is what this Mother of Pity evokes. By contrast, though desire and identification are similarly present in the scene between *father* and daughter, they are employed differently in the text, as the recognition scene between Ellena and Schedoni suggests. The scene where Schedoni (mis)recognizes Ellena as his daughter inverts the scene where Ellena first gazes at her mother. Taken together, these two scenes make explicit the threat which the maternal image presents and suggest the "cover" under which the woman writer might escape.

This scene is the novel's climax, depicting Schedoni's aborted murder of Ellena. What raises the emotion of this scene is its preparation in the text's preceding scenes: Ellena's imagination exerts its own terrifying force, supplementing the fears evoked by her real danger at the hands of the villains. The sequence of scenes works by inviting the reader, first of all, to identify with Ellena and similarly to invoke the imagination; its mechanism is voyeuristic and masochistic. When Schedoni enters the room where she lies sleeping, the access point for the reader shifts. Ellena becomes opaque, an object; and the reader's previous identification is partially replaced by scopophilic interest. Sadism supplements the masochism. Here, desire succeeds identification; what the reader undergoes is the reverse of the desire-identification vaccillation that we have seen Ellena experiencing earlier where the two characters involved were women. But in either case, psychological vacillation can be understood because we are reading a novel, a medium especially well adapted to depict interior states.

By contrast, when the scene of Ellena's murder really *is* a scene, in a play, the dynamics work differently. Boaden's adaptation of the novel, *The Italian Monk*, altogether avoids closet scenes, such as that depicting Ellena terrifying herself.[23] While the novel's text stresses Ellena's psychological state even above the real danger, the play centers its attention on the plotting villains; then it moves directly to the attempted murder. The play relies on a sadism that is less mixed with masochism, which has been given no opportunity to accumulate; it nearly by-passes any need for identification with Ellena, who remains opaque. She is merely the still, supine figure around which action circulates, a spectacle for the audience as for those would-be assassins who double them within the space of the stage—and who then as scapegoats bear off that audience's guilt.

In both novel and play, this tableau of Ellena's sleeping body is unlike other representations of the veiled woman's body that the text has described in that this scene makes explicit her vulnerability. However, even here Ellena is guarded. First, the representation of the father which she wears, and which here acts as a mirror for Schedoni, guards her. But her body also clearly exerts a certain strange power of its own in the context of this scene. The qualms of conscience which Spalatro and Schedoni express do not quite account for their fear in the face of Ellena's unmoving, unveiled body. After all, Schedoni has committed rape and fratricide; Spalatro has carried a dead body around in a sack. These are cutthroats and villains, accustomed to blood and death. Whence comes this power?

Part of the power unquestionably lies in her opacity, which the play stresses by refusing to allow the audience to maintain strong identification with her. In the play, she is never shown alone with her fears. By contrast, the novel submits that opaque body to its readers only after it has offered us Ellena's perspective. It gives Ellena a double role, as both an unreadable body and a transparent mind. As captive and potential victim of rape and murder, Ellena plays out another phase of that double function she acts elsewhere in the novel, as both subject and object. The relationship between Olivia and Ellena in that early scene where Ellena first sees her mother prefigures the relationship between the reader and Ellena: here unveiled and offering her unguarded breast to the assassin's poniard, she offers herself to her reader as object of desire as well as subject for identification. While she advances the plot of the text, her body serves to stop it momentarily, to offer a challenge. The figure of the veiled woman conveys a similar double function. If the veiled woman literally embodies repression, what she actually performs is its opposite, the revelation of a tale.

If the process of hiding structures the representation, representation allows escape under its cover. If explanations finally do not account for the villains' fears in Ellena's presence, no more do solutions account for the "uncanny" effect evoked by the novel's veiled figures and mysterious voices. Writing cannot convey an unrepresentable voice. *The Italian* rewrites the scene of a woman's body as a story of women's doubleness that undermines the authoritative, authorial gaze which that scene exploits.

CHAPTER 3

The Woman on the Bed (Frankenstein)

Frankenstein is obviously unlike Radcliffean Gothic in that masculine figures occupy its center, though they have been read to act as purveyors of woman-identified interests, such as childbearing (in Moers's reading) or women's anxiety of authorship (in Gilbert and Gubar's reading). But in *Frankenstein* the pursued woman as woman has not disappeared; she has just been moved to one side. Taking its cue from Radcliffean Gothic, going even a step further, *Frankenstein* conscripts the reader as voyeur, a conscription exploited by the many visual representations and reframings of the novel, in particular by the James Whale film adaptation (1931) that has been enshrined in popular culture. This novel invites and exploits the gaze. But in this text not only does the artistic gaze serve to freeze and exploit the woman's body; here, the woman artist exploits the spectator's gaze by mirroring it back with the body of a woman. In this text, the two halves of the structure of looking explicitly divide the role the author assigns herself; and the two halves serve both to illustrate the terms of a woman's confinement to the status of object and to follow the trajectory of her possible escape as artist.

NIGHTMARE VISIONS

As one critic of *Frankenstein* suggests, one of the dominant images of James Whale's film adaptation of the novel is "the image of the monster lurking ominously in the background with Elizabeth sprawled on the bed, an image profoundly phallic and profoundly violent, an unacceptable alternative to and consequence of the act of conception in the laboratory"[1] (figure 1). That the tableau to which he refers *is* one of the dominant

FIGURE 1
Still from James Whale's *Frankensein*, Universal Pictures (1931)
Copyright © by Universal Pictures, a Division of Universal City Studios, Inc.
Courtesy of MCA Publishing Rights, a Division of MCA Inc.

images of the film is remarkable, given the peripheral role of
Elizabeth in the novel and still more in the film. In the film narrative, this scene actually involves less violence than in the text.
In the film, Elizabeth has just fainted; in the text of the novel,
Victor Frankenstein rushes into the room to find her murdered
by the monster: "She was there, lifeless and inanimate, thrown
across the bed, her head hanging down, and her pale and distorted features half covered by her hair" (p. 195).

This scene assumes its status both because of its implicit
threat, its inner dynamics working within the confines of its own
space, and because of its intertextual associations that, for a
twentieth-century reader, work both forwards from the date of
the novel, to the film, and also backwards. The film tableau that
represents the scene does of course gesture towards Mary Shelley's description, though Elizabeth's features here are neither dis-

torted nor half-covered by hair. The woman's vulnerability is in fact emphasized by her exposed white neck and the blond hair that hangs down the side of the bed, giving us a clear view of her beautiful face. The film dwells on this frame for a few seconds, where the scene is so very carefully staged and composed. Elizabeth stands out because of her whiteness against the black background of the black-and-white cinematography; the whiteness cuts across the lower third center of the tableau to her body, and is echoed in the vase of flowers that leans askew but directly parallel to her arm. Body and vase indicate a line which continues to the whiteness that defines the edge of the monster's face.

In fact the movie scene adheres less to Mary Shelley's description than to Henry Fuseli's painting *The Nightmare*, on which it is surely based (figures 2 and 3). Freud evidently perceived this painting to have something in common with his own work on dreams (though he never discussed the painting in his writing), for *The Nightmare* hung on Freud's wall at Bergasse 19, Vienna.[2] What novel, movie scene, and painting share, however, is a visual game by which they all locate the spectator, a game that a careful look at the operations of the painting makes particularly explicit. The viewer, who stands where the painter must have stood, watches the woman in her disturbed sleep from a safe perspective. Her sensuous pose accentuates the lines of her body and deliberately provokes the (presumably male) viewer, who is invited to enjoy her discomfort, her powerlessness and her vulnerability.[3]

"One of the most unexplored region of art are [sic] dreams," states Fuseli's Aphorism 231. Although many of Fuseli's paintings "stage" a tension-filled dramatic moment in the theater at which the viewer gazes (from *Hamlet* or *Macbeth*, or from Greek tragedy, for example), *The Nightmare* "embodies" its subject on the canvas in rather a different sense than the stage allows, or than Fuseli himself uses in paintings of the theater. As dreamer, the woman might typically stage the dream herself in the space of her own dreaming consciousness. The dreamer views the dream; the spectators might look through her eyes. But here, the audience voyeuristically gazes at the woman rather than sees from her perspective; we don't actually see what she sees in her dream. Does she see anything at all behind her closed eyes?

Even the canvas on which the first version of *The Nightmare*

FIGURE 2
The Nightmare (1781), first version
© The Detroit Institute of Arts
Gift of Mr. and Mrs. Bert L. Smokler and Mr. and Mrs. Lawrence A. Fleischman

is painted suggests the woman's opacity. On the back of this canvas is the unfinished portrait of a young woman thought to be Anna Landolt, who rejected Fuseli as lover.[4] Critics suggest that this ill-fated passion may have been the motivating force behind *The Nightmare.* The individual features of Anna Landolt are here literally hidden behind a violently subjected neoclassical female figure. But also, the self-sufficiency of Anna Landolt suggests the opaque, unreadable quality of dreams themselves; she cannot be mastered any more than can a dream. Fuseli's phallic nightmare, with its two male sexual symbols, a horse and erect squat incubus,[5] appropriates the "phallus" of the powerful, self-sufficient woman and turns it against her. "Nightmare" not only acts as a mirror image, a reverse picture, of narcissistic self-sufficient femininity; here, it acts as revenge for it.[6]

FIGURE 3
The Nightmare (1782–91), second version
Reprinted with permission of Freies Deutsches Hochstift—Frankfurt-am-Main
Photograph by Ursula Edelmann

According to Powell's book-length study of *The Nightmare*, eighteenth-century Hobbesian and Lockean ideas about dreams suggested that dreams are not only unreadable; they actually have a physical basis and are associated with sexuality. The word *incubus* means both nightmare and a demon who has sexual intercourse with sleeping women; the word is derived from the Latin *incubare*, "to lie down." Art critics generally refer to the squatting figure in Fuseli's painting as an "incubus." Powell notes that women were thought to be inclined to have nightmares; Paracelsus (incidentally one of Victor Frankenstein's discarded intellectual fathers) explained that this tendency occurred because the menstrual flow engendered phantoms in the air.[7] Powell also cites a Dr. John Bond's case history of a fifteen-year-old pre-menarchal girl who, after being visited by an incubus who "stretched himself upon her," was afflicted with bleeding from mouth and nose; the next day she menstruated.[8] This striking case suggests an association among nightmares, hysteria, and the assumption of female sexuality. Evidently, nightmares were perceived as a kind of punishing self-directed internalized phallic weapon.

What *The Nightmare* suggests, however, is a classic case of *male* hysteria.[9] On a 1783 print of the *The Nightmare* appear four lines of a poem by Erasmus Darwin (of whose experiments Mary Shelley was to write). The complete text of the poem, *The Loves of the Plants*, was not published until 1789 and continues explicitly to describe Fuseli's painting. He describes the incubus:

> On her fair bosom sits the Demon-Ape,
> Erect, and balances his bloated shape;
> Rolls in their marble orbs his Gorgon-eyes
> And drinks with leathern ears her tender cries.[10]

What's especially provocative here is the description of the figure's "Gorgon-eyes." Literally, of course, the figure does not seem to be a Gorgon. The threat of the Gorgons was associated with their female sexuality; this figure—though if it has sex itself, its sex is ambivalent, hidden to the viewer of the painting—is associated with male sexuality. Nonetheless, Powell claims that as well as resembling certain phallic figures of antiquity, the figure also is reminiscent of Etruscan Gorgons that appeared on pottery vases. What is striking about it, in any case, is that it both possesses and represents sexuality; that it is evidently powerful and phallic; that it sits or squats on the abdomen of the sleeping woman; and that it fixes the spectator who gazes, frozen with horror, at the apparition.

At least in the Detroit Institute version, the figure, almost protruding from the woman's genital area, could actually be the erect phallus of the woman herself. This reading, bizarre though it seems, suggests a certain consistency with the Medusa theme. As Medusa was punished for her own sexuality, so, according to eighteenth-century ideas about nightmares, is this woman. For both women, the punishment takes the form of a phallic symbol—a mocking reminder of both the women's own sexual power and of the male domination that appropriates it: for Medusa, snakes; for the dreamer, the erect figure. And for both, the punishment produces a third party: for Medusa, the witness who becomes stone; for the dreamer, the horrified viewer of the picture, who is locked into a confrontation with the incubus. As Freud suggests, the spectator's petrification acts apotropaically to ward off the threat that the view of women's sexuality poses. Both the petrification of the spectator and the erect figure serve to deny the woman's threatening lack; she becomes a phallic woman.

Certainly Fuseli was no stranger to the Medusa theme. In one portrait (figure 4), Mrs. Fuseli, elaborately coifed, looks out at the viewer, while behind her stares a portrait of herself as Medusa. One of Fuseli's paintings for his Nibelungenlied series (XXXIX [1895]) uses as model ancient representations of Perseus with Medusa's head.[11] In any case, the glaring figure in *The Nightmare* sets up a relationship between himself and the viewer that by-passes the sleeping woman altogether. She lies discarded on the bed while she provides the occasion for the artist-spectator to confront the phallic demon. At the same time, her possession of a phallus (or its possession of her) relieves the spectator of the threat that the woman's lack poses.

The tableau in the James Whale film assigns to the film viewer a similar position, but it exposes the mechanism of its own sadistic voyeurism more explicitly. Here, as in Fuseli's painting, the spectator is invited to enjoy the sight of a vulnerable and beautiful supine woman. But the movie audience does not actually confront the Monster outside the window as the viewer confronts the incubus in the painting. Rather, the window in the tableau functions for the Monster in the same way as the camera functions for the film audience: the Monster doubles the audience, as each looks through a lens at the fainted woman.

FIGURE 4
Mrs Fuseli, Seated in Front of the Fire,
Behind Her a Relief Medallion wth Her Portrait as Medusa (1799)
Reprinted with permission of the Germanisches Nationalmuseum, Nüremberg

Of course the film tableau is a single moment in a moving narrative of pictures, a narrative that has already, as I have suggested, assigned the character Elizabeth to a peripheral role. In the film, the father-son relationship of the novel becomes central.[12] The creator of the Monster, here renamed "Henry" Frankenstein, has no mother; Elizabeth's function is to convey his father's wishes to him, and she is doubled (and reinforced) by a male friend, "Victor" (as Henry Clerval gets renamed). Whereas the novel creates an exchange of women among males (Elizabeth for the Monster woman that Frankenstein makes and destroys), to suggest a Girardian relationship among Frankenstein, Elizabeth, and Monster,[13] the film minimizes still more the importance of male-female relationships as such. The issue of the Monster's need for a mate is reserved for the film's sequel. "Sexual" relationships, insofar as the film alludes to them at all, exist to continue the patrimonic bloodline: for this reason do Henry's father and his two representatives, Victor and Elizabeth, urge Henry to get married. From the outset, creating the Monster threatens not female generative power but patriarchal succession. What Henry ought to do is produce an heir the proper way. The movie's triumphant conclusion is a toast "To the House of Frankenstein!" and more particularly, "To a son of the House of Frankenstein!" urged by the still-living father upon the servants of the house.[14]

In the film tableau, Elizabeth is even less important than Fuseli's dreamer, who splits the dark background with her white and light-colored body. In the film tableau, where Elizabeth is cast to the side, the viewer is already poised to move to the next frame, to chase the Monster with the already resocialized Henry. As the camera focuses on the recumbent figure of Elizabeth, our eye is attracted first by the movement of the Monster out the window, then by the movement of Henry and his friends from the door opposite. The control that patriarchal power exerts is always apparent in the film: even at the end when the mob of villagers pursues the Monster, they are first carefully organized by the burgomaster; and one party is led by Henry Frankenstein. The aristocratic patriarchal rulers, father, son, and the House of Frankenstein, preside.

In *The Italian*, marriage and family finally patch over the narrative's obsessive reaching for the unreachable past; they also substitute for the desire for the mother that transforms itself into women's narcissistic longing. That is, particular instances where the text momentarily defies the domination of the father are, by being subjected to marriage, forcefully restored to patriarchy. As I have suggested, Boaden's theatrical adaptation of Radcliffe even more forcefully recuperates and redeems the threat implicit in its literary source. The film version of *Frankenstein* similarly recuperates and redeems such defiance by subjecting it to the family. It also domesticates the aggression apparent in the tableau depicting Elizabeth on the bed. If female sexuality poses a threat to be neutralized, male aggression, similarly threatening, must be disguised and disarmed. The aggression against Elizabeth implicit in the Monster's and the audience's (double) position here becomes neutralized by a context that stresses protection of Elizabeth, depicted in terms that stereotypically confirm the male hero's "virility." The formulaic, almost ritualistic nature of this encounter highlights the sexual nature of the confrontation between the Monster and the woman. The male guards his mate; the female must rely on the male for protection against sexual predators—that is, rapists; by becoming the property of one male, one who shares her social class, she is guarded against attack.[15]

The frame depicting the fainted Elizabeth—"the nightmare"— is thrust here into a narrative context where "civilized" men seek to protect the supine woman: Henry Frankenstein locks the door to her room, which, like her, belongs to him (physical analogies here are not subtle)—but of course he forgets to lock the window, through which the monster enters and exits while Henry is searching other parts of the house for the Monster. The camera holds the "nightmare" tableau for several seconds, the audience in suspense about Elizabeth's state. But before the camera cuts away, we are reassured of Elizabeth's safety. Surrounded on the bed by a crowd of well-wishers (Henry, Victor, wedding guests, and servants), she murmurs deliriously, "Don't let him come here!" and Henry, patting her face to restore her to consciousness, soothes her: "It's all right."

Immediately the camera cuts away abruptly to the peasant Ludwig carrying the body of the little girl, Maria, whom the Monster has drowned, her hair and arms streaming down just as Elizabeth's were. The movie is clearly telling us that although

Elizabeth hasn't been killed (or, as the predatory sexuality of this image suggests, raped), she might have been—and here is proof. By killing Maria instead of Elizabeth, the movie can have both its domesticated happy ending and its implicit threat to women. And the implicit parallel between Maria and Elizabeth serves to underscore the adult woman's childlike status. Further, poignant though the scene with Maria is evidently intended to be, it allows the escape of the aristocratic woman at the sacrifice of the peasant girl; it emphasizes the importance of the class and gender structures that protect Elizabeth. A girl, adult or child, is more at risk without aristocratic chivalric protectors, their fortresses, and the peasant forces they can mobilize.

By coming down hard on the high side of class (upper) and gender (male), the film neutralizes much of the threat suggested by the novel, which invites the spectator's gaze but defies it. Its defiance is made explicit by the narrative's refusal of the domesticated "happy ending" and by its substitution of the image of the woman's body alone on the bed, as a perverted consummation of the marriage. In the novel, the reader is presented with the opaque, still body of Elizabeth, an image of death and a representation of that earlier scene where the unthinking, unfeeling monster woman lay before Victor. In the later scene, the horrible undead and unliving body of the female monster is revised to become the body of Elizabeth, beautiful but no less terrifying, though reassuring because dead. With the body of Elizabeth, the text exploits the spectator's gaze; yet in so doing it also establishes a manipulative vantage point for the woman as artist, while punishing (herself as) "woman" in the character of Elizabeth.

In the text of the novel, the Monster kills Elizabeth in revenge for Frankenstein's destruction of the female monster. In the movie, the Monster appears to be the "natural" enemy of the female sex: virtually without motivation, he kills a little girl (not a little boy nor a Frankenstein, as in the novel) and menaces Elizabeth. But this Monster, who cannot speak, ought to be the ally of the woman on the bed, who is also voiceless in the movie except as ventriloquized by the father. Such an alliance is of course impossible, because of the threat of the anarchy it would conveys, as Mel Brooks suggests in his parody *Young Frankenstein*. In the Brooks parody Elizabeth, who is sexually cold until her encounter with the Monster, ends up in bed with him;[16] her sexual awakening turns her into a bride resembling the Elsa Lancaster monster woman of Whale's 1932 sequel. Though her desire is (as always) a joke, she becomes not the submissive representative of the father but a wildly disruptive force. In the parody, the Monster finally speaks for himself at the end. But in the 1931 film, the unspeaking Monster, who momentarily defies the phallic order, must be held firmly in check, like the dreaming woman in Fuseli's painting.

THE ARTIST BEHOLDS

"The nightmare" constitutes one dominant icon from the film. Another, equally powerful, is the image of the scientist bringing the creature to life in his laboratory.[17] Mary Shelley's own nightmare vision from her preface, which depends in part on the same conventions of describing nightmares that Fuseli uses and may, like the movie, use his painting as source, ends up splitting in the novel into two parts: one is the "nightmare" scene of the woman on the bed[18]; the other is the scene of Victor Frankenstein's nightmare.

In the introduction to the novel, the "pale student" comes to replace the dreaming woman as "artist" (Shelley's term for him); in Mary Shelley's dream, the monster figures the dream itself. While the woman on the bed in the introduction (that is, Shelley herself) becomes the murdered woman at the climax of the novel, the same scene, with a gender change, is incorporated whole in chapter 5 of the novel. The film requires a great deal of literal machinery and a whole gallery full of spectators to replace the image of Mary Shelley's solitary "pale student of unhallowed arts kneeling beside the thing he had put together" (Introduction to *Frankenstein*, p. 9). Shelley continues on to describe "the workings of some powerful engine"—a vague description, but one that might, if exaggerated, suggest Henry's elaborate electrical apparatus in the film, exaggerated still further in the film's sequels.

While the introduction superimposes *creating* on *seeing* (the dreaming woman begins to plan her text just after her nightmare vision of the Monster), chapter 5 of the novel ("It was on a dreary night of November, that I beheld the accomplishment of my toils....") does exactly the reverse. Frankenstein has just finished his creation; then he contemplates ("beholds") it and sharply recoils in guilt and terror—clearly because he has seen something he shouldn't have. One might speculate here on the "primal scene" implications of this description[19]; but rather than attempting to decode *what* Victor Frankenstein sees, I would here like to draw attention to the specular relationship itself. My interest here is not so much in what is repressed but in what is represented and the implications the vision has for the spectator.

In the dream in the introduction, the relationship is tri-cornered: the scientist ("artist," Mary Shelley calls him) sees the Monster come to life, and Mary Shelley the dreamer sees both of them. In the text of the novel, identification between the creator of the Monster and the "dreamer" is literalized, while the dream is slightly displaced, to a point in time after the animation of the Monster. That is, what is dreamed in the introduction takes place as "real," not a dream, followed by a dream. What Victor Frankenstein sees in his dream is, first of all, the metamorphosis of Elizabeth into his mother's corpse, a transmutation that appears to be motivated by his kiss on her lips. As dreamer, his position is Mary Shelley's in the introduction; within the dream, what he does reverses what the "artist" does in Mary Shelley's dream. What Victor Frankenstein sees is the mirror image of his own previous action and the mirror image of what Mary Shelley saw in her own dream. While she saw him giving the Monster the spark that brought the Monster to life, he sees himself giving a "spark" to Elizabeth (a kiss) that turns her into someone who is already dead, his mother.

The horror of Victor's position is that, as in a dream, he is locked inside his own private world. He cannot emerge from his one-to-one relationship with the Monster. What Mary Shelley "saw" only briefly detached itself from a social context (i.e. at the moment of dreaming itself) and then reimmersed itself as writing, to become a story that could be presented to the friends who awaited it: "Swift as light and as cheering was the idea that broke in upon me. 'I have found it! What terrified me will terrify others; and I need only describe the spectre which had haunted my midnight pillow'" (introduction to *Frankenstein*, p. 10). But what Victor Frankenstein sees is literally unrepresentable in the sense that it cannot appear outside the context of relationship with him;

that is, it exists only in relationship to him, not otherwise. Critics have stressed that the Monster figures the text, and so he does, in his awkward embodiment of a weird assemblage of parts. But the Monster is unlike a literary text in that it cannot be separated from its creator. Often in the story the Monster seems to function not as something externalized but as something *within* Victor. After William's death, for example, Victor "knows" the Monster to be the murderer just because he has thought he might be: "The mere presence of the idea was irresistible proof of the fact" (p. 76). That is, there is not some external "fact" that Victor's idea confirms; his pronouncement of the idea, his putting the idea into language and not the Monster's existence or propensity for violence, constitutes the idea's becoming external. Putting his idea into language externalizes it, detaches it from Victor. The Monster is more intimately bound to him, less detachable, than his own utterance. Victor has no safe position from which to view the Monster; he "sees" him only in relation to himself.

When, in the final scene, the Monster appears to anyone other than Victor, he appears to Walton, Victor's double. His appearance here is also dreamlike (an "apparition," Walton calls it), set in the surreal seascape of jagged shapes and eternal light. Finally in this hallucinatory setting, reconciliation can be effected: the Monster returns to Frankenstein in a weirdly incestuous homoerotic *liebestod*. With this reconciliation, a social context can again be established. The Monster's appearance here figures Victor's narration, which, like the Monster, has Walton as audience. Victor's narration of the story externalizes, re-presents, what was internalized; and Victor, who sought to transcend death and thus to deny his humanity, dies himself and confirms it. Walton, as substitute for Victor, returns to his own social context, to England.

Like Radcliffe's horrors, Victor's unspeakably ugly Monster is more horrible than what can actually be shown; and any film visualization must inevitably fall short. "How can I describe my emotions at this catastrophe, or how delineate the wretch whom with such infinite pains and care I had endeavoured to form?" Victor asks (p. 57), a double question that links the physical appearance of the Monster to Victor's emotions. Though he does describe the Monster's yellow skin, black hair, shrivelled complexion, and straight black lips, the description misses the full horror of the reality; for when animated, the monster "became a thing such as even Dante could not have conceived" (p. 58); that is, he is well beyond representation. As in Radcliffe, horror is not so much represented as charted, here in its effects on Victor's body: "Sometimes my pulse beat so quickly and hardly, that I felt the palpitation of every artery; at others, I nearly sank to the ground through languor and extreme weakness" (p. 58).

Stage presentation, in any case, made a concession to its inevitable failure here, with its convention of leaving the Monster unnamed in the program. Mary Shelley responded to this concession with delight at her attendance at *Presumption, or the Fate of Frankenstein* (1823): "The playbill amused me extremely, for in the list of dramatis personae came————by Mr. T. Cooke: this nameless mode of naming the un[n]ameable is rather good."[20] The James Whale film suggests an interesting and provocative variation on the convention; in the credits at the beginning, "The Monster" (so named) is played by "?" though Boris Karloff gets credit when the cast list is run at the end of the movie. What appears to be unnameable here is not the Monster but the actor. For the audience of a 1931 Hollywood movie, nothing is really either unnameable or unrepresentable; but the fun lies in suggesting that the actor behind the Monster is himself possibly a Monster, or at any rate, not human. As in Radcliffe, here disguise appears to be indistinguishable from what is disguised.

As a creator bound to his monster even more closely than to the language which the Monster figures, Victor's position is similar to that of those recumbent women to whose nightmarish visions the text (after the introduction) obsessively recurs. The woman on the bed in the introduction to *Frankenstein*, the awakened Mary Shelley, is different from Victor and from these other women. As author, Mary Shelley represents her monstrous nightmare, figured as the Monster himself, *as* the text of a story—something that the murdered woman never has the option of doing. Elizabeth is no storyteller. At the one point when she does attempt to tell tales, in her letters to Victor which set up William's murder and Justine's trial, her story is fragmented and finally a failure, like the story of the woman she mentions, Justine.[21] Justine's story fails because it is incoherent; it cannot bridge its too-obvious gaps. The text of *Frankenstein* establishes that in general, created objects are not so easily separable from those who hold them as they are in Radcliffe. While the specular positioning of the artist serves to create a manageable distance, the separation between creation and creator is always threatened, too easily collapsible. If the creation of the Monster figuratively suggests the long and painful process of birthing a text, a separation never fully realized, the miniature portrait of Victor Frankenstein's mother represents other phases of the relationship between art object and its "owner," here figured as the literal possessor of the object. It is tempting to suggest a similarity between this portrait and similar paintings in Radcliffe (in *The Italian*, for example, Ellena's miniature of her father, or in *The Mysteries of Udolpho*, the portraits in the gallery at Udolpho), and they are in some ways analogous. Like the portrait, such paintings tend to signify gaps which the narrative must patch. But in other ways, clearly the miniature portrait here acts differently from such paintings in Radcliffe. In Radcliffe, where such little portraits become too easily detached from their owners, a question tends to revolve around *who* is represented in the portrait. When this question can be truly answered, certain key issues—for example, in *The Italian* the question of identity—can be definitively settled.

In *Frankenstein*, the identity of the woman represented is never long in doubt, but it is irrelevant. When the Monster approaches the child he will murder, what establishes little William's identity is not the miniature, which the Monster sees only after he has killed William, but, literally, the name of the father, which William invokes as a threat, though an empty one. In one sense, identity here *is* the name of the father, not only for William but also for Victor and his creation; and, far from acting to protect its bearer, the identity invoked serves to mark its bearer for destruction. But in this text, such identity seems to be reserved for men. Women, on the other hand, not only have been "birthed" into the families where they live by means other than mothers; they are also, unlike men, all easily detachable from their fathers. While the miniature portrait does not determine identity, it does appear to represent, though not possess, a certain negative power: it acts as badge of death. That is, while the name of the father *invokes* death, motivates murder (and, in the case of William, recoils and doubles back as a curse rebounding to its utterer), the portrait of the mother *represents* the threat. "Read" in turn by the Monster and the magistrates who will condemn Justine, in each case it reinforces murderous intentions. But like the murdered woman on the bed, it never tells its own story. Like Fuseli's painting, the introduction to *Frankenstein* places the reader in the position of voyeur. But here the reader gazes both at the dreaming woman and, unlike the spectator of the painting, also at her terrified dream surrogate, the "pale student of unhallowed arts." Within the text of the novel the reader is offered two coexisting alternatives: on the one hand s/he is encouraged to identify with that "pale student," that "artist," surrogate for the sleeping woman, here become Victor Frankenstein. On the other hand, in the later scene, the reader is invited, with Frankenstein, to gaze at the woman, who becomes opaque like Fuseli's dreamer, thrown across the bed. On the one hand, that is, the novel offers its readers narcissistic identification with the dreamer; on the other hand, fetishistic scopophilia.[22] If the woman on the bed, the dreaming author Mary Shelley, dreams the image of a man, that man, himself become now the speaking subject and dreamer, sees a woman, revealed to be both mother and lover:

> I thought I saw Elizabeth, in the bloom of health, walking in the streets of Ingolstadt. Delighted and surprised, I embraced her; but as I imprinted the first kiss on her lips, they became livid with the hue of death; her features appeared to change, and I thought that I held the corpse of my dead mother in my arms; a shroud enveloped her form, and I saw the grave-worms crawling in the folds of the flannel. (p. 58)

His later embrace of Elizabeth's corpse echoes this gesture: "I rushed towards her and embraced her with ardour; but the deadly languor and coldness of the limbs told me, that what I now held in my arms had ceased to be the Elizabeth whom I had loved and cherished" (p. 196).

Several points might be made here. First of all, in terms of the string of substitutions—Victor's mother for Elizabeth for Mary Shelley—the reader's vision of Mary Shelley's dream of the male "artist" becomes its precise inversion, its mirror image, a vision of the man's dream of the woman on the bed, Mary Shelley in her introduction. As in Radcliffe, in spite of the gender of the author and very possibly the reader, the spectator undergoes a somewhat surprising gender change; for the bearer of the look is evidently coded male, as Mulvey suggests is generally the case in film. The function of the object of (the audience/reader's) gaze also changes as its gender changes. Mulvey suggests that in film, the man as bearer of the gaze serves to advance action, while the woman as object of the gaze serves to stop it. This novel codes the function of gender similarly: because the dreaming Victor Frankenstein has already been established as teller of the tale and speaking subject, he can quickly resume that role even though momentarily we view him as dreamer; for we then see his dream through his eyes. But the body of the woman at the climax of the novel serves only to paralyze action. The film dramatizes this function of the woman's body in the set tableau where Elizabeth's body and the (carefully arranged) dishevelled room appear frozen, while the Monster moves off one edge of the film and Frankenstein and company move onto the other edge. Action appears to circulate *around* the large, still center of the room and the woman's body. But as in Fuseli's painting, the woman, displayed as the object of men's gaze, threatens to evoke the anxiety she signifies.[23] If, for the reader of Frankenstein, the dreaming man has come to replace the dreaming woman writer, the body of the woman remains on the bed as a threatening reminder of her sexual and physical presence.

In general, the body of "woman" on the screen becomes a fetishized object, a fetishizing that helps to neutralize the threat that that body suggests; and the supine body of Elizabeth in the *Frankenstein* film provides an excellent example of that. The novel charts a similar fetishizing as it traces the effect of the miniature portrait of the mother, the dead woman who has taken the place of the living Elizabeth viewed by Frankenstein in the earlier scene. As representation of the threat of death, even this miniaturized and fetishized object retains its power to evoke anxiety. In psychoanalytic literature, death and castration often become equivalents, substitutes for one another.[24] And the threat that the mother's portrait evokes is made manageable not only by reducing and objectifying it but also by reading it as a mirror image of the desires of male characters in the novel.

The fetishized woman in the miniature is the only mother within the inner narrative of this novel (Mrs. Saville, the recipient of Walton's letters, has "lovely children," according to Walton [p. 213]; but she is far removed from these events). More generally, she suggests that "mother" who in this novel is everywhere implied though rarely made explicit. While as fetish object, her represented form reinforces the desires of men, her implied but unrepresented presence elsewhere, both unspeaking and unspoken, haunts the novel, as its readers have often suggested. Critics who stress the presence of the author's mother in this novel tend to write in a different register from those who stress the presence of her father.

The presence of Mary Shelley's literary and biological fathers in *Frankenstein* is explicit, suggested by its strong male presence, not only in its male protagonist and narrators but also by the father-son relationships between Victor and his father, and Victor and the Monster. By contrast with the many stories told by men in the text, women seem unable to construct coherent narratives.[25] Critics have noted the significance of father-daughter relationships in terms of the author's relationship with her own father, explicitly worked out here in parallels between this novel and William Godwin's *Caleb Williams*.[26] Similarly, critics have noted the presence of Milton as Mary Shelley's literary father; a perverse reading of *Paradise Lost*, *Frankenstein* too is the story of the creation of life.[27]

Though Mary Wollstonecraft may have had a comparable influence on her daughter, readers have noted especially a "mother" in this text who is more generalized, less particularized than the presence of either Godwin or Milton, Shelley's biological and literary fathers.[28] The miniaturized mother exists as a ghostly presence, literally a ghost in Victor's dream just after the creation scene. Other women in the novel hardly exist as characters and, in terms of the plot, appear mainly in order to get killed; their very presence warns of impending death. Murky and phantasmal, the mother is rather a presiding, haunting presence than an active participant in the drama, perceptible in the implicit issues with which the novel deals: giving birth in both a literal and a literary sense.

The haunting presence of the mother, like "voice" in *The Italian*, suggests that unrepresentable, ineffable presence figured by *Frankenstein*'s nameless and unspeakable Monster. On the one hand, such an "ineffable" presence, like the voice, holds a certain privilege over what is representable, in the sense that it is less controllable precisely because unnamed; one cannot pin it down. While representation can be a strategy for fixing and confining (and thereby subjecting what is represented to the gaze of interpretation), what cannot be spoken retains its power by its very mystery. Besides, the body of the Monster, a distorted representation of the human figure, typifies representation generally in its imperfection. As in *The Italian*, here too storytelling itself is suspect. The Monster as narrator embodies and represents the psychic fragmentation of the next narrator, Victor Frankenstein; Walton, who frames Victor's narrative, is the least fragmented, but his firsthand narrative presents less of the story. Or, to look at the picture in reverse, concentric circles of narrative lead the reader only toward more fragmentation, figured finally by the body of the narrator in the innermost circle, the Monster; as the fragmentation of the story is patched by successive narrators, the fragmentation appears to become displaced onto the narrator's body. As in Radcliffe, the novel's method of insetting tale within tale suggests that the nature of narrative is fragmented, disjointed, incoherent. "Coherence" becomes a fiction that the reader imposes.

Given the imperfection of the physical world and the necessary limitations of representation, the mother's "ineffable" presence, which escapes such confinement, may appear in some respects privileged. Such privilege clearly limits itself. But if the outermost narrator, the "Mary Shelley" of the introduction, chooses the same course as that pale masculine student she has dreamed, she reminds us of her sexual and physical presence in that haunting maternal figure, the woman on the bed, whose subversive, threatening presence finally tells its own story.

CHAPTER 4

Charlotte Brontë's Post-Gothic Gothic

The novels of Charlotte Brontë obviously are not "Gothic"—nor for that matter is *Frankenstein*—if the term is strictly understood as an historical designation.[1] What has been understood as "Gothic" in Brontë has been vaguely associated with certain devices and conventions common to her work and the older genre: the dark, Byronic hero-villain, for example, or the maiden (sometimes as protagonist), or the presence of the supernatural (sometimes in the form of ghosts which are later explained, sometimes in the form of a prevailing presence hovering over the whole), or secrets (which often tend to concern the mistreatment of women, as has less often been recognized).[2]

How do we read Brontë's use of what we designate as "Gothic"? One traditional approach has been to argue that Brontë recasts such modes "realistically"—and hence subordinates Gothic conventions to a superior mode.[3] But critics who stress that Brontë pushes Gothic images and forms toward realism tend to construct arguments excusing or totalizing devices and techniques in Brontë that they more easily dismiss in the more extravagant, and less valorized, texts of Radcliffe or Shelley: her artistry is established at the expense of those Gothic mothers she invokes.

I would like to propose an alternative reading of Brontë's "Gothic." Her novels take advantage of the potential of earlier Gothic novels to call into question the authority of narrative vision, especially by foregrounding "vision" as a figure for narrative. This foregrounding is linked to certain thematic material in the texts, especially the issue of women's silence and self-effacement, against which the text juxtaposes another Radcliffean interest: performance. Nowhere are these concerns more evident, with this particular linkage of the formal and thematic, than in *Villette*.

Let me first suggest more specifically some of the limitations of such earlier discussions of Brontë's novels as an advancement toward psychological realism, in terms of an often-critiqued scene from *Jane Eyre*. When, pacing back and forth on the third story of Thornfield, Jane hears the strange laugh which she supposes to be Grace Poole at "high noon," she tells us that "no circumstance of ghostliness accompanied the curious cachinnation"; and when Grace appears, she says that "any apparition less romantic or less ghostly could scarcely be conceived."[4] Taken "straight," that remark recalls the moment from the brink of Gothic extravagance.[5] But to read this scene as an "advancement" toward realism reinforces a hierarchy which makes less visible the issues of reading and writing as a woman textualized here. Valorizing a "realistic" mode ignores the narrative's use of Gothic specularity and naturalizes the text as a kind of transparent window. It diverts attention from the narrative vision itself.

On the other hand, surely the eerie laughter that Jane hears, both at this point and a page or two later when she is looking out over the roof of Thornfield, is calculated to inspire both her and the reader with something like "Gothic terror," however much Jane attempts to reassure herself and us. The "apparition" of the ordinary Grace Poole in juxtaposition with the laugh which Jane has heard is precisely what places Jane in the position of spectator of the uncanny: Grace's homely appearance, witnessed by Jane, backs the scene into the un-homely—and blurs rather than asserts the division between "realism" and "Gothic."

If, then, Brontë conjures up an older Gothic mode, she writes that mode into a reinforcing juxaposition—not a depreciative opposition—of "realism" and "romance."[6] I would attribute the power of such scenes not to the subjection of an inferior Gothic cliché to a more authentic realism but to the uncanny disjunction between what is ordinary and familiar and what is strange and terrible, to the undoing of their opposition. Brontë defies easy confinement to conventional modes of writing because in her texts these two modes tend to deconstruct one another. The often-noted incoherence of *Villette* may have as much to do with its decentering of "Gothic" as with its plot.

Issues which both *Villette* and *Jane Eyre* thematize—the terms by which bourgeois women in nineteenth-century England (and Europe) can be seen to have been "oppressed"—suggest why writing as a woman under those circumstances was (and perhaps may continue to be) problematic. Unlike the novels of Radcliffe or Shelley, where anger at women's oppression is more heavily cloaked and coded, here it is explicit. This explicit anger is what Matthew Arnold recognized when he spoke of *Villette* as "disagreeable" because "the writer's mind contains nothing but hunger, rebellion, and rage,"[7] and what Virginia Woolf recognized when she echoed him in saying that *Jane Eyre* must have been written "in a rage."[8] In rewriting "Gothic" to impinge directly on this "rage," Brontë exploits visual metaphors for narrative which she represents as linked with gendered (power) relations. Self-consciously directing the "gentle reader's" attention to performance-as-text, Brontë's "Gothic" suggests how the text might be read as a kind of performance. The first-person narrators of *Villette* and *Jane Eyre* obsessively reflect on their own double relationship to the tale being told. They are driven forward by the issue of how a woman, who has been well taught by her cultural circumstances to link her gendered self-definition with silence and self-effacement, can speak, and what it might mean for a woman to (re)present herself (as a woman).

As I have been arguing, Gothic narrative teaches its reader specific modes of objectifying and interpreting "woman," while destablizing the readings it invites—as all texts destabilize themselves, but specifically here in ways which invoke a visual metaphor for narrative, then subvert the authority of the spectator and the gendered implications of that authority. If this mode provided a narrative vocabulary of thematic and formal possibilities which women writers almost immediately employed as ways of meditating on what it meant to write as a woman, then one might see such texts as *Jane Eyre* and *Villette* as clarifying and expanding the grammars within which such a vocabulary might be used by stretching the limits of these possibilities. Brontë's deconstruction of the opposition between "realism" and "romance" breaks this vocabulary out of its confinement to one particular kind of formula novel, written in one specific thirty-year period, and makes it—subject to other historical moments—available to other writers whose texts reflect on the issue of what it means to write as a woman. Sometimes gazing at the very same figures, images, and set scenes that Radcliffe's narrators observed—the convent, nightmare, woman-as-spectacle—Brontë's first-person narrators focus attention on the doubleness of their "vision," as they objectify themselves as part of what-is-looked-at. Observers observing themselves interacting with others, as well as observing eyes through whose vision the story forms itself, these narrators offer the issue of "vision" as a metaphor for narrative. And while Radcliffe and Shelley tease their readers by inviting them to read their texts as staged scenes, Brontë self-consciously plays with *self*-stagings. Like Gothic texts generally, these novels tend to function by allowing set tableaux to emerge from a swirl of narrative.[9]

This multi-positioned, multi-angled gaze of the individual narrator, who in these texts is gendered "woman," suggests how masculine authority might be both defined and defied. Repressive though this gaze may be, it is not unitary—and so opens up a space for resistance in its undermining of central authority.[10] As opposed to the panoptic gaze of Foucault, which must be dreaded even as it is internalized, the gaze of which I am speaking is itself passionately, desperately desired. Although Lucy Snowe calls herself "a mere looker-on at life," her phrase is doubly deceptive: first, because she is as much looked *at* as looking; and second, because the text repeatedly teaches its reader that the position of a "looker-on," while precarious, is hardly "mere."[11]

In *Villette*, two modes of storytelling compete with one another, public and private, both associated with spectacle and the position of the observer. Lucy Snowe holds her position of authority—and is enabled to be narrator—because she watches what goes on about her so closely. In perhaps the first feminist consideration of *Villette*, Kate Millett noted that Lucy is "a pair of eyes watching society"; she watches men and women alike.[12] But here the whole issue of watching and being watched is fraught with significance. The novel plays a game where power keeps changing, depending on who is being observed and who is doing the observing.

Lucy becomes conscious of the issue of surveillance practically from the moment she begins to head toward the town of Villette; and "surveillance" from the outset is linked with what is foreign and, it quickly becomes clear, Roman Catholic. On the boat bringing her from England to the continent, Lucy reflects:

> Foreigners say that it is only English girls who can thus be
> trusted to travel alone, and deep is their wonder at the daring

confidence of English parents and guardians. As for the "jeunes Miss," by some their intrepidity is pronounced masculine and inconvenant, others regard them as the passive victims of an educational and theological system which wantonly dispenses with proper "surveillance." (p. 48)

Proper "surveillance" here is perceived to have the effect of warding off such "masculine" characteristics as "intrepidity"; so Madame Beck's constant spying evidently is an important duty in bringing up her charges to be properly feminine. In part at least, this surveillance is evidently internalized (as Foucault would suggest) to place oneself under the guard of self-observation. A properly watched "jeune Miss," the passage implies, would find herself incapable of taking such a journey. But its internalizing is only partial, however; for Lucy testifies that (at least in the case of one of Mme Beck's young daughters) it fails to work "the whole cure." Surveillance begets more surveillance and lies. What is the "original sin"? Do lies make surveillance necessary? Or does surveillance generate lies? Though the novel does not answer these questions, it does make the point that the cycle of surveillance and lies is self-perpetuating, generating new patterns of surveillance and lies. Being part of society implies being contained within this self-perpetuating cycle. Lucy's gaze at Ginevra Fanshawe on the boat initiates contact between them and momentarily breaks Lucy's isolation.

Clearly Lucy is attracted to this whole system of surveillance, as she is attracted to the entire foreign "package" which includes Catholicism. Thrust into this world of ongoing espionage, Lucy plays the part of spy as well. Accustomed to having her belongings, her written letters, and her person constantly under the eyes of someone at the *pensionnat*, chiefly Mme Beck or Paul, Lucy herself does not scruple to open a letter which by accident finds itself at her feet, and which she (correctly) takes to be a *billet doux* (p. 103).

Lucy must be comfortable in her role as spy, for that is the role she must play in order to be a narrator. Her attainment of a speaking voice depends on her easy fit into the world of Villette, where confession and surveillance are part of everyday existence. Her horror at lies, spying, and Romanism mask her strong attraction to just these things, all of which become figures for narrative in the text. Lucy's contemptuous remarks about spying and lying fill out the pattern of anti-Catholic sentiment in the novel, one of the many themes connecting this novel with Gothic fiction of the late eighteenth century, where Catholicism is similarly associated with surveillance and lies; but as in the earlier fiction, here too such contempt hides fascination and attraction. As in Radcliffe's *The Italian*, the symbol in which these three terms converge is the confessional.

In *Villette* too, confession signifies a story; but the confessional appears humanized, less mystical—less a sign of an external and internal censor of behavior than a place which offers human contact. It acts as the sign of a story to be told, like the confessional in *The Italian*. But that one motivated the onlooker by titillating him or her with the chance to gaze voyeuristically at a private sin and to participate in turning that sin into a public shame. Here an audience is not the dread of the "penitent" Lucy, but rather a hope which this confessional offers. As a paradigmatic instance of the relationship between the narrator and reader of a text, the confessional suggests a mode of storytelling—an intimate relationship which plays against the "public" mode suggested in *Villette* by acting. The confessional suggests an "oral" mode of storytelling, alternative to the "visual" metaphors elsewhere employed; it also acts as the locus where the one is transformed into the other as "surveillance" is here turned verbal.

Attempting to convert Lucy, the old priest to whom Lucy wanders during her night of delirium evidently recognizes her attraction to the religion she disdains. But Lucy goes to confession not to confess a sin but to find sympathetic human contact through the telling of her own story. This is what she achieves in her narrative as a whole. The dark of the confessional figures that internal split in Lucy that enables her to become a narrator. Lucy begins her confession by telling the priest that she is a Protestant, as if that is the sin she has come to confess. In a sense it is, because her Protestantism acts as a sign of her Englishness in a foreign world, a symbol of that Otherness that isolates her, relegates her to the outside. But just as she easily slips into her role as spy, she similarly finds herself attracted to the position of the one being spied upon; she is almost desperate to be the focus of someone else's gaze.

The prototype of this scene is that scene in *Frankenstein* where the Monster, alienated and alone, having learned over a period of time how people act in the society he wishes to join, approaches old Mr. De Lacey. Another analogue to both scenes is of course the moment in *Jane Eyre* when Jane seeks admittance to the Rivers family. In all three instances, a period of observation is followed by an attempt to gain admittance; for Brontë, both attempts result in a family discovery which would appear to be overly coincidental. But perhaps the clue to the logic of these scenes is to be found in that careful watching, which both reveals and conceals a secret relationship. Appropriately, the Frankenstein Monster, who has not been conceived in the usual way, fails to find any relationship when he approaches the family.

In *Villette*, Lucy finds a more compassionate greeting than had the Monster; and she herself decides not to follow up her contact with the priest. But her bid to find human solace is rewarded; her contact with the old priest leads indirectly to her discovery by Dr. John and to the revelation of her real connection with his family. If the theological purpose of confession is the reconciliation of a broken bond, Lucy's confession achieves that purpose, no matter what coincidences this plot needs to devise for the sacrament's efficacy to be attained.

If confession is the signifier of a story, so too is the nightmare that provokes it. The mysterious scene of Lucy's confession, which acts as a pivot in the plot by concluding with Lucy's reuniting with the Brettons, also prefigures the later climactic scene where, half-drugged, she again dream-walks through the streets of Villette to see the bizarre festival where all the principal characters assemble. The significance of Lucy's confession becomes especially evident in terms of its association with sleep and dreaming. In the scene where Lucy makes her strange confession, she is driven by a delirium announced by one of her nightmares, one of those she describes by a sea image: "a cup was forced to my lips, black, strong, strange, drawn from no well, but filled up seething from a bottomless and boundless sea" (p. 148). Lucy describes her dream as suggesting a sense of isolation, alienation, and despair about her future: "Methought the well-loved dead, who had loved *me* well in life, met me elsewhere, alienated; galled was my inmost spirit with an unutterable sense of despair about the future." Lucy's nightmare rewrites the scene of the woman on the bed, but with a difference. Like Mary Shelley's dream, Lucy's gives impetus to the telling of a tale, which here in itself is clearly recognized as an act fraught with terror.

This association of storytelling and nightmare, and the stakes it entails, become clarified in terms of the similar association of the two in *Jane Eyre*. For some time, readers of *Jane Eyre* have been aware of Bertha's doubling of Jane,[13] a doubling emphasized in the scene where Bertha assumes the bridal veil which Jane is to wear. The moment of (mis)recognition which takes place as Jane looks into the mirror at Bertha's face—like Perseus, she sees only the reflected face of the monster—allows Jane to dissociate herself from the "fearful and ghastly" face she sees, to split it from herself rather than to identify herself with Bertha's face. Jane has similarly dissociated herself from the image of her own face in the mirror in the earlier red-room scene. That scene, like this one where she sees the reflected face of Bertha, suggests a refusal of self-mastery and "identity," which—in Lacanian terms—ought to be established through (mis)recognition.[14] A similar moment of non-recognition occurs in *Villette*, when Lucy catches a glimpse of herself in a mirror, dressed up, in the company of Mrs. Bretton and Graham, as "a third person in a pink dress and black lace mantle" (p. 197). Thus by the logic of Lacanian theory, as well as of earlier Anglo-American feminist criticism (which suggests how boundaries between characters are blurred), we understand how this instance undercuts rather than supports the possibility of Jane's definition of a "self."

Awakening from her nightmarish faint after her night of confession, Lucy Snowe also sees herself in a mirror, looking spectral in the uncanny setting of her godmother's living room. Here, a mirror provides the entrance for her step back into her childhood world. Later, when dressed in her pink finery, Lucy catches a reflected sight of herself and her party as strangers, she finds the experience disconcerting (p. 198). Lucy's view of herself is consistently a disclaimer which splits her into a speaking subject and an object; she is not a "self," as Ginevra suggests by describing her only in terms of what she is not (she is not Ginevra, though her double, just as Jane Eyre is not really Bertha), surveying them both in "a great looking glass in the dressing room" (p. 134). "Who are you?" Ginevra asks her at one point; and Lucy echoes the same question to another of her doubles, the ghostly nun: "Who are you?" Lucy might similarly echo Ginevra's next question: "Are you anyone?" But if mirrors in these texts deny a self, they also establish sufficient distance for commentary—the ground on which an author can stand—as well as proximity.

Bertha is put in place as Jane's double not only in terms of their similar positions in the marriage plot, their similar roles in Rochester's life, but also through the image of the nightmare, which becomes a fluid medium through which they exchange positions. And "nightmare" acts as signpost to repression. According to Blanche Ingram, governesses (with Jane as prime example) are "incubi" (p. 205). The dissociation which Jane affirms between herself and the spectacle of woman-as-horror—in contrast with the reading shared by Blanche Ingram and the twentieth-century reader—is clearly marked by a sexual difference: Jane's virginal purity contrasts with the voracious lust Rochester imputes to Bertha. And this dissociation, particularly if read through the slippages and substitutions current criticism indicates, suggests the terms under which Jane is allowed to tell her own story. If Bertha as nightmare represents the repressed embodiment of Jane's erotic desire and animal nature, Bertha's repression, and her very existence, indicate the only terms under which the Gothic maiden might be allowed a voice: what she personifies is explicitly repressed, later killed off, as a sacrifice to Jane's position. Rochester's attempt to make Jane his wife by denying his first marriage doubles within the plot of the narrative a movement of the text itself: Jane is permitted to hold a subject position at the expense of Bertha, who assumes the position of spectacle for Jane, and through Jane for Rochester, who as the audience to her story doubles the reader within the text.

But Jane as the woman-on-the-bed is no opaque figure like *Frankenstein*'s Elizabeth, nor is she the fetishized supine figure which stops narrative action. As she resisted Rochester's attempt to bedeck her with clothes and jewels—his desire to see her "glittering like a parterre" (p. 296)—she actively refuses to be appropriated to the male gaze.[15] And at the apparition of Bertha, hers is the narrative voice which sees and attempts to read.

Jane's nightmare vision of Bertha is presented as a narrative within the narrative: Jane is recounting the story of her nightmare vision to Rochester, as the climax of a series of bad dreams she has had, this one breaking the sleep boundary which safely confines dreams. The text insists on Jane's position as narrator by giving her a double function as such: Jane here is not only the text's narrator but also the teller of the inner story. Within this context, Bertha functions as symbol. More than she represents herself, she represents the series of bad dreams Jane has had, the literal embodiment of "nightmare" itself, like the Frankenstein Monster. Read in the context of Jane's other haunting dreams, the vision which Jane confronts functions much like the spectre which haunts the woman in Fuseli's painting. But this time not only the dreamer but also this nightmare is gendered a woman. Like a nightmare, the vision of Bertha invites, even demands, the interpretation which she defies. Besides terror, Jane's reaction is to demand an explanation—a "reading" from Rochester, whom she takes to be the authoritative reader. But like Fuseli's *Nightmare,* Bertha as nightmare vision is not quite readable. Or, more accurately, she can be read (to Jane, to us at that point) only as something female which inspires terror. In some detail Jane describes Bertha's "ghastly" appearance, her "red eyes" and "fearful blackened inflation of the lineaments" (p. 311). The point of this description is not to differentiate her as a character (with a narrative of her own) but to make her readable as woman and monster. And while the text later "explains" her significance for Jane and the reader by providing her with a narrative context, she retains for Rochester the significance with which she was first invested. (Mis)read by Rochester, she never becomes more than the embodiment of entrapment and terror.

Over a hundred years later, another woman writer, Jean Rhys in *Wide Sargasso Sea,* would finally permit Bertha Rochester to tell her own story. Rhys's novel acts in obvious ways as a twentieth-century critique and reading of Brontë's: a rewriting of Gothic (re)vision which stresses Bertha/Antoinette's oscillating roles as both object of vision and subversive narrator, rather than Jane's.[16] But I think that Brontë's move here is similar to Rhys's, though less obvious: a rereading, critique, and rewriting of Radcliffe in particular, and perhaps of other writers (such as Shelley) who followed in her path.

This scene clarifies the enormous stakes at work in the repression of storytelling and sexuality (the two of them linked) that are at work here—and, I think, in *Villette*. Tremendous psychic energy is at work in burying the narrative. Brontë anticipates Freud in seeing sleep as the window on narratives which would otherwise be entirely inaccessible. The role of the father-confessor is obviously analogous to that of a psychoanalyst.[17] In both *Jane Eyre* and *Villette*, the story is told to a man whose job is to interpret and defuse terror, though neither Jane nor Lucy remain satisfied with the masculinist response, which in both cases clearly serves only the special interests of such masculine readers as the priest or Rochester.

What appears, then, to be a merely associative relationship between confession and nightmare becomes more than that, as the two are clearly linked through their relationship with storytelling. Read as a psychoanalytic narrative (rather than through a theological register), Lucy's confession leads to a kind of cure, a rebirth for her, but only through a regression to an infantile state. Helpless and childlike, she is cared for by Mrs. Bretton, her surrogate mother from the novel's earlier chapters; and by the end of the chapter, she makes another confession, this one to the reader only, of her infantile voraciousness: "'Do not let me think of them too often, too much, too fondly,' I implored; 'let me be content with a temperate draught of this living stream'" (p. 167). Lucy has awakened from one nightmare into an uncanny dream, where people and objects from her past are oddly reconstituted; and her recognition strikes her with a sense of the *heimlich* made *unheimlich*.[18] "Reader, I felt alarmed!" she tells us, because "these articles of furniture could not be real, solid armchairs, looking-glasses, and washstands—they must be the ghosts of such articles; or...there remained but to conclude that I had myself passed into an abnormal state of mind" (p. 158). One (perverse) way of reading the novel might be to suggest that the whole narrative acts as a frame for that later "nightmare" moment when the fevered and delirious Lucy wanders the streets—a discursive explanation for the figure of a woman unaccountably wandering alone at night. She awakens to, and by means of, a psychoanalytic reconstruction of her own childhood which "explains" how she has gotten to that point. At the novel's end, the image of Lucy walking alone motivates a surreal confrontation, just as it had earlier, at Mrs. Bretton's home, where Lucy visually again confronts her own past.

These tableaux of the characters who have dominated her life at Villette—one tableau composed of the De Bassompierres and the Brettons, the other of Mme Beck, Mme Walravens, and their relatives—act as a sort of operatic finale to the narrative at this point. These tableaux reveal to Lucy "the TRUTH" (p. 438), which she here describes as "a homely web" (p. 435)—a description she herself suggests to be fraught with significance, since she stops over it to suggest that the girl Justine Marie, who embodies this deceptive "truth," is anything but homely. The materialization of the young Justine Marie resembles the apparition of Grace Poole in the scene where Jane hears Bertha's eerie laugh: for both Lucy and Jane, women are introduced who literally "embody" deceptively obvious answers to the question plaguing the narrator. Both are evidently "homely" answers—and yet both suggest how the homely, as Freud suggests, backs into its opposite.

If Justine Marie embodies "the TRUTH," at the same time she both answers and refuses another question Lucy ponders: who or what is "the NUN" Lucy keeps seeing? The other "Justine Marie," for whom she is named and of whom she is the uncanny representation, is the obvious answer, if only the register of the narrative shifted ever so slightly to allow for spiritualistic possibilities. And in fact, the apparition of the real Justine Marie just barely precedes the revelation of the answer to the second question. Her "homely" appearance, as part of Lucy's sleepwalking dream vision, clears the way for revealing the identity of the nun Lucy has seen—ironically, lying in Lucy's bed. What seems to be going on here is a kind of dance, where "TRUTH," "NUN," "nightmare," "Justine Marie," all slide into and out of each other.[19] These terms act as interchangeable signifiers of one another; and while the narrative proposes no "transcendental signifier," what they finally point to is the emptiness where a woman's body should be but which is, in fact, here a blank space.

But the intrepid Lucy confronts this blankness unblinking. Lucy creates a terrific parody of the masculinist move to fragment the woman's body physically or visually or both. As she puts it: "I tore her up—the incubus! I held her on high—the goblin! I shook her loose—the mystery! And down she fell—down all round me—down in shreds and fragments—and I trod upon her" p. 440). Her very sentence structure is fragmented, as the text participates in literalizing what might elsewhere, in other texts, be figurative. In a comic reversal of the move that creates a fetish to substitute for woman's "lack," Lucy literally dismantles the space that contains it, as she also comically revises our "nightmare" scene by going to sleep, finally, with the nun's clothes under her pillow.

If *Jane Eyre* achieves her speaking voice at the sacrifice of another woman (who becomes the feared object of vision), *Villette* in some ways is more subversive, both because it undermines the expectations set up by its adherence to several narrative modes at once and also because its mode of subverting these expectations depends directly on the relationship set up between the narrative gaze and what it sees. If *Jane Eyre* could find her voice at the expense of Bertha, Lucy struggles much harder to find a way to deal with the women she watches so intently, a struggle that figures the textual movement of how women negotiate the space between being appropriated by the gaze and discourse of others (on the one hand), and (on the other) being the gazing spectator and the generator of discourse. *Villette* may be most subversive in its struggle around this issue.

The scene where Lucy acts in M. Paul's "vaudeville" wonderfully suggests the complexity of this problem. Lucy has just been relating how her dress for Madame Beck's "fete" has been calculated to make her into a kind of shadow—not for her the gossamer white dresses of the students. Her choice of a "dun mist" dress for the day makes her less conspicuous by making her look different from the others—for she *is* different; she is not a young girl or a student. Her colleague Zélie St. Pierre, dressing like her young charges, in the eyes of Lucy and Madame Beck makes herself conspicuous, ironically, by attempting to fit in, by dressing like the girls. We have to see Lucy as different from the others in order to understand the implications of that "difference"—which we can read as what makes a woman-as-writer "different," both from other women (who are not writers) and from other writers (who are not women)—to see how her part in the play is not the same as the parts of the others, who are girls acting the parts of girls. But they are not producing an art or representing themselves; they are acting as they are expected to act in a play which is the conception of a man, M. Paul. Lucy's part characterizes a woman's problem in producing art in contrast to the roles played by the other girls and women in the text: Mme Beck as audience, the young students, or even Zélie St. Pierre, whose role is to carry out men's orders.

The situation under which Lucy produces her "art" is instructive: she prepares it confined to a prison, exiled from all company and half-starved. Circumstances that are treated with pathos in Lucy's life—she is alone, isolated; she actually could starve to death—are treated comically here. Of course Lucy's boldest move, and the most telling, is her donning of men's clothing on stage from the waist up, while she adamantly refuses such a costume from the waist down. Lucy's ambivalently gendered dress is not really androgynous or bisexed but alternately sexed, like a reversing figure. The audience sees a woman dressed partly as a man and partly as a woman wooing a woman.[20] She retains the accoutrements of her female sexuality in the lower half of her body while taking on a man's character in the upper part.

Lucy's acceptance of ambivalent sexuality in the art of drama remarkably resembles her creator's assumption of her androgynous pseudonym. As Brontë describes it:

We had very early cherished the dream of one day being authors.... We agreed to arrange a small selection of our poems, and, if possible, get them printed. Averse to personal publicity, we veiled our own names under those of Currer, Ellis, and Acton Bell; the ambiguous choice being dictated by a sort of conscientious scruple at assuming Christian names, positively masculine, while we did not like to declare ourselves women, because—without at the time suspecting that our mode of writing and thinking was not what is called "feminine"—we had a vague impression that authoresses are liable to be looked on with prejudice.[21]

Like "Currer Bell," Lucy refuses to put herself before the public as a man. Why? Because it would be dishonest? One gets the sense that any "conscientious scruple" that Lucy might have, like Brontë, is more likely to be concerned with its being indecent than dishonest. But what's more important still is that Lucy—

again, like her creator?—fears looking ridiculous by posing as a man. As a woman donning a man's clothing or a man's name, a woman becomes simply silly, someone trying to resemble what she cannot be, attempting to fool the public but becoming instead the fool herself. But the exigencies of the situation, for Brontë as for Lucy, require the accoutrements of a man. Lucy and Brontë retain a measure of control by acquiescing to this requirement, saying in effect to their audiences: "You know and *I* know that I'm not a man; I'm not trying to be; but you see that I must take this role for now. We are in on this joke together." Rather than the fool, she becomes instead the comic. The compromises which both Brontë and Lucy effect have not always been perceived as altogether happy—both have occasioned much distress for readers—but are perhaps the best that might be expected under the circumstances. Is this a "woman's art"? As Lucy's costume and Currer Bell's name indicate, possibly neither man's nor woman's: neither Lucy nor Brontë is either man nor his mirror image. That is to say, in her very ambivalence, she may perhaps escape being confined to a gender which can only define itself in terms of the other. And the "art" that Lucy invents provides a wonderfully paradigmatic instance of how subversive feminist art might constitute itself.

Choosing this comic role immediately liberates Lucy to indulge the wit she diplays in the text far more to the reader than to the characters in the novel. She turns upon her sneering colleague St. Pierre, who has attempted to force her to look ridiculous by wearing the masculine attire, telling her "that if she were not a lady and I a gentleman, I should feel disposed to call her out" (p. 129). Her transformation into an ambivalently gendered person gives her a measure of liberation especially in dealing with women; and she is freed not simply because she is disguised and playing a role but because the role is that of a man, however fatuous. Lucy avails herself of certain masculine codes of behavior that empower her, not as a man but as a woman playing a man's role. In the person of her "fat" character, she makes love to Ginevra Fanshawe. In her outrageously flamboyant performance, Lucy in effect rewrites the script as the product of two women who appear as lovers in a parody of a play which originally was the conception of a man.

In their scripted but script-defying lovemaking, Lucy and Ginevra defy hierarchies implicit in heterosexual romances. Directing attention to the artifice of what she is doing, Lucy's performance resembles Luce Irigaray's mimicry of patriarchal logic in *Speculum de l'autre femme*: imitating and marked by male discourse, she makes available a "feminine" logic in its blank spaces. Fostered by imprisonment and starvation, scripted and directed by men, Lucy's performance triumphantly becomes a woman's art which rewrites the terms into which women are forced, not by ignoring or transcending masculine discourse but by using it deliberately and calling attention to its fictiveness.

While Lucy is the author of this artistic victory, Ginevra Fanshawe's supporting role is important, not only in enabling its success but also in illustrating how Lucy's (read: a woman's) function as artistic creator differs from a man's. Ginevra, whose behavior under ordinary circumstances aims at pleasing men, here becomes neither an object nor simply malleable material but a co-author with Lucy. Ginevra always has a penchant for play-acting, which she enlists in her and her lover's reenactment of the nun's story for the purpose of carrying on their affair—a comic revision of the "Bleeding Nun" episode in *The Monk*. On stage with Lucy, Ginevra gives Lucy the cue which Lucy can use to turn her unpromising materials into an artistic achievement. Typecast as the coquette, Ginevra breaks through the boundary of the proscenium arch to suggest how the roles she plays both on and off the stage are similarly scripted; and this is the move which is Lucy's cue, to make Dr. John—a man, not another woman as in *Jane Eyre*—the sacrifice to the performance, and to the artistic alliance of Lucy and Ginevra. In this guise, Lucy reverses the conventional move of much masculine-authored fiction of making a woman the sacrifice to the bond between two men in their competition for that woman's affection.[22] Here the same triangle leads to a bond between two women, specifically as artists. Emotionally, this is the closest Lucy ever gets to any of the women in the novel, though her feelings toward Ginevra are ambivalent. In spite of the narcissism and self-absorption she mocks in Ginevra—Lucy's mockery of her seems at once a pretense and a dramatization of her actual distaste for the girl—the younger girl becomes "a sort of heroine" for her, as she remarks during "The Long Vacation." The terminology

Lucy uses is instructive because it suggests that Lucy sees Ginevra as a (masculinist) fictional creation, woman as defined by man, as reflecting man. But as fellow artists, the two are colleagues and friends. They are lovers.

"But it would not do for a mere looker-on at life," Lucy comments afterward (p. 131). Acting becomes an excellent metaphor for a woman's role as artist because as actor, a woman becomes both the object to be looked at and the creative artist. Although Lucy can be an artist who creates herself as object of vision, elsewhere in the novel she reverts to her role as unobtrusive spy. She again becomes observer, not only of women and of men, but also of women cast specifically as art. Readers have commented that in the scene where she visits the museum, she critiques men's conception of what women should be like in the painting of *Cleopatra*, as well as in the didactic series *La vie d'une femme*. But it is also worth remarking that the *Cleopatra* acts for Lucy as a kind of touchstone, provoking responses in men for Lucy's observation. Read that way, the female object of art becomes another ally of Lucy, allowing her voyeuristically to observe an interaction between her and the men provoked by a (representation of a) woman—that is, her provocation of an aesthetic response which is also certainly erotic.

M. Paul is the only spectator analogously interested in the interaction between the painting and a woman-as-spectator, Lucy; his focus is on the same kind of interaction that produces Lucy's interest. Paul sees Lucy's perusal of the painting as evidence of her "temerity"—like that "intrepidity" which English girls have, evidence of her lack of femininity. While she has the "sangfroid" to gaze at the *Cleopatra*, he notes with disdain that she fell ill while caring for the *cretin* left in her charge over the vacation (in complete isolation, he fails to note), an indication of a deficiency in feminine character. She does not have the strength to do what a woman "worthy of the name" ought to do; but she has the temerity to do something only men should be permitted. In vain does Lucy inquire whether he himself could have looked after Marie Broc and note that he too is looking at the painting. Paul thinks the *Cleopatra* to be "une femme superbe," but he would not like her to be his wife or his daughter or his sister. He cannot see her as a woman without casting her into the roles to which he attempts to confine Lucy herself—but which Lucy can usually evade.

Although the foppish elegance of Colonel de Hamal is obviously incapable of making much of the painting at all, because he is a man and the spectator, he can "titter" at *Cleopatra's* threatening sexuality. As with the fop Lucy played in the "vaudeville" (imitating De Hamal), De Hamal's very fatuousness becomes a weapon deployed in diminishing what threatens him. By contrast, Lucy admires Dr. John Graham's reaction to art; his is a refined sensibility. But he too fails the test, as he will fail it at Vashti's performance later. Like Paul he can only compare *Cleopatra* to the women's roles to which he is accustomed. He reduces her threat by domesticating her to the status of women he knows, and by finding her inferior. We know that Lucy is aware of the deficiency of his taste because of the irony with which she reports his remark implying that Ginevra Fanshawe is somehow the evidence of *Cleopatra's* inferiority: "Compare that mulatto with Ginevra!"

Graham's use of the term "mulatto" to describe the *Cleopatra* reveals a facet of the painting only hinted to the reader previously, when Lucy describes her as a "dark-complexioned gypsy-queen" (p. 189). Evidently the painting holds a double threat, racial as well as sexual; and evidently her darkness is directed at emphasizing her sexuality. As with Bertha Mason Rochester, the dark (though "White") daughter of a Creole mother, Brontë buries a racialist issue in the image of a sexy woman of whom her narrator nominally disapproves.

"Nominally," because as with Bertha Mason, the dark woman here shares a bond with the narrator. As she conspired with Ginevra on stage earlier, here her observations of the reactions of the men who look at the picture amount to a tacit conspiracy between the woman in the picture, who becomes her ally, and her. Reporting the reactions of these masculine spectators, Lucy evidently sees them all as lacking in perceptiveness. They are evidently threatened by the sexual power the painting conveys, which they neutralize, every one of them, by trivializing and reducing its large proportions. If a painting serves the function of fetishizing what is threatening, the indistinguishable interpretations of these spectators go a step further in diminishing the vision before them.

Lucy's objection, by contrast, is that it is not large enough—an objection clarified when she reflects on this and other paintings in her observation of the actress whom she calls "Vashti."

This scene makes clear why she has mocked the proportions of the painting: not that they were too large, but that size as a medium at the visual artist's disposal was inadequate for this representation and could only serve the purpose of diminishing, no matter how large it might be. The paintings serve the purpose of fetish objects in Freud's sense. Lucy's disdain for physical proportions as a measure of value acts as a critique of foolish masculinist assessment, like penis measuring. No matter how big the artist has painted his Cleopatra, no matter how many feet of draperies he has placed around her, these proportions are not capable of doing the job of representing the power of a powerful woman, who really eludes size as a measure of greatness:

> Where was the artist of the Cleopatra? Let him come and sit down and study this different vision. Let him seek here the mighty brawn, the muscle, the abounding blood, the full-fed flesh he worshipped: let all materialists draw nigh and look on. (p. 243)

By contrast with the power of a woman whose art is in the process of being acted, a woman painted on a canvas, mighty though she is painted to be (that is, as represented by the gazing man), is merely part of an "army of his [the masculine artist's] fat women." One is tempted to remark the pun on "fat" as used earlier in the novel (as "fatuous")—that is, the "fat" (in the sense of "large") woman becomes a sign and symbol of masculine fatuousness.

Lucy is shocked to find that Graham judges the actress "as a woman, not an artist" (p. 244). I don't think that we are to read Lucy's judgement as evidence that she perceives Vashti to lack femininity—that she does *not* perceive her "as a woman." Lucy means that Graham judges her, as he and Paul (and the "tittering" de Hamal) had judged the *Cleopatra*, in terms of conventional women's roles. But Lucy's remark also suggests a mutual exclusiveness of the terms "woman" and "artist" which doubles the problem of her roles as woman and storyteller.

The actress is "a spectacle," monstrous like the Frankenstein Monster. Like the Frankenstein Monster also, she remains mysteriously nameless; Lucy tells us: "What I saw was the shadow of a royal Vashti: a queen, fair as the day once, turned pale now like twilight, and wasted like wax in flame" (p. 242). "Vashti" is the name Lucy (and Brontë) confer on this powerful actress out of awe, as if her name dare not be spoken. Often read as Brontë's reaction to the French actress Rachel—who would also be the original for the Princess in Eliot's *Daniel Deronda*—Lucy's response to Vashti surrounds her with mystery.[23] The original Vashti, Ahasuerus's queen from the Book of Esther, refused to show herself to the crowds at the behest of the king "to shew the people and the princes her beauty: for she was fair to look on"; the king punishes her by giving her "royal estate unto another that is better than she," and by choosing a new queen. But the biblical passage (Esther I, 1) makes clear that what threatens the king is not only her own disobedience, but also the fear that her insubordination will motivate other women's defiance of their husbands: "For this deed of the queen shall come abroad unto all women, so that they shall despise their husbands in their eyes when it shall be reported." Read into conventional women's roles by Graham, the actress read by Lucy as "Vashti" is a sign of the power of a woman who does as she pleases ("I acted to please myself," Lucy told us in the earlier scene); and in her own self-determination, her very existence becomes a sign of defiance of a patriarchal order. The aborted ending of her performance, often read as an eruption of the passion she has displayed into a literal fire, might also be read as a sign of the threatened chaos which might erupt as Ahasuerus and his "wise men" feared. Vashti's unruly disobedience, which here becomes figured in a woman's performance which defies conventional notions of womanliness, has no end but anarchy.

In that sense, the actress Vashti's performance doubles the movement of the text itself, which invites our interpretive gaze as it defies it. At one point near the beginning, Lucy issues an invitation to the reader: "I will permit the reader to picture me, for the next eight years, as a bark slumbering through halcyon weather, in a harbor still as glass" (p. 31). For Lucy, "the nightmare" is a dream of shipwreck (at this point evidently figurative, though retrospectively we see that the nightmare must be of the literal shipwreck of Lucy's lover Paul): "it repeats the rush and saltness of briny waves in my throat, and their icy pressure on my lungs." Here as elsewhere (especially at the ending), Lucy teases the reader to imagine what s/he will—an invitation which hands authorial authority to the interpretation of the reader. In the erotic tease between Lucy and the reader, Lucy finally surrenders, abdicating her own power as narrator—but in that very move, she escapes the reader's gaze and asserts the power of retaining knowledge to which the reader has no access.

Jane Eyre, despite her resistance to being read by Rochester, finally surrenders to a conventional role, once Rochester's sight has been dimmed—as critics have often noted in a reading that suggests the equivalence of his gaze and the phallus by suggesting that his blinding is a symbolic castration. But by contrast, Lucy manages to have it both ways. Like Vashti's performance, which is not allowed the conventional authored ending but is disrupted, so too is *Villette*. And by inviting the reader to fill in the gaps, Lucy pushes him/her into a "dominant" position which enables her slippery escape, inviting readings attempting to "correct" the incoherence of her narrative. To take a lesson from Jane Eyre, we might instead refuse the invitation and let the incoherence stand.[24]

At one point the text of *Jane Eyre* presents a parable of reading and interpretation, where women's bodies are texts to be read. Rochester as the gypsy attempts to read Jane's physical features. He is baffled by her palm, but he finds her face more legible, especially her eye: "soft and full of feeling...susceptible... where it ceases to smile, it is sad; and unconscious lassitude weighs on the lid: that signifies melancholy resulting from loneliness" (p. 230). Rochester moves to dismantle Jane's threatening gaze; her eye, read by Rochester, becomes something to be read rather than the agent of interpretive vision. Jane and the reader recognize the limits of his reading. Meanwhile, although Jane's eye deceives her about the gypsy's identity, she correctly reads her as a fraud and retains some measure of control because she resists Rochester's invitation to fill in the narrative gaps of the scenes he plays, as she also refuses to be drawn into the narratives which confront her, preferring instead to assimilate them to her own narrative. She refuses the alliance that his woman's dress seems to offer, seeing his clothes as the illusion they are. Although the novel's "happy ending" depends on her (and our) final acquiescence in playing a conventional (male-authored) role, at this point she is a "resisting reader,"[25] deliberately refusing the readings offered by a man—and here a man disguised as a woman.

Offering women the two alternatives of public and private art, *Villette* suggests that ideally a "public" mode best suits a woman who can create herself as art object. Writing, by contrast, seems a poor second-best, confessional, which must do under the intimate circumstances which confine most women, at any rate all that is available to a Jane Eyre, a Lucy Snowe—or a Charlotte Brontë, who are "lookers-on." And it might seem perverse to imagine the sad story of poor Lucy Snowe's life as a mode of comedy. But the double position that writing requires, like Lucy's parodic performance, allows a space to open between the woman's two roles, as artist and art object. Millett called *Villette* "one long meditation on a prison break." Precisely by imitating confinement, Lucy Snowe manages to break out of the prison of language and art—a break which the text of *Villette* does not so much meditate on as perform, by rewriting Gothic to imitate, parody, and foreground the issue of what "Gothic vision" might be.

PART II

Gothic Undone

CHAPTER 5

Eva's Curl
(Uncle Tom's Cabin)

In "A Child Is Being Beaten," Freud specifically names *Uncle Tom's Cabin* as one of those books read during adolescence that reactivate sado-masochistic fantasies of beating.[1] As usual, Freud proves to be an acute and provocative reader of literary texts as well as psychoanalytic narratives. *Uncle Tom's Cabin* supports ideas in his essay evidently beyond Freud's reason for mentioning this novel. First, in this essay, Freud here stresses the constitutive nature of representation,[2] a point relevant not only to the fantasies he recounts but also to the literary texts he mentions; for the history of *Uncle Tom's Cabin* graphically illustrates how literature reproduces the ideology in which it is inscribed. And, as I have noted, he suggests how the viewing subject and the object of fantasies become gendered in relation to one another: when the little girl as psychoanalytic subject produces the fantasy, she changes her own sexual identity and the sexual identity of the adult figure in the fantasy. The structure Freud describes indicates a relationship among readers and texts relevant to *Uncle Tom's Cabin*, a novel by a woman writer addressed to the "Mothers of America" and taking as its main focus a suffering man and a dying little girl. But I will especially depend on Freud's suggestion in this essay of a shift between "identification" (necessary, the essay indicates, in order to produce sexual gratification) and desire, that very shift which specular structuring defines and employs—and which Gothic fiction generally makes use of.

Like *Frankenstein*, this novel is haunted by an iconic female presence, that of little Eva, which becomes fetishized at several levels, both within the pages of the text and, finally, outside these pages in an image that has become textualized in adaptations. As in *Frankenstein*, this image is balanced, here by a narrating voice that clearly presents itself as that of a woman and that doubles itself as women characters who assume the role of "author." While at first glance *Uncle Tom's Cabin* may not seem very "Gothic," to read it under this rubric places it in a line of romanticism that has been appropriated by women.[3] It also puts Stowe in the company of writers to whom she felt akin—with Charlotte Brontë as literary "mother," for example, but also with Lord Byron, as real-life model for the Gothic hero-villain. To see this text as "Gothic" also emphasizes the novel's visual quality. In addition, Stowe's use of Gothic conventions casts light on the novel's status as a feminist tract. Critical discussion of *Uncle Tom's Cabin*, like much critical discussion of Radcliffe's novels and of *Frankenstein*, has concerned itself with how the text supports or subverts dominant discourses and the patriarchal culture it depicts. To describe such novels merely as supportive of the status quo[4] risks reinstating a new myth of feminine weakness (in terms of political tactics), as it fails to account for what is genuinely subversive; but to describe them as completely subversive[5] fails to account for the oppression to which they bear witness formally as well as thematically.

I would like to consider more closely the terms in which *Uncle Tom's Cabin* has been read as a "protest novel," the description ironically applied to it by James Baldwin in his burning critique.[6] My intention is to suggest that understanding the textualizing of "woman" in this novel, as well as the uses to which the novel has been put, sheds light on the function and status of this text as "protest novel," both as fetishized icon and as "author" (in the sense of "generator") of its own meaning. The relationship between "woman" and "text" as metaphors is reciprocal: if women function as texts (as bearers rather than producers of meaning, as something to be read), texts often function culturally like women. And as Harriet Beecher Stowe has been reclaimed by feminist critics as a "major writer," critics' attempts to place *Uncle Tom's Cabin* as "feminist" or possibly "anti-feminist" text have roughly paralleled critical notions of how the text can be situated regarding racial issues.

The operation of "Gothic" conventions in *Uncle Tom's Cabin* suggests how the novel both complies with conventional structures of representation and subverts them. Gothic structures provide a model for allying ethnic (or "racial") darkness and femininity; they also provide a way of understanding those structures of looking which this text exploits; and they suggest that here these two issues are related, through an anti-slavery moral framework, coded as feminine. But while the text obviously protests slavery, it also "obviously" speaks from a perspective that might be (and often has been) characterized as "racist."[7] It also obviously protests white women's powerlessness (and therefore is "feminist," at least in one common understanding of that term), at the same time it "obviously" sees women's potential strength as "different," perhaps even naturalized as different, from that of men (and is therefore "sexist" or at least "anti-feminist"). What an understanding of Stowe's Gothicism allows is a purchase on the double function of the framing of sexual and racial "otherness," as both confinement to conventional structures and escape from them.[8]

SENTIMENTAL HERESIES EXPOSED

Ann Douglas's *The Feminization of American Culture*, probably the best known and most clearly articulated statement of the "anti-feminist" reading of the novel, perceives it to be *the* outstanding example of the sentimental fiction that colluded in the oppression of women—possibly, it is true, because written by women damaged by the very culture whose values they articulated. Douglas suggests that though we may not blame these writers for failing to place themselves outside prevailing cultural values, the role of the twentieth-century critic becomes to expose what was reprehensible in their fiction rather than to perpetrate what she sees as the "sentimental heresy."

In *Sensational Designs*, Jane Tompkins has confronted Douglas to suggest the radically conservative subversiveness of Stowe's text. Tompkins perceives the novel to be a revolutionary argument for a cultural restructuring based on matriarchal values. In Tompkins's view, the sentimental novel spoke feminine strength rather than women's weakness; and her own role as critic becomes to suggest a reading to counter the "normative" set of aesthetic guidelines critics tended to use with the American canon which, until recently, was perceived as "standard"—and predominantly white-male authored. The position which Tompkins assigns to Douglas finally becomes analogous to the one into which Douglas casts Stowe. And in general, while Douglas claims for herself the position of "feminist critic," feminist critics of her work have claimed the contrary.[9] Like Stowe, Douglas is cast as a critic of patriarchy who is perceived to be "siding with the enemy"—precisely as Douglas fears she will be read, in a curiously confessional passage.[10] Tompkins indicts Douglas for resting her case on values presumably shared by her readers, values that are not shared by such a reader as Tompkins. This is exactly the same case that Douglas makes against Stowe: "sentimentalizing" evokes values presumed shared, but the response is not earned. Tompkins holds that sentimental novels are both conformist and subversive; nonetheless, in her view, they are not self-contradictory.

Both Tompkins and Douglas have been curiously race-blind reading a novel that deals most centrally and obviously with white oppression of black women and men. Though their debate in some respects parallels an analogous debate regarding how this novel deals with race, they themselves never address that issue. Does the domestic revolution that Tompkins suggests Stowe proposes offer merely a revision of the oppressive racial power relations that the text describes? It could be that the "feminine strength" Tompkins reads in the novel proposes a way of rewriting the dominance of a master race as a race of mistresses. If so, *Uncle Tom's Cabin* might well be the manifesto of the very sort of white bourgeois ideology that much feminist protest has been often accused of being.

James Baldwin's impassioned critique remains, I think, one of the most powerful indictments of the novel as racist. Baldwin objects to more than simple stereotyping—the creation of such offensive figures as Stowe's "lively procession of field-hands, house-niggers, Chloe, Topsy, etc."[11] and the figure of Uncle Tom himself, who had already, by the time Baldwin's essay first appeared in 1949, long since detached himself from the pages of the novel to become widely recognized as the image of the subservient black man, a significance far different from what the character Uncle Tom has in Stowe's text. The categories on which the protest novel relies take on their own life, a life that ends up usurping the place of the "life" they are supposed to represent: "The failure of the protest novel lies in its rejection of life, the human being, the denial of his beauty, dread, power, in its insistence that it is his categorization alone which is real and which cannot be transcended."[12] Baldwin understands literature as a manifestation of ideology,[13] an infinitely appropriable representation of conditions of existence that becomes one of the tools of society, which has "the force and the weapons to translate its dictum into fact," in Baldwin's words. Baldwin declares:

> We take our shape, it is true, within and against that cage of reality bequeathed us at our birth; and yet it is precisely through our dependence on this reality that we are most endlessly betrayed. Society is held together by our need; we bind it together with legend, myth, coercion, fearing that without it we will be hurled into that void, within which, like the earth before the Word was spoken, the foundations of society are hidden. From this void—ourselves—it is the function of society to protect us; but it is only this void, our unknown selves, demanding, forever, a new act of creation, which can save us— "from the evil that is in the world." With the same motion...it is this toward which we endlessly struggle and from which, endlessly, we struggle to escape.[14]

The simile that Baldwin employs—"like the earth before the Word was spoken"—suggests that language takes its place along with its uses, "legend, myth, [and] coercion," as a structure that acts as a stay against the void, a structure that defines the "shape" we take. Baldwin would appear to be anticipating later notions of "ideology" (in particular, Louis Althusser's "interpellation of the subject") in suggesting that we inhabit our culture through linguistic and representational structures which determine all that we are and do. To rethink Baldwin's metaphors temporally, they imply how Baldwin sees inscription in representation ("legend, myth") as marker of a division between two threatening states: one state might be read as prelinguistic—but here it is recalled not nostalgically but with terror, though also with hope—and the other describes a "reality" which betrays. The series "legend, myth, coercion" sounds odd: coercion seems out of place but in fact is astonishingly right here. All three use language to define "our" shape. This "our" is generalized; the suggestion here is that both the oppressed and the oppressor rely similarly on defining structures.

To speak of a novel's "escaping," as Baldwin does, or to imply a kind of "enslavement" to a dominant ideology is to use as metaphors the material that Stowe chose as her themes. Unlike Baldwin, Stowe does appear to view a prelinguistic state, identified with the maternal, nostalgically; and here would seem to lie perhaps the most important issue for which Baldwin, from his multi-determined perspective, takes her to task. But in fact, Stowe too evinces the same terror of this state, this "void." I would like to turn to the novel at this point, to begin to address these issues in the terms that Stowe suggests. While *Uncle Tom's Cabin* certainly addresses the social problem of slavery, it can be read also as using the terms of this problem as metaphors for the dilemma of a woman writer. In writing of the terms in which a man is made into a "thing,"[15] Stowe frames the issue of "objectifying" in terms of race, an issue equally pertinent to her own situation as writer: under what terms can she as a woman assume the position of speaking subject? And while considering the novel in these terms momentarily deflects attention from the racial issue, I think that it finally leads back to it in terms that begin to address the complexity of this very issue.

GOTHIC PICTURES IN *UNCLE TOM'S CABIN*

Like novels conventionally recognized as "Gothic," *Uncle Tom's Cabin* relies heavily on the "pictorial," the set scene or tableau— as Stowe herself recognized. "My vocation is simply that of a *painter*," she wrote to Dr. Bailey of the *National Era*, "and my object will be to hold up in the most lifelike and graphic manner possible Slavery, its reverses, changes, and the negro character.... There is no arguing with *pictures*."[16] Tompkins's reading implicitly stresses this pictorial method, this privileging of the frozen tableau over the sequential narrative. She stresses how scenes in the novel mirror one another and become interchangeable representations, where the sequential nature of narrative is subordinated to its potential for figuration. Doubling, rather than sequence, becomes privileged, because of its possibilities in a political enterprise which in Tompkins's view "both codifies and attempts to mold the values of its time."[17] In other words, the individual scene detaches itself from narrative as a "flow" in order to attach itself to another "flow"—that of history, which it attempts to direct. Though Tompkins does not specifically deal with visual representations *of* the novel, her discussion of set scenes *in* the novel ends up implying that the pictorial method Stowe uses for her typological narrative is, on a formal level, just as subversive as the novel's thematic content. In Tompkins's reading, the association of "feminine" content and pictorial method, two aspects previously counted to the detriment of the novel as art, are shown to be intimately associated and reassigned a positive value.[18]

While I think Tompkins is right in implying that Stowe's method subverts the conventions of linear narrative, I also think that her reading of it as "typological" fails to account for all the doubling and recurrence the text presents. The text to which *Uncle Tom's Cabin* repeatedly refers, the Bible, becomes a kind of discursive excuse, a way of explaining what might otherwise be inexplicable; but as "explanation," the Bible does not stabilize the text as much as Tompkins implies. *Uncle Tom's Cabin* makes use of doubling and recurrence much as Gothic fiction does: obsessively, as if to suggest a repressed content. Stowe's novel employs the Gothic convention of figuring inset narratives as interior spaces, ranging from the modest dwelling that gives the novel its title to the Shelby and St. Clare mansions.[19] As in the Radcliffean Gothic mode, these interior spaces provide a "dream space" for the drama, as becomes especially evident in the Red River scenes at Legree's plantation and within Legree's decaying mansion itself. The mise en scène of the dream takes on an uncanny cast; the plot makes use of such Gothic conventions as ghosts, which, as in Radcliffe, can be explained in "natural" terms. *Uncle Tom's Cabin* also suggests a terrifying fixation on the maternal that reveals a covert counter-text to the novel's glorification of mothers.

Within the text's climactic heart of darkness, Simon Legree, the novel's Byronic Gothic villain, is cast as spectator. Legree becomes witness of suggestively "uncanny" representations of his own past. The demonic slave Sambo brings him the first of these, the lock of Little Eva's hair, which Sambo recognizes as a "witch thing"—as indeed it is, for Legree. Engaged in exchanging taunts with the witchlike Cassy, Legree is interrupted by Sambo, who brings him a piece of paper. When Legree unwraps it, there drops "a silver dollar, and a long shining curl of fair hair,—hair which, like a living thing, twined itself round Legree's fingers,"[20] like the charnel worms that wrapped themselves around the fingers of the fallen nun Agnes in *The Monk*. In *The Monk*, these worms feed on the flesh of Agnes's dead baby: "Often have I at waking found my fingers ringed with the long worms which bred in the corrupted flesh of my infant."[21] One is tempted to speculate on Lewis's "influence" on Stowe, especially since Agnes is found in the dungeons below the deceptively fine-looking convent of St. Clare—in fact, the entrance to the dungeon is disguised by St. Clare's statue, an ineffective stay against the portals of horror. If such influence exists, one can only assume that the religious forces that censored Stowe's reading list were largely unsuccessful. But more to my point is not this text's use of details or descriptions from specific Gothic novels but Stowe's use of Gothic devices to inscribe the reader as spectator and to rewrite that relationship in terms that suggest where a "woman" might place herself.

Superstitiously, Legree reads the hair as belonging to his mother, who had, it becomes apparent, sent him a lock of hair as emblem of her love and her prayers for his salvation. But Legree's apparent misreading really is accurate, considering that Eva holds a maternal position in the novel and that, like his own mother, she prays for the salvation of everyone. The hair of Legree's mother and the hair of Eva convey the same significance and in effect *are* the same; and through a synecdochic and metonymic relationship (Eva's hair equals Legree's mother's hair; hair stands for its owner; Eva therefore equals Legree's mother), so too are Eva and Legree's mother, as two of the many interchangeable mothers in this novel.[22]

While Eva's lock of hair had been sent with beneficent intentions, it has now become fetishized and "petrifying" like the hair of Freud's Medusa. Like the Medusa, this fetish represents femininity as terrifying; but also like the Medusa, it acts apotropaically: Legree's response is a kind of "stiffening," an assertion of his sexuality and the power that accompanies it. After his initial terror, he seeks the young slave Emmeline, presumably to rape her. But once again frightened by the imagined ghost of his mother, he contents himself with asserting his power through homoerotic voyeurism; he sends for the slaves Sambo and Quimbo as entertainers, to sing and dance or fight like cocks before him.

This sequence of events also makes clear not only that there is an alliance between femininity and racial darkness (as the friendship between Uncle Tom and Eva also suggests); it also implies that the two are allied in acting as threats. Making its appearance as a "middle term" between Cassy and Legree as they bait one another, Eva's curl is associated with Cassy's power over Legree, a power that is clearly sexual but that invokes superstitious notions of "black" magic, in a double sense—both racially black and associated with demonic power. The entrance of the curl interrupts Legree's threats to torture Uncle Tom further; the curl acts literally to protect Uncle Tom from Legree's threats (and possibly from carrying them out at this point). The fiendish Sambo is the purveyor of the curl, an unwitting ally of Eva in bringing her "power" to rebound on the head of Legree. He brings the curl to Legree because he sees it as a token, not of femininity (as Legree reads it) but of African voodoo. Eva's curl acts as signifier of both blackness and femininity.

As object of vision, Eva's golden curl figures the narrative method of the novel. In her originary vision of the novel, Stowe saw what she reports to have been the first (in order of composition, in this account[23]) of the "pictures" that compose it, as a detached, isolated entity. The lock of hair is similarly detached; like Stowe's vision, it invites the spectator to provide a context for it but mysteriously refuses to reveal its origin. Ironically, the position that Stowe assumes in the tale of her vision becomes recast here as the position of Legree, the villain; and while visions may be inspiring, they may also be terrifying. Like Eva's curl, the vision may be assumed to be beneficent, sent by a redemptive God or His representative; but this vision *could* be just as terrifying as the curl can be—as indeed it became in other cultural adaptations of it, as I will suggest.

Legree's terror at the lock of hair suggests that the curl itself is powerful, and, through a chain of synecdochic and metonymic associations, that Eva herself, his mother, mothers generally hold such power. But the curl actually demonstrates the reverse—that is, how completely the object of vision is subject to the appropriating gaze to be interpreted. Though the fetishized object seems to carry within it its own power, such power manifests itself only as the object is read; and the object might instead be misread. It "embodies" and "represents" only through what is imputed to it. This reading provides a figurative account of how fear of the maternal becomes transmuted to hatred, not only of femininity but also of racial darkness (because within the novel this fear of the maternal is cast as explanatory myth of Legree's debased character. Evidently Legree displaces this hatred/fear of the feminine onto the slaves).

But the power of the curl is not *only* a function of the spectator's visual acuity but of its own status as "vision." As Freud suggests in "The 'Uncanny,'" ghosts are frightening precisely because they are revenant; that is, returning. Such a vision as the one Stowe reports may be terrifying, not only because of its content but because of its status as "vision."

Metonymically, the lock of hair re-presents Eva; and its status as fetishized object suggests not only the scene of her death within the novel but those stagings of Eva's death scene that became a generalized emblem of the "Tom shows." And even as represented in the pages of the text, the image of the dying child is already a detached image, broken off from other Gothic/romantic contexts. Dickens's Little Nell from the *Old Curiosity Shop* is an obvious precursor of Eva, but Dickens did not originate the type.[24] Thomas De Quincey's *Suspiria de Profundis* is haunted by images of dying girls that function, like Eva, as pictures to be looked at. Little Eva resembles De Quincey's dying children rising through the clouds in their beds. Eva is recognizably trustworthy when she talks of God, in part because her status as dying child places her close to the Divine Presence in terms that cultural symbology makes explicit. De Quincey reports:

> Such a child, having put off the earthly mind in many things, may naturally have put off the childish mind in all things. I thereby, speaking for myself only, acknowledge to have read

with emotion a record of a little girl who, knowing herself for months to be amongst the elect of death, became anxious, even to sickness of heart, for what she called the *conversion* of her father. Her filial duty and reverence had been swallowed up in filial love.²⁵

De Quincey's two sisters Jane and Elizabeth, particularly Elizabeth whom he remembers more clearly, are evidently the original models for these haunting presences for De Quincey. In trying to come to terms with her death, De Quincey compares the possibility of never having known his sister (and so having escaped the pain of her death) with Milton's postulation of the possibility of "a second Eve, one that would listen to no temptation."²⁶ De Quincey's description of the "second Eve" clarifies an important implication of this stock theological/literary convention: the second Eve herself is a representation (of the first Eve). Though she is intended to be recognized as superior to the first Eve in terms of virtue, in terms of the emotion she evokes, she can never take the place of the original she represents: "If God should replace him in his primitive state and should condescend to bring him again a second Eve, one that would listen to no temptation, still that original partner of his earliest solitude...could not be displaced for him by any better or happier Eve." In other words, the second Eve is an emblem and representative of something, an original that is no longer present. She is the place-keeper of a loss that has always already occurred, a reminder of absence. As "second Eve," Stowe's Eva bears such associations. But in addition to being "Eve," she is also "Evangeline" (her full name), a doubly significant appellation: "evangel" can mean either the writer of the gospel (an evangelist) or the gospel, the text itself.²⁷ Her name thus indicates that she is author, text, and character. In Little Eva, who becomes the center of one of the text's central icons, the differences among these functions collapse.

Whether or not Stowe had De Quincey in mind when she created her, the character she did create was already a representation of this recognizable icon when placed in the pages of *Uncle Tom's Cabin*: a pretty, frail, and consumptive female child, full of religious and filial virtue, who redeems her father by her death. The image of the dying Eva functions like the image of the dead Elizabeth in *Frankenstein*, a break in the forward motion of the narrative, an emblem of stasis, and a threat to narrative coherence. And the narrative does break off at this point, with Eva's death forming a climax to the New Orleans section; St. Clare's death follows as denouement; and the narrative resumes as a new section, taking Tom to Legree's plantation. Eva's death literally stopped Stowe in her composition. Though as a rule extraordinarily reliable about meeting her deadlines, Stowe missed the next installment in the novel's serialization in *The National Era*.[28]

The death of the girl/woman, both here and in *Frankenstein*, has a dual function in the narrative: it lends a narrative "reason" for the freezing into a still body (necessary to the image's iconic function) as well as contributing a narrative means (on the level of plot) of neutralizing the threat the female poses; that is, the female body becomes both a still body (and hence a fetish, an icon) and a dead body (what feminist critics have sometimes termed "punishing the heroine").

The maternal power that *Uncle Tom's Cabin* seems to celebrate[29] (and at one level *does* celebrate) is also presented as not only powerful but threatening and terrifying, certainly to Legree, but also implicitly, and through the operation of the narrative, to any spectator. Uncle Tom's beneficent vision of little Eva is doubled by Legree's visions of his mother's ghost, a doubling emphasized by Eva's maternal function. As representation of the mother, Eva's image becomes a link in a chain of substitutions that neutralize the threat the body of the mother presents: she is only a child, a diminutive of an adult woman; then her image becomes that of a small dead body. Finally a fetish object, the lock of hair, comes to substitute for her.

But though domesticated, made into a child, killed, and fetishized, as sign, Eva threatens; she evokes the anxiety she signifies. She also regenerates herself, as do so many other monstrous maternal presences represented in Anglo-American texts, a series that might be traced from Beowulf's mother in the English epic to Jason's mother in the slasher movie *Friday the Thirteenth*. Her curl ascends from the grave. It is the powerful survivor of multiple attempts at death: Eva's own death, Legree's mother's death, and the destruction of Legree's mother's lock of hair, which Legree has thrown into a fire (as another "witch thing"). Repressed, it returns.

By contrast, another character in the novel, Eliza, suggests the value of miming masculinity, more practical if less radically subversive and terrifying. During the course of her escape, Eliza dresses as a man. Eva's lock of hair sharply contrasts with Eliza's tresses, shorn to give her the appearance of a man as she takes her final steps toward liberty: "Eliza turned to the glass, and the scissors glittered as one long lock after another was detached from her head" (p. 545). Eliza's hair does not take on the fetishistic value of Eva's. One thing here suggested is the difference in the narrative mode between the "realistic" Harris sections of the novel as contrasted with the progressively more Gothic sections of the "Uncle Tom" sections. But also, Eliza's transvestism implicitly underscores by contrast the significance of Eva's locks. On an imagistic level, by imitating a man, Eliza implicitly recognizes and hides the threatening "lack" that her femaleness suggests; that is, a cross-dressed woman literalizes, even parodies, the notion that woman's self-representation must express itself in male terms. And while she proposes to flaunt her new adopted identity as a white man—"I must stamp, and take long steps, and try to look saucy"—her husband George advises her to become even more covert: "There is, now and then, a modest young man; and I think it would be easier for you to act that character" (p. 547). Having become a white man to hide her identity as a black woman, Eliza is forbidden to express the idioms of her newly adopted personality.

On the other hand, in terms of character motivation, Eliza hides not her femininity but her identity as a slave. Her son Harry similarly cross-dresses, but as a girl, for the same reason. But like Eliza's disguise, Harry's also is multiply significant. From the outset, Harry appears to be ambivalently sexed. He always looks like a little girl: "His black hair, fine as floss silk, hung in glossy curls about his round, dimpled face, while a pair of large dark eyes, full of fire and softness, looked out from beneath the rich long lashes" (p. 43). Harry may already be cross-dressed. We must recall that "A Child Is Being Beaten" works through sexual transformations: the (girl) child comes to watch a little boy, with whom she identifies, being beaten. Identified as a little boy who escapes both being beaten and being sold, Harry/Harriet late in the novel reveals her sex by dressing as a girl. Perhaps in little Harry/Harriet the white woman author as spectator not only covertly peeks out into her text, but also frames herself as object, as a little boy who is black—a reversal of the collapse that occurs with Eva.

The images of the hair of Eliza and Eva metonymically suggest what these two female characters represent in this novel. Eliza achieves the results she seeks, though she subverts the system rather than directly challenging it. Unlike the startlingly direct and vulnerable Eva, to effect her escape Eliza becomes duplicitous—thereby confirming the stereotype of blacks as devious and shifty (a label which white majorities have conventionally applied to groups racially or ethnically different from themselves, including Jews and Orientals). By way of contrast with Eliza, Eva is indeed personally "ineffective," as Douglas has suggested; she actually *does* very little. But as image, she is radically subversive (as Tompkins and others suggest)—because, as I am arguing, she embodies the threatening lack that the feminine represents.

If Eliza's haircut is "simply" a haircut, though with its own implications, her disguise functions as "simply" a way of hiding. At Legree's plantation, the mechanisms for concealing and revealing operate in a more dreamlike fashion (as Freud described the stagings of dreams); that is, something hidden actually makes its appearance through representations by which it can be perceived and known. Cassy and Emmeline do not merely hide in the garret; their presence there is hidden by their own sounds and appearance. "O, don't speak a word!" Emmeline protests to Cassy; but Cassy replies: "No danger; we may make any noise we please, and it will only add to the effect" (p. 484). As in a dream things—and, here, people—are hidden *through* their own representations.

Further, Legree's plantation makes clear the terms under which a woman can hold the position of storyteller in the face of her position as object. If Eliza is duplicitous in her assumption of a man's identity, she foreshadows the duplicity suggested by women's authorship that in this novel is typical of black women. *Uncle Tom's Cabin* resolves the dilemma of the woman writer by making her black. It asserts a double "objectifying": a thing because black, and an object (rather than a speaking subject) because a woman, the black woman eludes this categorization by virtue of her double assignment to it. Black women tell stories;

and the character Cassy comes to fill the dual role of both representation *and* author. The narrative comes to suggest a blurring of the line between the threatening mother of Legree's imagination and the living Cassy; and Cassy becomes a representative of Legree's nightmare visions, a figure for the text that resembles the Frankenstein Monster in Mary Shelley's dream. Here, the narrator is close to the consciousness of Legree; and the reader sees through his restricted vision:

> Well, he slept, for he was tired,—slept soundly. But, finally, there came over his sleep a shadow, a horror, an apprehension of something dreadful hanging over him. It was his mother's shroud, he thought; but Cassy had it, holding it up, and showing it to him. He heard a confused noise of screams and groanings; and, with it all, he knew he was asleep, and he struggled to wake himself. He was half awake. He was sure something was coming into his room. He knew the door was opening, but he could not stir hand or foot. At last he turned, with a start; the door *was* open, and he saw a hand putting out his light.
>
> It was a cloudy, misty moonlight, and there he saw it!—something white, gliding in! He heard the still rustle of its ghostly garments. It stood still by his bed;—a cold hand touched his; a voice said, three times, in a low, fearful whisper, "Come! come! come!" And, while he lay sweating with terror, he knew not when or how, the thing was gone. He sprang out of bed, and pulled at the door. It was shut and locked, and the man fell down in a swoon. (p. 596)

Like Shelley, Stowe presents a tableau of a dreamer on the bed; here, as opposed to the Fuseli painting and the similar tableau in *Frankenstein*, the dreamer is a man, Legree. But Cassy does not simply represent and embody the dream, though she does that, as the "something dreadful" that hangs over Legree; she also controls it, presenting to Legree his mother's shroud. Finally, not only Legree but also the reader is left uncertain as to where the operations of Legree end and those of Cassy begin. Is she really there or is his imagination (overheated by Cassy's suggestions) simply conjuring her?

We learn a few paragraphs later that the morning following that night, "the house door was found open...and some of the negroes had seen two white figures gliding down the avenue towards the high road." Are we then to surmise that Cassy was simply putting the finishing touches on her terrorizing of Legree, to ensure that she and Emmeline would not be followed? Or could it be that both apparitions, the shroud revealed by Cassy and the "cold hand" with its ghostly voice, were the products of his mind? Either suggestion is plausible; the latter implies that the escape takes place when his terror is at its peak and that Cassy need no longer supplement his fantasies. Was the "confused noise of screams and groanings" part of Legree's nightmare? Or was it the sound of Cassy and Emmeline in the garret? In the narrative, Cassy has almost completely, if only momentarily, merged into a dream figure. Like a character in a dream, she both hides and represents herself.

While suggesting the dreamlike function of visual representation *within* narrative, Cassy's story is less "visual," more "narrative" itself than certain key scenes of the novel that more easily and quickly became adapted to a visual mode.[30] In George L. Aiken's adaptation of the novel, the version most often played on American stages throughout the nineteenth century and on into the twentieth, none of the visual dramas in which Cassy appears are actually staged. The story of Legree's mother, however, is *narrated*, in a dialogue between Cassy and Legree; Legree is the principal narrator, motivated by Cassy's questions. At the end of the scene Legree soliloquizes the apparition of "something white rising and glimmering in the gloom" before him. In this scene, Cassy takes on the voice of the narrator in the novel, commenting at the end: "Yes, Legree, that golden tress was charmed; each hair had in it a spell of terror and remorse for thee, and was used by a mightier power to bind thy cruel hands from inflicting uttermost evil on the helpless!"[31]

Cassy also has her own story to tell and she tells it, a story of her own respectable upbringing which was followed by rape, infanticide, and subsequent madness, a tale that in its Gothic horror easily matches those of Agnes or Antonia in *The Monk*. Like the appearance of other women characters in *Uncle Tom's Cabin*, her appearance signals and generates a narrative separate from the main plot but tied to it. In her narration of her own story, Cassy implies what Aiken's theatrical adaptation underscored, that her role is doubly that of the novelist and the object of vision, a doubleness she turns to her advantage. While Eva's curl generates a story only by being read, Cassy generates stories *both* as storyteller and by being "read." Cassy's simultaneous concealment and revelation as dream specter depends on Legree's perception of her, but his perception is conditioned by what she as storyteller has previously shown him. The novelist as both speaking subject and object of vision can evidently control her own appropriation, the use to which she is put.

THE FATE OF MRS. STOWE'S PICTURE

Uncle Tom's Cabin finally suggests how women, functioning as both icons and authors, threaten the very power relations they accommodate. As this novel suggests, accommodation and threat are not mutually exclusive; indeed, they are mutually necessary. In the novel, Cassy maintains sufficient control to escape Legree. But if Cassy's story suggests that the role of storyteller gives a woman control over her own appropriation, Eva's curl suggests how that control is undermined by the appropriating gaze, as does the subsequent history of *Uncle Tom's Cabin*. Like *Frankenstein*, *Uncle Tom's Cabin* passed from a "vision" to a written text and thence into popular culture (to achieve a kind of "folk" status) through visual media. In the process, it has become "immortal" but at some cost.

In *A Small Boy and Others*, Henry James tells us: "We lived and moved at that time, with great intensity in Mrs. Stowe's novel," which he recalls as his "first experiment in grown up fiction."[32] In James's terms, "Mrs. Stowe's novel" is construed as a space that one can inhabit. But it is not Stowe's text at all; it was "much less a book than a state of vision," induced by the "Tom plays" based on the novel:

> Letters, here, languished unconscious, and Uncle Tom, instead of making even one of the cheap short cuts through the medium in which books breathe, even as fishes in water, went gaily roundabout it altogether, as if a fish, a wonderful 'leaping' fish, had simply flown through the air. This feat accomplished, the surprising creature could naturally fly anywhere,

and one of the first things it did was thus to flutter down on every stage, literally without exception, in America and Europe. If the amount of life represented in such a work is measurable by the ease with which representation is taken up and carried further...the fate of Mrs. Stowe's picture was conclusive.[33]

But of course, as James's irony implies, "the amount of life represented in such a work" is *not* measurable by the ease with which representation is taken up. On the contrary, such a quality condemns the work to the same category as the spectacles of P.T. Barnum, in whose company James discusses "Mrs. Stowe's novel."

For James, finally, "Mrs. Stowe" merges into the figures of the actresses who played the roles of Cassy and Eliza, such as Miss Emily Mestayer, off the stage appearing as "a worn and weary... *thing* of the theatre" (James's emphasis), just as "Mrs. Stowe's novel" merges into not only its own theatrical representations but into circuses and museums and finally into spectacle generally. Mrs. Stowe is Cassy and Eliza (just as Cassy is Eliza); so is Emily Mestayer, the actress, and so is she also not only Cassy and Eliza but also Mrs. Stowe. Not only are all the women here interchangeable; also, as with certain other novels by women, a peculiar sort of fluidity appears to mark the boundary between a text and an artist; and not only between a character and a writer, but also between a character and a different real-life woman artist, an actress, who is perceived to be interchangeable with fictional characters. While novels by both men and women are frequently read in terms of autobiographical doubling (for example, *Frankenstein* is often read this way[34]), James's reading of *Uncle Tom's Cabin* suggests a different sort of "doubling."

As a text whose boundaries seem to include real-life women, *Uncle Tom's Cabin* has predecessors in Gothic fiction. For example, the actress Sarah Siddons has been seen as a model for Radcliffe in creating Emily St. Aubert in *The Mysteries of Udolpho*.[35] Vashti in Charlotte Brontë's *Villette* and Alcharisi in George Eliot's *Daniel Deronda* have been perceived to have shared a real-life model, the actress Rachel.[36] An odd displacement takes place: a real-life woman becomes translated to the pages of a text; the text may become adapted for the stage; and that actress (or another actress as her substitute) may play that part; in turn, that stage adaptation may influence the writing of another novel or be influenced by one.[37] In these examples, one need not assume that the text of a novel is co-terminous with the lives of its author and readers in order to describe a relationship between "literature" and "life."[38] Here, the frame—the stage or the text—becomes the signifier of priority. If "Sarah Siddons" equals Emily, that "Sarah Siddons" is a construction of the stage on which she appeared, not just a "real-life" woman. Like Radcliffe's fictional character Emily St. Aubert, "Sarah Siddons" too is determined by the space that confines her. And it's clear that for James, "Mrs. Stowe," Cassy, Eliza, and Emily Mestayer all become cultural institutions, public property. All women, whether textual or physical, look pretty much alike. The reader/spectator is implicitly male (in the Stowe example, explicitly Henry James), and the object of his gaze is the woman character as determined by a text, even though marked by a real flesh-and-blood woman. Her physical presence has no real meaning except as determined by the appropriating eye. And as James describes it, so does the author become the property of the reader; she is indistinguishable from both the actress and the character. James's account suggests both prophetically and nostalgically how the novel's visual quality became a way of denying integrity to the text of the novel and its author.

But more important, James forcefully articulates the extent to which scenes in the novel, like Eva's cut curl (mis)read by Legree, did indeed detach themselves from the narrative, for the first generations of readers of the novel who became audiences for the Tom plays, and not only in terms of anti-slavery propaganda. If these scenes from the novel had anything to do with directing the course of history (as Abraham Lincoln, in the famous anecdote about his meeting with Stowe, suggested that Stowe's writing of the novel had), history likewise directed them. Baldwin's critique suggests why—why, that is, the novel itself has cut loose from its linguistic moorings to send its characters floating free in the culture that produced them. Stowe's insistence that she acted only as a kind of medium in transcribing the text for God can be read as a statement of how the authority of the author is undermined by her operation as an agent for cultural ideology; that is, authors are written as they write, and they serve as mediums for

the ideology that speaks through them. If Stowe became a
medium for either God or cultural ideology, so too did the theater and, later, film—not just movies of *Uncle Tom's Cabin* itself
but films that reappropriated and adapted tableaux from "Mrs.
Stowe's novel."

Baldwin had suggested that "the spirit that breathes in this
book, hot, self-righteous, fearful, is not different from that spirit
of medieval times which sought to exorcize evil by burning
witches; and is not different from that terror which activates a
lynch mob."[39] This statement can be understood in view of critical
discussions that have perceived Stowe's novel as the predecessor
and mother text of such popular film images as those in *Birth of a
Nation* and *Gone With the Wind*.[40] Stowe's novel gave birth to
Aiken's play which adapted the novel; the play gave birth to
Thomas Dixon's *The Clansman*, the novel adapted for D. W. Griffith's film. In beginning his trilogy (with the novel *The Leopard's
Spots*), Dixon evidently was motivated by a theatrical performance of *Uncle Tom's Cabin*.[41] The cultural myths, thematics, and
imagery of all these works are similar: relations between blacks
and whites; sexual predation; the sanctity of the home and of
motherhood.[42] But in becoming detached, like Eva's hair, they
take on different significance; and because this novel juxtaposes
discrete, individual scenes, such detachment is so easily effected.

For example, Eva's death scene replays in the novel as the
death of Uncle Tom, Stowe's originary "vision." The relation
between the two scenes was made even more explicit in Aiken's
play, which ends with an allegorical "vision," where Tom rises to
glory to be greeted by Little Eva. Both deaths depict innocent
victims, doubles of one another in the novel, past all pain at the
moment of death itself and surrounded by weeping friends
whose conversion and deliverance from evil they have sought to
effect; both scenes reenact and draw their meaning from the Biblical scene of the crucifixion of Christ.

But earlier, the scene where the recumbent Uncle Tom lies
surmounted by the torturing figures of Legree and his demonic
henchmen suggests a nightmare inversion of that scene, like the
scene of Legree's nightmare. Thematically, this scene resembles
Fuseli's *Nightmare*, but it operates inversely. Here, the narrative
center of the tableau is the suffering Tom with whom the reader

is invited to identify. Such a mechanism of identification was undoubtedly what Freud referred to when he suggested that this novel could remotivate beating fantasies. If the scene operates sado-masochistically, it emphasizes the sadistic reversal of masochism; and sadism depends on narrative context—unlike Fuseli's painting, where the central figure is opaque and stops the action. By contrast, the dying Eva provides an instance of fetishistic scopophilia, which does indeed freeze the action. But what has been set up here is an identification between a black man and a white girl that allows a way around the opacity of the female figure in the tableau. While the dying girl insists on her status as "other," the suffering black man invites identification. And by suggesting an inversion of the "dying woman" scene, the parallel between Tom and Eva suggests other possibilities, invites further revisions.

For example, the scene depicting the black man and the white girl may be transmuted into a less benevolent picture. In the novel, Eva is depicted in the arms of Uncle Tom on the days shortly before her death. Here, the figure surmounting the reclining victim is, of course, perceived to be beneficent. But as Fiedler points out, the image of the black man carrying the white virgin changes in later transmutations of the scene (chiefly in movies), becoming the image of the black rapist. As the scene changes, it becomes more clearly analogous to the death of Uncle Tom scene. Eva becomes Tom in the later scene; Tom becomes Legree; and in later representations of the scene, the black man carrying the white girl becomes another tormentor and violator, a black Legree in relation to women, resembling Legree in his exaggerated embodiment of predatory maleness.

But these scenes, detached from their context in the novel, have not become the exclusive property of racists. While Dixon, whose project is to redeem the South, uses the images one way, another possibility is suggested by Richard Wright's deliberate use of the same material, producing *Uncle Tom's Children* and another descendant in *Native Son's* Bigger Thomas. Wright produces a metareading of Stowe through Dixon, not simply depicting these images as traitorous but suggesting *how* these images betray. Baldwin perceived the relationship of Wright's images to Stowe's as well as the similar affect of the two. With as much criticism of Wright as of Stowe, Baldwin described the two as "locked together in a deadly timeless battle; the one uttering merciless exhortations, the other shouting curses."[43] Baldwin saw Bigger Thomas as having accepted "a theology that denies him life." Bigger clearly has written himself in the terms that the dominant ideology that surrounds him has prescribed. Early in *Native Son*, Wright makes clear how dependent Bigger is on the movies for his own self-image and the image of the world he lives in. Bigger and his friends go to see a double feature at the movies. The first film gives a distorted impresssion of how "rich white folks" live, in particular the white woman, sexually loose and hungry. Commenting on the movie, Bigger's friend Jack says to Bigger: "Man, if them folks saw you they'd run.... They'd think a gorilla broke loose from the zoo and put on a tuxedo."[44] Bigger and Jack find this image funny—largely, no doubt, because it suggests how easily the stereotypes white culture creates can be turned back on the culture that produces the stereotypes. The second movie, which Wright describes less completely, depicts "naked black men and women whirling in wild dances."[45]

Later, during his trial for the murder of white Mary Dalton, Bigger Thomas sees himself rewritten in the newspapers as an ape-like wild man:

> His lower jaw protrudes obnoxiously, reminding one of a jungle beast. His arms are long, hanging in a dangling fashion to his knees.... His shoulders are huge, muscular, and he keeps them hunched, as if about to spring upon you at any moment. He looks at the world with a strange, sullen, fixed-from-under stare, as though defying all efforts of compassion. All in all, he seems a beast utterly untouched by the softening influences of modern civilization.[46]

The newspaper reports a "terrified young white girl" to exclaim: "He looks exactly like an ape!"

In Baldwin's terms, Bigger is betrayed, inevitably, by the myths on which he depends. Bigger Thomas and Jack imagine themselves to be perceived as gorillas because of such movie images as those Dixon made available to film; and although they mock these images and the white culture that produced them, in the hands of that culture, these images wield power over them.

The image of Eva in the arms of Uncle Tom turns threatening in terms that suggest the fear of blacks harbored by the white establishment; it offers another instance of the spectacle of a woman's violation for visual enjoyment. It allows the (white, masculine-coded) spectator to indulge both sadistic fantasies toward women *and* horror of racial darkness. Read through the terms in which Bigger and Jack see themselves, it resembles the image of King Kong carrying off Fay Wray.

The history of *Uncle Tom's Cabin* makes graphic the instability of the positioning of the author, as of any spectator. A posture that assumes "control" is bound to be undermined. At the same time, the *fiction* of a controlling position is necessary for any story to be told. Eva's curl appears to be powerful but in fact is so only in terms of the "readings" it evokes; by itself it is inarticulate. It depends on the discourse that interprets it. In that way, it resembles another figure for narrative in *Uncle Tom's Cabin*. I wish to stress the (finally) unstable nature of the balance of power between interpreter and image; and to illustrate, I wish to make use of one final image from the text of *Uncle Tom's Cabin*.

An image recurs in the narratives of both Cassy at Legree's plantation and of Prue, a slave in New Orleans, who eventually dies mysteriously, a result of her ill treatment. Both Prue and Cassy are haunted by the cries of children of their own. The cries of these children echo the actual telling of their own stories; the cry reaches only their ears, as their stories reach only the ears of the maternal Uncle Tom. But while their response to the cry is to block out the sound, Prue by drinking and Cassy with her insanity, Tom's response is to read their stories into a theological context. His response to Cassy and Prue suggests not only the typological nature of narrative that *Uncle Tom's Cabin* employs; it also suggests how completely narrative depends on prior discourse to be interpreted. The cry of the child becomes "readable" as the narrative cry of Cassy and Prue, whose stories, like that of *Uncle Tom's Cabin* itself, become understandable through the image of Christ's crucifixion and death. But through this "readable" interpretation sounds that inarticulate cry, just as the iconic, silent figure of Eva appears through the narrative that domesticates her.

CHAPTER 6

Exorcising the Mother
(Daniel Deronda)

Perhaps more than in any of her other novels, in *Daniel Deronda*, a text thoroughly obsessed with mothers at a thematic level, George Eliot thinks back through her (literary) mothers, to use Virginia Woolf's phrase. As in *Jane Eyre*, the existence of an earlier liaison, with a woman reputed to be dissolute, delays an anticipated marriage. Grandcourt advises Lydia Glasher that if she likes, she can "play the mad woman" to the extent of disrupting the marriage ceremony itself,[1] as did Bertha Rochester. As in *Pride and Prejudice*, a family of five daughters constructs matrimonial prospects from the knowledge that an unmarried man is coming to take possession of a nearby mansion that has been vacant. In *Daniel Deronda*, the narrator reports: "Some readers of this history will doubtless regard it as incredible that people should construct matrimonial prospects on the mere report that a bachelor of good fortune and possibilities was coming within reach" (p. 123); and, while such speculation may not be "human nature," "the history in its present stage concerns only a few people in a corner of Wessex"(p. 802). These observations twist the famous opening of *Pride and Prejudice*, which plays similarly on the irony of the idea "that a single man in possession of a good fortune, must be in want of a wife" as "a truth universally acknowledged."[2] The plot device of *Pride and Prejudice* is also echoed in the Mallingers' situation of producing only daughters and no son to inherit the estates. And Eliot's novel inverts the premise of Austen's, that a wealthy but unpleasant prospective suitor must turn to good account.

Such use of her literary mothers might suggest a special concern with women's authorship; and reading *Daniel Deronda* through the lens provided by *Villette* reveals several points where such concern is evident. Most obvious may be the character of the Princess, who is usually taken to be modeled after the real-life actress Rachel, the model for Vashti in *Villette*.[3] Like Vashti, Alcharisi (the Princess's professional name) is an actress who enflames her audience with her own passion. On a formal level, *Daniel Deronda* also resembles *Villette* in its intense attention to visual perspective. Presenting its two central characters in its opening scene, the text traces Daniel's gaze at Gwendolen;[4] their relationship is first of all a matter of visual teasing. As I have suggested, visual positioning, and acting as a special instance of it, work as metaphors for the double positioning of "women writers."[5]

But the differences in the ways the two texts handle these devices are also instructive. While both Vashti and Alcharisi similarly are secondary characters in both texts, who nonetheless lead the text to a climax around which the action turns, Vashti is presented in *Villette* as an actress, actually on stage, while Alcharisi, past her prime, has almost been swallowed up by the other roles she has played by the time she actually appears in the pages of the text. For Daniel and the reader (who sees through his "eyes"), her acting is secondary to her "role" as his mother—ironically, since such assignment to conventional women's roles is precisely what she had sought to avoid. And while *Villette*'s metaphors of vision work through the eyes of a woman who watches women and men both, *Daniel Deronda* exploits visual perspective chiefly through the perspective of a man, who watches mainly women.

These differences are instructive in that they suggest that it is Eliot who more successfully represses the mother in her text, on a formal as well as a thematic level; that is to say, not only the mother as that phantasmal presence which tends to haunt Gothic-marked texts, but also "mother" as that feminine-coded object which may not act as speaking subject. Another way to put this is to suggest that *Daniel Deronda* more safely maintains that near collapse of specular distance always threatened in *Villette*. Nonetheless, *Daniel Deronda* summons its "mothers" as well as banishing them; and it finally expends so much textual energy in repressing mothers that the absence becomes palpable enough as to be a kind of presence. While Alcharisi may not represent the woman-spectacle who stops the text's action (as Vashti does), she imports into this novel the same set of issues that Vashti had focused, though fractured and dispersed in this novel's "realism" in different form. Eliot's use of texts by other women in this novel might be imaged as a long-distance correspondence, sufficiently close, but far enough away not to be threatening. And in fact this image becomes literalized with one more of *Daniel Deronda*'s literary mothers. The relationship between George Eliot and Harriet Beecher Stowe in both letters and novels suggests the significance of literary "mothering" in *Daniel Deronda* more generally.

EXODUS VERSUS ASSIMILATION: DISTANCING GHOSTS

Early in the correspondence between Harriet Beecher Stowe and George Eliot, Stowe mentions to Eliot the novel which she is completing, *Oldtown Folks*. In her first letter to Stowe, Eliot anticipates that novel's reception in England: "I have good hope that your fears are groundless as to the obstacles your new book may find here from its thoroughly American character."[6] Soon Stowe sends Eliot a copy, which Eliot quickly reports to Stowe that she has read (V, p. 48). Over the course of the correspondence, Stowe comments on Eliot's work (sometimes rather presumptuously); and she is particularly taken with *Daniel Deronda*, which she read as it was serialized in *Harper's*. She discusses the novel at some length, in a long letter in which she also speaks with passion about her brother and the scandal involving him.[7] Stowe tells Eliot that the serialized novel is "as good as a letter." Like a letter, the novel evokes the presence of its writer, whom she calls as witness and comfort for her own situation. She cites what has evidently been to her a comforting sentence from the novel she has been reading: "The sense of injury breeds, not the will to inflict injury but a hatred of all injury,"[8] a sentence applied to Daniel in the novel but that, through a sort of literary magic that releases the sentence from its context, Stowe here applies to her brother and implicitly herself as well. Eliot's novel, like her letters, becomes a substitute for Eliot's supportive presence.

In her response (May 6, 1876), Eliot writes that she hopes that "the Professor" and Mrs. Stowe will continue to be interested in her "spiritual children." On Stowe's situation she comments: "I make a delightful picture of your life in your orange grove—taken care of by dear daughters" (VI, p. 246). Eliot's equation of her books and children fits in with a number of other similar metaphors in her letters.[9] Here, Stowe's "dear daughters" resemble Eliot's "spiritual children" in that both are evidently perceived as extensions of their mothers, who proudly watch how others perceive their offspring.

However, neither author comments on the extent to which Eliot has clearly borrowed from Stowe's work in this last novel.[10] Most strikingly, a central plot device from *Oldtown Folks* contributes to Eliot's novel: a central character learns about the illegitimate children of her husband. Tina in *Oldtown Folks*, however, makes this discovery immediately after her marriage rather than before, unlike Gwendolen Harleth in *Daniel Deronda*; for Stowe is less concerned with moral ambiguities than Eliot. Tina appears in the pages of *Oldtown Folks* first as a child, one of Stowe's little innocents like Little Eva. Though always virtuous, as a child she is at least capable of petty lies on her own behalf and defiance of adults (who are generally in the wrong). But she grows into a woman who, like Mirah in *Daniel Deronda*, is a paragon of innocent virtue. One form her innocence takes is that, like Gwendolen Harleth, she cannot imagine anything beyond her own boundaries. Stowe is less explicit in suggesting the dark side of this innocence (though she hints at it), which in Eliot often comes to some bad end, Hetty Sorrel of *Adam Bede* being perhaps her best example here. In *Daniel Deronda*, Eliot ends up splitting Stowe's Tina into Mirah, who possesses Tina's innocence, and Gwendolen, who acts in a plot resembling Tina's story.

But not only does *Oldtown Folks* appear in the pages of Eliot's novel; *Daniel Deronda* also performs some of the textual moves of *Uncle Tom's Cabin*. Like that novel, *Daniel Deronda* can be read as typology[11] but finally denies such a reading as a final "explanation." *Daniel Deronda* consistently undercuts faith in the authority of other, "master" texts, which propose to act as a solution to the text as a kind of puzzle; while it may rewrite (and thus evoke) other texts, it finally subverts the authority of texts altogether. What *Daniel Deronda* finally offers may (once again) be closer to "uncanny" doubling—which also suggests similarities between events separated in time but reveals only the figure of the mother rather than a "solution." While a prior text might seem to "explain" the events of this text, or a later time might appear to give significance by fulfilling a prophecy that is made here, such interpretations are only provisional.[12] Anterior time becomes associated with femininity and Jewishness, which are subordinated to a present which neither completes nor fulfills but rather, is uneasily haunted by this past.

Let me illustrate Eliot's undercutting of her typological method with an example late in the novel where she clearly qualifies the prophetic vision of Mordecai, who is sometimes taken to be a spokesman for Eliot's claims for history.[13] To the contrary, Mordecai, while saintly, is not entirely reliable—nor perhaps is his "vision," which is a product of his admirable though half-mad mind. Mordecai resembles a Wagnerian "wise fool," Parsifal, for example: while he is clearly a hero activated by a divine light, his vision is private. The light is not visible to other mortals, nor is his vision the motivating force in the rest of the world. This example also stresses how the novel's prophetic vision of history is undermined by women. Eliot's novel (like *Uncle Tom's Cabin*) deals with a question that is characterized as one of "race"; and the racial issue doubles questions about gender in the text.[14] In this scene, an apparently insignificant conversation between Mirah and Mordecai, the novel also offers a way of reading the association it suggests between race and gender.

Here Mordecai suggests a way of perceiving Jewish identity and its relationship to the larger culture. As he contemplates seeing Deronda again, Mordecai meditates in the tradition of Jewish mysticism, which leads him to speak to Mirah of "divine Unity" and to tell her: "See, then—the nation which has been scoffed at for its separateness, has given a binding theory to the human race. Now, in complete unity a part possesses the whole as the whole possesses every part" (p. 802). Mordecai suggests that with his death he himself will merge into a greater "unity." To Mirah's protest that her mind is too poor to understand what he is saying, Mordecai suggests that women are particularly equipped to understand the renunciation of which he speaks; and he illustrates this suggestion with the story of a Jewish maiden whose love for a Gentile king led her to sacrifice herself for the life of the woman the king loved. In this story, the Jews are represented by the "Jewish maiden" who opposes the "Gentile king," and whose sacrifice of herself for love Mordecai reads as womanly, while he also makes her representative of the Jews.

The intention of Mordecai's spiritual sense of unity is evidently to change the terms of the contestation between the dominant culture and the minority, so that sacrifice transforms the struggle between them. But, as his subsequent conversation with Mirah suggests, his idea is based on misconceptions and, like the wish for assimilation which their friends the Meyricks express, a similarly wistful desire. In response to his story, Mirah objects that the maiden's goal was not renunciation but self-assertion: dying for her love, she would gain him as she could never do by living. She reads the story as a case history of passive aggression, where the rejected maiden uses renunciation and her own status as "outsider" as weapons. Both sexual and racial difference are deployed. Mirah exposes the power struggle that Mordecai attempts to read away. In her reading, the parable as a wish differs from the Meyricks' wish only in giving the victory to the Jews, represented by the maiden.

Mirah interprets the parable in light of her own situation, which lends credence to her reading. What undercuts Mordecai's interpretation is his misjudging of hers. He perceives it to be (mis)guided by dramatic literature, "where the writers delight in showing the human passions as indwelling demons" (p. 803), in contrast with Mirah's own heart, which, he believes, is like their mother's. By his comment, he silences Mirah, who well knows the "indwelling demons" in her heart, and disallows her desire, which cannot be admitted. One point to make here is that Mirah's silence acts to echo the Jewish maiden's self-sacrifice in the terms of her own reading; in the reader's eyes, Mirah's "victory" is clear. That is, Mirah sacrifices herself just as the maiden did, by allowing herself to be silenced. But while Mordecai remains unaware of her sacrifice, the reader is not. Here is an implicit answer to Mordecai's objection: "But if she acted so, believing the king would never know?" (p. 803). A witness to the sacrifice, whether king or reader, renders it meaningful.

But also, Mordecai's stance as spokesman for the mother's "heart" as well as Mirah's suggests how heavily veiled the mother is, as misread and misrepresented as is Mirah, and at even further remove. Mordecai's identification of Mirah's "heart" with that of their mother has the effect of silencing both Mirah and her mother, replacing both their desires with Mordecai's words, because it also suggests the extent to which women generally are viewed as symbolically interchangeable. Individual women's desires are not recognizable (or admissible) because individual women are replaced by Woman, who becomes assimilated to Mother. "Assimilated" to Mordecai's view, what remains of the desires of Mirah and her mother is a residue of silent self-assertion.

If Mirah, in allowing herself to be silenced, repeats the action of the self-sacrificing Jewish woman in the parable, her identification with her mother suggests a three-way identification: the Jewish woman represents the Jews in the story, but she also represents Mirah, who represents both the Jews and her mother. The wish that Mordecai has voiced, and that keeps returning in different guises, is to make the Jews one with Christian society. But while Mordecai's status as reliable interpreter of the novel's apocalyptic vision is undercut by Mirah and their absent mother, his reading that femininity and Jewishness function analogously is supported within the novel. Both are associated with the past; and the desire for assimilation refigures another desire which the text keeps reiterating: a desire for reunification with a (lost) mother. Like *Uncle Tom's Cabin*, *Daniel Deronda* stresses mother-child reunions. Gothic plots often operate toward a reunion (for example, Ellena in *The Italian* is finally reunited with Vivaldi; Emily in *Udolpho*, with Valancourt). But, like the reunion of the dead with the living, this meeting may be feared as much as it is desired; and that is the case here as well.

The key issue that marks the letters between Eliot and Stowe is the concern explored in *Daniel Deronda*: the presence of the mother, an issue that becomes associated with both writing and Gothic language and structure. Reunion and assimilation are both ways of dealing with a past, of connecting a past to the present, an impulse in this novel that is both desired and feared; for countering this desire is a drive toward achieving distance.

For Eliot, describing the relationship between the Jewish and Christian cultures offered an opportunity to deal with the relationship between past and present. In a letter to Stowe, Eliot says about *Daniel Deronda*:

> There is nothing I should care more to do, if it were possible,
> than to rouse the imagination of men and women to a vision of
> human claims in those races of their fellow-men who most dif-
> fer from them in customs and beliefs. But towards the Hebrews
> we western people who have been reared in Christianity, have
> a peculiar debt and, whether we acknowledge it or not, a pecu-
> liar thoroughness of fellowship in religious and moral senti-
> ment. (October 29, 1876; VI, 302)

In this passage, "difference" and "similarity" play off against
one another. Eliot wishes "to rouse the imagination...to a vision
of human claims" of people who are different from the white
Gentile culture which she herself represents—and to share this
desire with an author who had roused a nation to a vision of
human claims in a different "race." But she sees "the Hebrews"
not as "different" but as sharing "a peculiar thoroughness of fellowship." Eliot goes on to comment on the relation between
Christians and Jews, on "the history which has prepared half our
world for us." "The Hebrews," in other words, are both similar
and different from Christians as ancestors. In the sense that Jews
are the predecessors of Christians, in the novel Jews become
aligned with other "predecessors" who have become part of the
present. A problem Eliot poses in terms of aesthetics, culture,
and gender identity is how to reclaim a predecessor *without*
being assimilated. Mordecai's wistful vision had suggested a wish
for "unity" without losing cultural identity.

By contrast, a metaphor of organic growth in this text, a
recurrent metaphor in Eliot's writing, exposes a lie that suggests
a related wish in a different guise. In "The Natural History of
German Life," for example, Eliot states: "The nature of European men has its roots intertwined with the past, and can only be
developed by allowing those roots to remain undisturbed while
the process of development is going on, until that perfect
ripeness of the seed which carries with it a life independent of the
root."[15] She follows this statement with a long quotation from
John Ruskin's *Modern Painters* (IV, Part V, ch.1, section 5)
which describes a ruined building of the eighth or tenth century
that has been incorporated into the daily life of European children and adults and that acts as a figure for the continuity that
Ruskin (and implicitly Eliot) professes to see in the culture. In

Daniel Deronda, architecture similarly appears to suggest a sort of "organic" cultural growth; but the whole idea of "organic" growth is clearly deceptive.

Readers of Gothic novels have long noted the recurrence of the Gothic habitation—the castle or convent or church or abbey, sometimes more than one of these, and often presented in ruined form. Varma, for example, suggests that the Gothic motif of the ruined castle suggests the "symbolic collapse of the feudal period" and the triumph of chaos over order.[16] In *Daniel Deronda* "the Abbey," the most magnificent of the "family seats" the novel depicts, suggests the opposite: that is, a triumph of order, which has incorporated the ruin into its structure, over chaos; as well as a victory for feudalism, which has likewise evidently been incorporated into the reformed social structure in the terms of an intensely patriarchal system based on economic class. Like Ruskin's ruined building, but guided by the planning of wealth rather than being haphazardly appropriated by peasants, the Abbey has been incorporated into modern life.

But the appearance of continuity is clearly a deception. What the Abbey actually suggests is disruption and a nostalgic wish for a lost world. It is in the cloisters that Daniel comes to suspect that he is the illegitimate son of Sir Hugo; although he is mistaken, his suspicion marks the end of his childish innocence and initiates his quest to find the truth of his birth. Rather than testifying to the idea of "organic growth," the Abbey bears witness to the disruption between one generation and the next: while it represents nostalgia for the lost world of Daniel's childhood, it also becomes associated with the issue of legitimacy, an issue that suggests the replacement of biological generation with legal inscription.

The Abbey finally comes to suggest what is neither natural nor organic but constructed and artificial, in a strikingly positive sense. And although in the scene between Mirah and Mordecai the text has warned us against investing texts with undue authority, in this scene it also suggests that in practice texts accrue authority through the power that might be imputed to them. The Abbey here acts as the text which instructs the reader about the function of representation: as a child, Daniel was taught to observe nature through representations of leaves on the capitals of the cloister. As an adult, Daniel claims to carry with him the image of the place (p. 476). "The Abbey" is less an entity than a process, a lesson in observation and memory. What Daniel comes to see in the leaves of its capitals becomes what he retrospectively "sees" in nature; his mental image of the place becomes the place itself. The Abbey suggests how completely "nature" and the past are governed by what is imposed on them—by Daniel's mental representations as well as the legal and economic system that disposes of the Abbey. In that sense, "the past" becomes a kind of raw material to be appropriated and acted on by various human agencies; appropriated by memory and reshaped by the mind, it is assimilated to "the present," which retains mastery. Though Mordecai's vision suggests a wish for the presence of the Jewish past in the predominantly Christian present, in Daniel's attitude toward the Abbey, longing for the past is firmly consigned to its status as a wish, while this past is relegated to the controllable status of a mental image.

ABJECTING MOTHER THE MONSTER

If desire for assimilation in *Daniel Deronda* is countered by an impulse toward exodus, those impulses toward the mother— toward Daniel's and Mirah's mothers in particular—are opposed by a revulsion from her. As recent feminist theory has suggested, the absence of the mother, notable in such diverse but key explanatory texts of cultural foundation as the book of Genesis, *Paradise Lost*, and *Totem and Taboo*, appears to make Western culture possible.[17] And *Daniel Deronda* makes explicit the necessity for this "abjection," to use Julia Kristeva's term for it, in the climactic scenes between Daniel and his mother.[18] The terms that describe Daniel's mother associate her with the Gothic tradition of demonic madonnas. In folk and fairy tales, the demonic madonna appears as the evil stepmother, one of our most familiar cultural stereotypes. In drama, Lady Macbeth is her prototype. Among Gothic novels, Matilda in *The Monk* serves as model: first loved literally as the Madonna, in a picture on a wall, she then undergoes successive metamorphoses as a young novice monk, a seductress, and finally a demon. The Marchesa

Vivaldi acts as the evil mother in *The Italian*. In all of her guises, she is amoral and unloving; she is to be read as horrible because unnatural; that is, she belies the loving "nature" of women—or, even worse, the "natural" love of mother for child.

From the beginning, Daniel's desire to know his mother is "constantly haunted with dread" (p. 246); she is from the outset invested with a secret loathing as well as longing and assumed to be evil, an evil that spreads to Mirah's mother as well: "It was the habit of his mind [Daniel's] to connect dread with unknown parentage, and in this case [Mirah's] as well as his own there was enough to make the connection reasonable" (p. 247). That Mirah's lost mother remains dead acts as a countering force to the resurrection of Daniel's. Mrs. Meyrick's remark, "a dead mother is worth more than a living one," (p. 411)[19] is true in more than one sense here. And although Daniel does meet his mother in a climactic scene that realizes the longed-for reunion of the dead with the living, she also must soon be consigned again to the shades, in what Neil Hertz has appropriately termed an "exorcism."[20] At the end of her second visit with Daniel, "she looked like a dreamed visitant from some region of departed mortals" (p. 730).

One issue focused by the meeting between Daniel and his mother is the contrast between the desired resurrection of the dead and the reality that Daniel confronts; as his mother remarks to Daniel, she is not like what he thought she might be. Even more to the point, "he had lived through so many ideal meetings with his mother and they had seemed more real than this!"(p. 687). If the sculpted leaves of the columns in the Abbey have taught Daniel to look at leaves, they have also presented an "ideal" leaf to which the real thing must aspire lest it disappoint. A controllable mental image made possible by the absence of its referent may well be more satisfying than the real thing; what is internalized can more easily be dealt with.

But also, the scene where Daniel confronts his mother makes clear the extent to which the story she tells of her own life acts as coda to the women's stories that have been told to this point. Her story acts as negative image of Mirah's: like Mirah, the Princess fled her father, but toward the theater instead of away from it, and away from her Jewish heritage instead of toward it.

Gwendolen's desire to be an actress, and her evocation of the actress Rachel, are echoed during the appearance of the Princess, who herself acts as literary incarnation of the same actress. Like Gwendolen, though with more strength of will, the Princess thought to rule her husband; and in spite of her will, her father, like Grandcourt, attempted to fetter her into obedience, to mold her in the image of "the Jewish woman" as firmly as Grandcourt wishes to mold Gwendolen into the image of his wife. Her earlier life as an artist took the course that Gwendolen had imagined her life taking. Like Gwendolen she "could not endure the prospect of failure and decline" (pp. 702–03) and married a wealthy man to avoid sinking to a role she saw as beneath her; both women married their wealthy suitors because of the failure of their talent as artists. As the life of the Princess recapitulates that of Gwendolen, so too do her roles as mimetic artist, whore, and wife coalesce, as they do for Gwendolen. At the end of the novel, Gwendolen is "sent packing" with her.[21] At one point Mirah compares Gwendolen to the Princess of Eboli in Schiller's *Don Carlos*—an appropriate comparison because that character too is finally banished.

The resemblance between Gwendolen and the Princess is heightened by the similar images in terms of which the two are conceived. Both are characterized as monsters. The Princess is described as a "Melusina" just after she meets Daniel, in one of those passages so typical of Eliot, where she modulates between what is evidently in her character's mind and in the narrator's: "Her worn beauty had a strangeness in it as if she were not quite a human mother, but a Melusina, who had ties with some world which is independent of ours" (pp. 687–88). When Daniel first sees Gwendolen at the gambling casino, observers describe her as a "Lamia"; and the narrator's description of her twisting neck and green clothing identify even the narrator's perspective with that of these spectators. The images of the Melusina and the Lamia are similar: both are reptilian women who hide something from their men; and when they are found out, they disappear.[22] Both are female monsters destroyed by the gaze of a man.

A clue to the significance of the Melusina and Lamia legends in this novel is suggested by one more reference to a monstrous woman-as-mother. Lydia Glasher, whose disruptive influence in the novel's plot is entirely due to her motherhood, appears to Gwendolen as a "Medusa-apparition" (p. 668). And the similar feature of the three myths is not simply the recurrence of monster women but that in each case the gaze of a man implicitly denies the reality of what he has seen, finally neutralizing and disarming it. In the novel, the monstrousness of the three women appears to be particularly associated with autonomous actions, of which men disapprove; and in all three instances, the woman displays herself as spectacle.

The two scenes where Lydia appears to Gwendolen present remarkable instances of woman-as-spectacle: Mrs. Glasher presents herself for the express purpose of being viewed, by one particular audience. She is an actress playing the role of herself, her own body becoming a text and her children acting as stage props. At her first appearance at the Whispering Stones, Gwendolen "felt a sort of terror: it was as if some ghastly vision had come to her in a dream and said, 'I am a woman's life'" (p. 190). Her designation as a "Medusa-apparition" the second time she appears, on the path where the Grandcourts are riding, seems particularly appropriate. Here, her appearance with her children, whose presence suggests their origins in her womb, seems even more obviously than the first instance an occasion of deliberate exhibitionism. The revelation of her maternal body is intended as an aggressive act.[23] And her uncanny reappearance along the bridal path suggests an implicit pun that emphasizes the repetition in her appearance by literalizing the circumstances of her earlier appearance to Gwendolen, disrupting Gwendolen's course on a different sort of "bridal path." No wonder, then, that Gwendolen and the Princess are cast as monsters who can be destroyed by a man's gaze.

In this scene Lydia mimes both herself and the generalized "woman-as-mother." As "creative artist," she wields power. But Gwendolen, and not a man or boy, is the intended audience; and while Lydia's appearance has its desired result, its effect goes beyond what Lydia has intended. Lydia has failed to grasp that Gwendolen's reading of the scene might be different from her own. What strikes Gwendolen is not merely the appearance of Lydia but the interaction, or lack of it, between Lydia and Grandcourt. Grandcourt becomes part of a second spectacle for

Gwendolen, a subplot to the story that Lydia's appearance with her children tells, a story told by silence. And though Gwendolen appears to be passive in her role as spectator, subject to Lydia's artful presentation of herself, she does possess a certain power over Lydia; that is, the power to interpret her, though this power is limited to what Grandcourt allows her.

For the powerful gaze that threatens and disarms belongs to men. Later, when Gwendolen wears as a bracelet the necklace which Daniel had redeemed for her, Grandcourt warns her not to make a "spectacle" of herself and compares her to "a mad woman in a play" (pp. 502–03). The effect of his interpretive gaze is to divest her of power. And if he is part of the tableau vivant spectacle Gwendolen witnesses, he must also be another spectator to the same scene, though the text never notes his reaction. The opaque presence in this scene is not a woman (as in the Fuseli painting) but Grandcourt's. But the text does note that in assuming her position, Lydia is "daring Grandcourt so far" (p. 668). And while Grandcourt acts as spectator of the monstrous woman here, in the opening scene and in the scene where the Princess appears, Daniel is the witness to those two other monstrous women, Alcharisi the Melusina and Gwendolen the Lamia; and his is the gaze which fixes and interprets the women.[24]

Symbolically, with the exorcism of the Princess, women-as-monsters—that is, women acting autonomously, as a challenge to men—are cast out of the novel. The casting-out of the Princess is a true exorcism, performed by the traditional exorcist of Gothic novels, the Wandering Jew, who bears a special significance here. The Wandering Jew traverses much Gothic literature.[25] In *The Monk*, the Wandering Jew is the exorcist of the spirit of the Bleeding Nun, who suggests a clue to the maternal nature of the exorcized spirit in that text. Because the ghostly nun has usurped the place of Raymond's intended bride Agnes, Agnes's live burial, the punishment for her pregnancy, acts as a perverse and dreadful inversion of that childbirth through which Agnes herself becomes a bleeding nun. Haunted by the Bleeding Nun, Raymond appeals to the Wandering Jew, who happens to be wandering by and who fortunately obliges him by performing an exorcism.

The musician Klesmer claims the role of Wandering Jew early in the novel, but his claim is spurious.[26] The function of the Wandering Jew in the novel is filled by a minor character, Joseph Kalonymos, friend of Daniel's grandfather. Kalonymos sees Daniel early in the novel, but Daniel recoils from him; typically in legend, people shrink in horror from the Wandering Jew. Bearing the chest of Daniel's grandfather, Kalonymos represents the law of the father which exorcises the spirit of the mother.

The name "Kalonymos" is suggestively overdetermined. Literally, it means "having a beautiful name" (from the Greek *kal*, the good or the beautiful; and -*onymos*, having a [specific] name). The good name that this character possesses is not only his own, but the name that he can finally confer on Daniel—that of Daniel's father, which in effect Daniel claims when he takes possession of his father's papers. *Kalonymos* also anagramatically flirts with the Greek *kalymnos*, or veil, mentioned in the Bible by Paul in a passage specifically concerned with reading. The *kalymnos* of which Paul speaks covers the Old Testament as read by the Jews; *apocalypse*, which means "to uncover," is its inversion.[27] In his function as exorcist, Kalonymos performs the function of a nearly impenetrable veil: for Daniel, he replaces the mother with the documents of the father. Kalonymos's power to name Daniel by giving him his father's papers performs the double action of erasing Daniel's mother while inscribing him in his father's law. What Daniel finally inherits is the language of his fathers, a language he must learn to read.[28]

THE (QUALIFIED) TRIUMPH OF THE TEXT

Although the novel invests the casting-out of the mother with special energy, for much of its length the novel moves *toward* mothers. Such movement is characteristic of Radcliffean Gothic: in *The Italian*, for example, what appears to be random movement in separating, then joining the lovers, actually moves Ellena and Olivia closer in a fairly steady motion. *Daniel Deronda* maintains a tricky balance among its major characters: the first part of the novel plots Gwendolen's course away from her mother, toward her marriage; about a quarter of the way into the book we are told of the mystery around Daniel's birth, on which follows his desire to learn of his mother; and shortly thereafter

Mirah appears, looking for her mother. That is, the opening presents one character moving away from the mother, while two others move toward theirs. With the final resolution we see the reverse: one mother reinstated, while two others have been banished. Gwendolen has been reunited with her mother (her last words in the novel, other than her letter to Daniel, are "tenderly" addressed to her mother), while Daniel and Mirah appear to have accepted ultimate separation from theirs. But as in Radcliffe, the good mother is aligned with an "ineffable" language of presence—once again (as in Radcliffe), associated with voice.[29] This presence finally can be admitted only as a nostalgic memory (for Mirah) or as a regression (in the case of Gwendolen). What I wish to indicate here is instances where the novel suggests the replacement of the mother with highly self-conscious structures of representation.

To Mrs. Meyrick, the best of the novel's "good" mothers, Mirah pours out stories of her idyllic childhood with that mother whose place Mrs. Meyrick takes; and in these stories, Mirah stresses what is unrepresentable in writing—that is, what is purely the experience of her mother's presence. Mirah remembers best her mother's voice and her face; and her brother comes to recognize Mirah from the lilt in her voice as she says his name, imitating their mother. Mirah recounts, and later sings, her mother's Hebrew hymns (p. 250) in words less important than the nonsensical, babyish sound of them. The mother's presence is equally important to Gwendolen, who, in spite of her air of superiority to her mother (and her mother's submission to it), expresses her most intense passion toward her mother, a passion that appears in her dealings with no one else, not even Deronda. "Are you there, Mama?" she cries in the middle of the night, wishing to be reminded of her mother's presence, after Grandcourt's death (p. 824); she is comforted by the sound of her mother's voice.

By comparison with the mother's "ineffable" presence, the issue of legitimacy is concerned with the "unspeakable." In this novel the relationship between the two, and the distinction between them, is more clearly marked than in earlier Radcliffean Gothic. Daniel's own possible illegitimacy is the "unspeakable" secret between him and Sir Hugo. This secret acts as a veil over

Daniel's mother and the real circumstances of his birth, until Daniel, the novel, and the reader are ready to receive them. Grandcourt's illegitimate children are the "unspeakable" secret between him and Gwendolen; one of its effects is to suggest to Gwendolen a bond with Deronda. The issue of "legitimacy" focuses a set of problems concerned with the father's absence and the mother's presence. Legitimacy means inscription in the name of the father, *law* and *name* here becoming equivalent. This issue testifies to the necessity for a "fiction" to establish the identity of the father—that is, a story that only the mother can tell with certainty, whose narrative truth is known only to the very person whose identity as mother needs no such intermediary.

While the "ineffable" is associated with what is prelinguistic and unconscious (that is, the world of union with the mother), the "unspeakable" is associated with the repressed. Unlike the "ineffable," which has no language (though the absence of the mother makes possible the figuration that attempts to represent it), the "unspeakable" has its own language and grammar, a language of repetition and recurrence, such as is characteristic of the "uncanny" in Freud's sense. The "unspeakable" does get spoken—not directly but through structures that indicate its presence, such as repetition. I have mentioned Lydia Glasher's uncanny reappearance to Gwendolen. The reappearance of Gwendolen's necklace, associated with her father, is another instance of uncanny recurrence. Repurchased by Daniel, the necklace acts as a reproach; later when she attempts to use it as a silent language for Daniel, Grandcourt uses it as a psychological weapon against her; transformed, it reappears as the "poisoned" diamonds, emblem of Lydia's illegitimate children. In each case, it reminds Gwendolen of suppressed shame at having transgressed limits of being a "lady."

The moment invested with more "uncanny" effect than any other in the novel is the tableau vivant scene near the beginning of the novel. In this scene, as Gwendolen plays Hermione from *A Winter's Tale*, her entrance is interrupted by the accidental opening of a panel depicting a dead face and a fleeing figure:

> Everyone was startled, but all eyes in the act of turning towards the opened panel were recalled by a piercing cry from Gwendolen, who stood without change of attitude, but with a change of expression that was terrifying in its terror. She looked like a

statue into which a soul of Fear had entered: her pallid lips were parted; her eyes, usually narrowed under their long lashes, were dilated and fixed. Her mother, less surprised than alarmed, rushed towards her, and Rex too could not help going to her side. But the touch of her mother's arm had the effect of an electric charge; Gwendolen fell on her knees and put her hands before her face. She was still trembling, but mute, and it seemed that she had self-consciousness enough to aim at controlling her signs of terror, for she presently allowed herself to be raised from her kneeling posture and led away while the company were relieving their minds by explanation. (pp. 91–92)

This scene rewrites a scene often depicted in Gothic novels, where a protagonist, usually a heroine, sees something terrible, whose effect is not entirely accessible to the audience. The prototype of this scene occurs in *The Mysteries of Udolpho*, where Emily raises a curtain in an art gallery to see—what? She faints dead away. Hundreds of pages later, the reader learns that she thought she saw a decaying corpse; but the corpse turns out to be only a wax figure. The reader experiences no uncanny effect from what has been revealed; what is important is that the reader *witnesses* the reaction of a fictional character to something that has an uncanny effect on that character, which causes a bodily hysterical reaction. The physical reaction of the spectator-heroine makes this effect visible to the reader.

In the scene where the panel reappears, spectator, object of art, and artist merge one into the other. Though Gwendolen has claimed for herself the position of the artist-spectacle actress, she becomes instead a terrified witness. Playing the role of Hermione playing the role of a statue, she herself fuses with the inner role of the play, the statue played by Hermione, as she resembles "a statue into which a soul of Fear has entered"; the panel she witnesses assumes the role of Hermione, in coming to life. Even as spectator, Gwendolen remains the object of vision, the woman whose person terrifies because she is terrified.[30] The panel has a mirroring effect, evidently returning to Gwendolen her own terrifying vision of herself as monster.

For the audience of the tableau, the scene offers a moment of voyeurism, where the stage becomes a window opening on real emotions rather than an act.[31] Momentarily, art ceases to mediate between the representation and what is represented; the emotion floods through its own representation. Such moments when the fictiveness of the theatrical presentation broke down evidently fascinated Eliot; Lydgate's story in *Middlemarch* of a real stage murder provides another example. Finally, as in *Udolpho* (and *Villette*), the text "explains" what has been revealed—as a retrospective clarification of Gwendolen's fate.[32] Later the novel suggests that she becomes that fleeing figure in the panel, escaping the dead face that would appear to be Grandcourt's. The oddity here is that the sight of the picture is not a representation (as Freud suggests the uncanny is generally) but a presentiment—and yet the experience (for Gwendolen) is clearly that of the uncanny. If the sight of the dead face is uncannily familiar, it is as a vision of what will be, not what has been; the future appears to be implicit in the past; the dead face is uncannily "recognized" because it is always (already) familiar—perhaps because, like the dead woman in other Gothic scenes, the effect of its opacity is to mirror back the face of the spectator. Like Daniel's Jewish identity, Gwendolen's identification with the fleeing figure appears to be a way of confirming something that has already been identified as her fate. The recurrence of the "dead face" as Grandcourt's repeats this uncanny sight yet again.

Gwendolen herself has been responsible for locking up the panel: "How dare you open things which were meant to be shut up, you perverse little creature?" she says to her sister, who first discovered the painting and who is responsible for its reappearance (p. 56). Gwendolen takes control of this art object—imperiously—by ordering it locked and taking possession of the key; what the panel represents belongs to her. Her words to Isabel have the effect of suggesting that propensity for repression which is especially characteristic of Gwendolen. Later, while visiting the Abbey, when Sir Hugo imagines the ghosts of monks there, Gwendolen suggests that "they should know their place and keep underground" (p. 461). Gwendolen is a study in repression, as her fear of sex suggests. But she is also a study of a woman who is never permitted access to power because she is always divested of control over the art which she claims. Like Grandcourt's later withering gaze, the panel turns her attempt at representation into something to be ashamed of.

By contrast with Gwendolen's method of acting, where the scene opens a window on her own real emotion, Alcharisi acts by interposing art as a mediation of real emotions, an inversion of what Gwendolen does in this scene. In Gwendolen's scene, while her emotion is framed by a theatrical apparatus, the audience sees the emotion raw, unmediated by art. Gwendolen has no control over it. Alcharisi, on the other hand, has no access to feeling *except* through her conversion of it by acting. Like the leaves on the capitals of the Abbey, the Princess converts "experience" into something both accessible and controllable. Her acted emotions also serve to make the Princess herself remote and untouchable. Protesting to Daniel that, though unlike other women she is not "a monster," she delivers a speech that the narrator terms "sincere acting": "this woman's nature was one in which all feeling—and all the more when it was tragic as well as real—immediately became matter of conscious representation: experience immediately passed into drama, and she acted her own emotions" (p. 691). While her "sincere acting," is not outright dishonesty (the narrator also calls it "double consciousness"), it is suspiciously artful. Gwendolen evidently understands the nature of art, which interposes itself as a mediation; the scene she "acts" does precisely the inverse, removing the mediation. The Princess herself is a repressed vision, covered by the "unspeakable" secret between Sir Hugo and Daniel, reappearing as a representation of herself—she acts what she is—but only to be more forcefully repressed.

If highly mediated structures of representation stand in for feminine presence, one resemblance art bears to women is that both are suspect and likely to deceive. Early in the novel, acting is perceived negatively and associated with falsehood and prostitution.[33] Mirah sees acting in terms of her father's lies to her: "My father taking me on his knee and telling me that my mother and brother were both dead seemed to me now nothing but a bit of acting, to set my mind at rest" (p. 255). Mirah's acting evokes unwelcome applause and attention, that eventually translate themselves literally into the rewards of harlotry, what they have figuratively been all along. Acting is an art that quickly becomes commodified; hence its appeal to Gwendolen when she needs money.

If the scene between Daniel and his mother figures the casting-out of the mother in terms of a discourse suggested by spiritualism, as the "exorcism" which Hertz reads in the scene and which the function of Joseph Kalonymos suggests to be explicit, in another scene Eliot suggests the dynamics that allows the substitution of specifically a *text* for the presence of the mother. Here "apocalypse," also known as "Revelations," might be read ironically.

In the scene that immediately precedes Mirah's presentation to the Meyricks, the family is depicted in their little parlour, the mother reading aloud from a recent French novel, *Histoire d'un Conscrit*. At the conclusion, Mab Meyrick exclaims that "that is the finest story in the world"; and comments:

> Call it a chapter in Revelations. It makes me want to do something good, something grand. It makes me so sorry for everybody. It makes me like Schiller—I want to take the world in my arms and kiss it. I must kiss you instead, little Mother! (p. 239)

For Mab, the text of the novel they have been reading functions as a transitional object, in the terms suggested by object relations theory. To read her sequence of substitutions backwards, a kiss for her mother substitutes for a kiss for the whole world; and her love for the world (that is, as a substitute for her mother) is displaced by love of an author, Schiller. That Schiller is not the author of the text they have been reading does not matter, just as the particular text itself does not matter; like the text, which can be called "Revelations" rather than "Histoire d'un Conscrit," the author is similarly a representative of a group, all of which Mab loves. And that the text the Meyricks are reading substitutes for that of the novel in which they appear (in a sort of *mise en abyme*) is apparent in Mab's designation of the Book of Revelations as substitute for the French novel; for *Daniel Deronda* is explicitly a book of "revelations," a careful rewriting of the Old Testament Apocalypse, the Book of Daniel.[34] I read Mab's near-hysterical ecstasy (she also expresses her enthusiasm physically, throwing down her needlework) to be a serious comment on the possibility of enacting on the mother's body an emotion generated by a text, an action that hints at possible reciprocity: that the presence of the mother may be replaced by a written text, as the letters between Stowe and Eliot suggest. The exorcism of Daniel's mother makes possible the apocalyptic ending of the novel. But Apocalypse rests finally on belief in its efficacy, on the driving out of demons; as a way of sweeping out what is old, this apocalypse sweeps out only to veil yet again. Finally, and ironically, this text is less a book of "Apocalypse," of Revelations, than it is an anti-Apocalypse, a *kalymnos,* which veils not only the mother but also any "meaning" in its own typological references. Its "revelation" is highly qualified and finally no revelation at all. Perhaps it is here, in the text's insistent indication of veils, its refusal to allow a final authority, that this novel most clearly suggests its veiled "mothers."

Daniel Deronda's obsession with maternal relationships may finally indicate Eliot's concern about her own relationship to her literary "mothers," those woman-signed texts which—in designating an empty maternal space—attempt to circumvent the paternal law of language. Of course, as the Princess suggests to Daniel: "A great singer and actress is a queen but she gives no royalty to her son" (p. 697). Art cannot be inherited, nor (under the law that pertained at this time) could inheritance be passed down except from father to son. But this very drawback of art may at least be one more way of evading a paternal model. And literary predecessors can provide a haunting presence to be dealt with, like that image of "woman" such texts rewrite. What the presence of Gothic narrative does in *Daniel Deronda* is provide an entrance and an exit for the maternal presence around which George Eliot shapes her narrative. The haunting presence of the mother here must be dealt with explicitly. Although George Eliot reinstates a story of women's exclusion, her veiled use of Gothic becomes a site of muted protest, a rewriting of the marginal position the mother still holds, as she continues to haunt the novel.

CHAPTER 7

Tableau Mort
(The House of Mirth)

Edith Wharton has come to be perceived as one of this country's greatest novelists of manners. In no conventional sense was she writing "Gothic" fiction; yet her densely social "realism" defined itself through and against other established genres, including one closely related to Gothic—the "Romance." In *The House of Mirth*, the novel which established its author as a professional writer, the text's authorial voice positions itself in terms of scenes rewritten from Charlotte Brontë, particularly by way of George Eliot.[1] This text especially recalls those scenes of Eliot's *Daniel Deronda* which concern themselves with visual structuring and with a thematics of gender. Both novels, for example, open from the perspective of a man engaged in observing and mentally making notes about a beautiful woman moving through a crowd. Gwendolen Harleth and Lily Bart both engage in gambling, an activity that becomes a metaphor for the courtship and marriage game, as well as a microcosm of the financial transactions in the stock market or foreign trade that covertly control the social worlds of both novels. Gambling and the greater financial games which gambling suggests are ways of illustrating the instability which characterizes the protagonists of both novels, as well as the literary modes of the novels themselves.

But the relationship between *Daniel Deronda* and *The House of Mirth* moves beyond the matter of "literary influence." It suggests that Wharton, on the verge of a mature understanding of herself as a professional writer, read Eliot's novel as a text which clears an ambivalently coded fictional space for her as (a woman as) reader and writer. That Wharton understands the stakes here is evident in the way she rewrites key scenes in Eliot's text where the positioning and gendering of the viewer and the object of his gaze plays out most explicitly.

Much recent feminist criticism of Edith Wharton has focused on the question of how to classify and understand the literary tradition to which she belongs. According to Elaine Showalter, for example, *The House of Mirth* revises a tradition of women's domestic fiction, complicating its conventions with the issues of a more mainstream literary heritage.[2] Other readings have stressed Wharton's use of conventions other than "realistic," particularly those used in fairy tales.[3] Read as critiques of fairy tales, Wharton's novels suggest how certain imagistic, character, and plot conventions limit depictions of women and their lives, and replace such "illusory" tales with the greater "accuracy" of realism. But such approaches assume that one set of literary conventions can be replaced by a more direct representation of "life," as if "realism" were not another set of literary conventions. And while Wharton does imply that confusing fairy-tales with life has disastrous results—for example, in *The House of Mirth*, *The Custom of The Country*, and *The Reef*—she also employs similar conventions. Reading *The House of Mirth* in such terms, one can hardly escape one critic's conclusion that Wharton herself is seduced by the very fantasies she critiques.[4] This novel in particular appears to waver between enchantment with romantic fantasy and indictment of it.

I would suggest, rather, that in rewriting Eliot, Wharton shows her awareness of realism's "literary" nature. The "realism" of both novels works by framing another literary mode, "romance." Gwendolen Harleth's appearance as Hermione, for example, foregrounds her dissimilarity from that heroine as much as any resemblance to her. Likewise, Lily Bart is no dryad, although she is often compared to one in the text and appears as such in her tableau vivant. The impersonation by these nineteenth-century characters of their older fictional counterparts acts to limit the lives of both Gwendolen and Lily. Both novels suggest that the convention itself must be examined for the way it fixes what it frames. But in her use of Eliot (and texts signed by other women), Wharton never implies the superiority of a realistic mode for representing the lives of women. Rather, her use of Eliot suggests the complexity of the issue of representation for a woman writing, the problem of finding a mode ("realism" or "romance," or any alternative one might imagine) and a perspective for writing (as a woman) the life of a woman.

If the narrative voice in *The House of Mirth* appears at times to argue against the "illusions" of romance, it offers in its place only an alternative fantasy of the "real." The novel flirts with the possibility of different modes of representation—for example, in the scenes toward the end of the novel which depict the protagonist Lily Bart in her boarding house or working in the hat factory— which, as they nod toward either the sentimental realism of other women writers or toward that "grittier" sort of realism of a Theodore Dreiser,[5] purport to be more "accurate," but depend just as entirely on other sets of conventions. But this text's rewriting of *Daniel Deronda* finally offers no single adequate perspective. For both Eliot and Wharton, multiple perspectives undermine the authority of narrative voice.[6] Both texts present sensitive men, not only as sympathetic love interests for their protagonists but as their commentators and interpreters; but in both, the women protagonists offer alternative points of view. Similarly, multiple narrative modes, mutually undercutting one another, suggest another kind of multiple "perspective." If Lawrence Selden represents the perspective of romantic fantasy, he is balanced in *The House of Mirth* by the character Simon Rosedale, whose perspective is certainly "realistic"[7] and in that respect more nearly matches that of Lily herself. Yet Rosedale's understanding of Lily Bart's plight, though it has the merit of being "truthful," is clearly also found wanting by both Lily and the narrator.

But the joint perspective of the marginalized Jewish Rosedale and Lily also creates a partnership which raises the novel's self-consciousness about form to another level. For example, in the second proposal scene between Rosedale and Lily—when Lily actually proposes to Rosedale[8]—the conversation makes several theoretical points about fiction itself: first, that stories have their own power (as the stories ciculating about Lily demonstrate); and, second, that "realism" may not be so very subversive after all, because it does not necessarily change anyone's actions (Rosedale's knowledge of the "truth" does not release him from the social bind created by the stories). As Rosedale puts it, "truth" may actually matter more "in novels" than in "real life." And resorting finally to "stage talk" ("'You see I know where you stand—know how completely [Bertha Dorset's] in your power,'" he tells Lily), he demonstrates that "'there's a lot of truth in some of those old gags'"; that is, in melodrama and sentimental conventions.

In my discussion of *The House of Mirth*, I wish to suggest how the text's wavering toward romance works to affect our reading of the novel's feminism(s) in a novel where any literary conventions are bound to proffer women only as representative and bearer of paternal law. Thus, the very source of power in this haunting novel of a woman's decline and death lies not in successfully replacing one father-marked code of conventions with another (for that does not take place), but in its oscillation between modes, figured within the text as Lily Bart's longing, tentative glances toward an "ideal" which must always be denied even as it surfaces. The novel thus puts its reader in the very position of its protagonist, though it offers the visual perspective of the man looking at her. Just as Lily is denied both the solace of her wealthy suitors' money and also the rarified air of her lover Lawrence Selden's "republic of the spirit," so too is the reader disallowed both the lofty vantage point of satire and the consolation of romantic tragedy. If *Daniel Deronda* rewrites Brontë's double-written visual perspective to "abject" the mother and affirm the Law of the Father, what emerges from *The House of Mirth* is a rewriting of a similar post-Gothic, double-written vantage point as doubly *dis*allowed.

I want to consider *The House of Mirth* as an extended meditation, first of all, on the significance of art generally for women—how art represents women, their bodies, their desires, their lives—and, more particularly, on the problem of writing for a woman. *The House of Mirth*, so pivotal to its author's career, is centrally a novel about art and language, both spoken and written. Establishing a context from which to read Wharton's novels biographically, Cynthia Griffin Wolff has written of Wharton's early awareness of herself as an object to be looked at. Wolff describes how Wharton learned of her society's preoccupation with feminine beauty, as, for example, in her mother's annual box of dresses from Paris. Wolff recalls the confessional pages of Wharton's "Life and I," where Wharton speaks of her own desire "to look pretty"; and she envisions the seventeen-year-old Wharton as wondering whether Paris would find her attractive.[9]

If her mission in life was to be a beautiful object, why and how could a woman *create* art? *The House of Mirth* thematizes Lily's awareness of herself as object and indicates that she is so perceived by others, especially but not exclusively Selden; it also constantly alludes to the relationship between feminine beauty and art. In addition, the images and central scenes of *The House of Mirth* reveal it to be a novel about novels, a text which—in its frequent, almost-obsessive rewriting of scenes and images from other novels—concerns itself not only with its own place in literary tradition(s), but also with the nature of textuality itself.

Before I embark on such a discussion, I'd like to clarify one point about the genre of such conventions that I have termed "romantic" in *The House of Mirth*. While such critics as Cynthia Griffin Wolff, Elizabeth Ammons, and Joan Lidoff have discussed Wharton's use of "fairy tale" conventions, I think that "romantic" might be a more accurate term for those elements of fantasy used by Wharton. But I mean "romance" in a specific sense, one different from the way the term is often used in regard to American literature, where "romance" resonates with the use to which it is put in Hawthorne's prefaces. Such critics as Richard Chase have argued what has become a critical commonplace (though much disputed): that the American tradition is predominantly a "romantic" tradition. This American Romantic tradition comprises the very canon which, until the second half of this century, had systematically excluded the work of most women (of all races) and writers of color (of both sexes).[10] (By contrast, in the British tradition, where realism tends to be privileged, "romance" has often been synonymous with "Gothic" and perceived as a lesser forerunner of the "realistic novel"; and the gendering of the two genres has been almost symmetrically reversed, along with their relative status.)

While the mainstream American romantic tradition undoubtedly was one of the strands in the complex matrix from which Wharton wrote, I wish to consider her use of "romance" in the older, more typically continental European sense of fantasy stories, which often incorporated legends from traditional European folklore or from classical mythology—the sort of "romance" which, before the two strains diverged, coincided with what we now call fairy tales. For example, it is well known that the stories—the "romances"—of Charles Perrault were originally written for a sophisticated court audience. In the nineteenth century, not only did "childhood" become established as an institution on both sides of the Atlantic; some of these stories, often expurgated and sanitized, became its property, while others, still directed toward adults but often with a revised status as "art," were rewritten or adapted to other artistic modes, such as painting or music (for example, in opera or ballet).

In her autobiography *A Backward Glance*, Edith Wharton remarks, "Fairy tales bored me."[11] Evidently, however, she was less bored by the greater sophistication of the romance. In *The Custom of the Country*, Edith Wharton specifically makes use of one such rewritten romance, Friedrich, Baron de la Motte Fouqué's immensely popular and widely translated *Undine* (1811).[12] Such a romance as Fouqué's *Undine* makes use of complexities of plot and character not generally associated with fairy tales, which are often assumed to be a "simple" literary genre. But the real sophistication of the romance resides in the nostalgia such tales deliberately evoke. They are self-consciously reflexive by virtue of their mode. Pointing their reader/audience's attention to their own dissociation from realism at a time when realism was becoming the dominant mode of fiction, they call attention to their own fictiveness, their location in a dreamlike space, their "framed" quality—and hence their identity as "art." Late Victorian British art, for example, just earlier than the composition of *The House of Mirth* (1905), suggests a nearly obsessive concern with medieval romance, which provided a focus for late Victorian and fin de siècle meditations on the nature of art—for example, in Tennyson, in the pre-Raphaelites, and in the aesthetic movement. This deliberate recollection of the medieval points to the fictiveness of such texts. And "romance" as rewritten in the nineteenth-century works from, and contributes toward, the establishment of certain rewritten conventions of representation. If *The Custom of the Country* exploits the legend of the naiad, or water sprite—the undine, as recreated by Fouqué—*The House of Mirth* makes use of legends of dryads, or wood spirits.[13]

In the novel's opening chapter, viewed from the perspective of its negative hero Lawrence Selden, Lily Bart appears (to Selden) "as though she were a captured dryad subdued to the conventions of the drawing-room"; and Selden reflects "that it was the same streak of sylvan freedom in her nature that lent such savour to her artificiality" (p. 11) But the description of Lily Bart as dryad suggests not so much sylvan freedom as artistic convention, convention underscored in later chapters that emphasize how otherwise appropriate Selden's reflections are. Like Lily's first name, her identification as a dryad deliberately evokes nature (or "sylvan freedom") only to refocus attention on the force of the mediation that intervenes. This protagonist is no Lily of the fields; she is the stylized flower of art nouveau.[14]

The entire opening establishes Lily's status as an artist whose chief creation is herself, at least as viewed by Selden, who watches her first from a distance at the train station and then closer at hand. As a "spectator"—the term is specifically used—Selden not only enjoys the spectacle of Lily's sexual attractiveness; he appropriates her to his own interpretation; and finally, he justifies his own status as appropriating spectator precisely by attributing to her the role of artist, a role dangerous because seductive. In effect, (Lily as) the artist invites his appropriating gaze; she "asks for it." To Selden, "her simplest acts seemed the result of far-reaching intentions" (p. 1); he guesses that "the crisp upward wave of her hair" is brightened by "art" (p. 3); in fact, "he could never be long with her without trying to find a reason for what she was doing" (p. 9). But when he muses that "In judging Miss Bart, he had always made use of the 'argument from design'" (p. 3), the problem implicit in Lily Bart's duel status emerges. Whose design is it, anyway? Presumably, Lily is the designing woman as designing artist; and the pun suggests what is dangerous about women's artistry, particularly in this context where Selden's analogy suggests the artist's quasi-divine status. But what Selden also implicitly assimilates, but cannot acknowledge, is that even as artist, Lily may wield only limited power, driven by other cultural forces, perhaps economic and social.

Lily is not entirely unaware of her own ambivalent status as subject and object: she tells Selden, for example, that she is "'horribly poor—and very expensive'" (p. 8)—a phrase which links her double status as subject and object in economic terms. A woman who is a thing, she cannot afford to buy herself. But she is especially aware that she is an art object: her clothes are her "'background, the frame, if you like'" (p. 10). To buy herself, she will "have to go into partnership." Selden, amused, answers only that "there must be plenty of capital on the lookout for such an investment," and suggests that she'll meet her fate at the Trenors—an ironic suggestion, since that is precisely what happens. The problem is that Lily attempts to make the "partnership" literally no more than that in her deal with Gus Trenor. What Selden means is quite different and involves the sale of her only asset—herself. But Selden, whom many readers like better than the other men in the novel, is here no different from Trenor, who will also expect Lily's partnership to involve the sale of herself in a transaction which comes to motivate a giant step downward in Lily's decline.

In *The House of Mirth*, as in *Daniel Deronda*, a scene where the protagonist creates a tableau vivant illustrates the problem of the relationship between a work of art and the "reality" that the work of art purports to depict. Both texts rewrite the problem as the relationship between a woman as the subject matter of art and a woman as an artist. Eliot suggests that the two are separated by a thin permeable border, in the moment when Gwendolen catches sight of a "dead face" in a painted panel. Gwendolen's horror is written on her face and body; and later, as a tactful way of repressing her horror, guests read it into her performance. If for Gwendolen the performance embraces the moment of real emotion, so that the "real" becomes part of the tableau, for Lily Bart the reverse happens: her image as tableau grafts itself to the image she becomes outside its frame; it determines the shape of that image. Like Alcharisi, she performs "sincere acting." In both texts, the "tableaux" scenes focus the problematics of becoming a woman artist, in the face of a society where woman's proper role is to be looked at.[15]

In *The House of Mirth*, this scene assumes a central position in the text. Lily takes part in a tableau vivant entertainment hosted by her friends the *nouveau arrivées* Wellington Brys, where she demonstrates not only how dryadlike she is, but also how the dryad image appropriately transfixes representations of femininity which constitute the web out of which she emerges, both as representative and scapegoat of the society of fictional characters within the novel and as fictional character herself. (See Figure 5.)

Here there could be no mistaking the predominance of personality—the unanimous "Oh!" of the spectators was a tribute, not to the brush-work of Reynolds's "Mrs. Lloyd" but to the flesh and blood loveliness of Lily Bart. She had shown her artistic intelligence in selecting a type so like her own that she could embody the person represented without ceasing to be herself. It was as though she had stepped not out of, but into, Reynolds's canvas, banishing the phantom of his dead beauty by the beams of her living grace. The impulse to show herself in a splendid setting—she had thought for a moment of representing Tiepolo's Cleopatra—had yielded to the truer instinct of trusting to her unassisted beauty ...her pale draperies, and the background of foliage against which she stood, served only to relieve the long dryadlike curves that swept upward from her poised foot to her lifted arm. The noble buoyance of her attitude, its suggestion of soaring grace, revealed the touch of poetry in her beauty that Selden always felt in her presence, yet lost the sense of when he was not with her. Its expression was now so vivid that for the first time he seemed to see before him the real Lily Bart, divested of the trivialities of her little world, and catching for a moment a note of that eternal harmony of which her beauty was a part. (p. 131)

As in the opening scene, which almost as explicitly as this one stresses Lily's appearance as an object of art, the reader again views Lily from the position of Selden. I want to stress, first of all, the "artistry" suggested in her appearance here; she is a "self-creating art object."[16] This description, which seems simply and gloriously to describe the moment of Lily's triumphant artistry, reveals on closer examination how her two roles cancel each other. Within the oxymoron collide two contradictory terms. The medium of the tableau vivant perfectly allows a woman, conventionally assigned to the position of the object which is viewed, to occupy from that very position the role of creating artist, the traditional prerogative of men. But it allows for, and insists on, the collapse of the distinction between artist and art object. If the artist holds a certain amount of power, while the art object is powerless and appropriable, what sort of power might a "self-creating art object" have?

Second, the text here makes explicit something the novel repeatedly implies: that though Selden's gaze holds power over Lily, and though her image exerts a certain power over him, the reciprocal play of the interchange between them works through a

FIGURE 5
Joanna Leigh, Mrs R. B. Lloyd
Private Collection, London. Reprinted with permission.

language of presence only ("The noble buoyancy of her attitude...revealed the touch of poetry in her beauty that Selden always felt in her presence, yet lost the sense of when he was not with her"). For Selden, Lily often appears to be a readable text; and his ability to interpret her gives him a vantage point over her. But Lily herself does not have the power that a written text might have to check interpretation. Unlike written language, Lily is a text whose effect resides in her physical presence.[17] As a structure, specularity simultaneously both distances and summons. For Selden, who wishes to enjoy the appearance of Lily erotically but to reduce the threat that she suggests, such a relationship is perfect.

If this scene explicitly recalls the tableau vivant scene from *Daniel Deronda*, it more subtly rewrites the museum scene in *Villette*. Just as Gwendolen hesitated over which fictional character to impersonate (pausing over the captive slave Briseis before settling on the statue of Hermione), so too does Lily, who is tempted not by women held captive by men but by a picture of the very character that Lucy Snowe contemplates, the royal Cleopatra. In *Villette*, the Vashti scene acts as corrective to the museum scene—but there a woman is the spectator: "Where was the artist of the Cleopatra?" Lucy Snowe asks gleefully (p. 243), sharing the actress's triumph. *The House of Mirth* rewrites the museum scene in terms of the Vashti scene; but men are still the spectators. What if, this scene asks in revising the earlier text, a woman painted herself? For one thing, she might reject the terms the earlier image used in order to convey grandeur—but still, woman in the image of man: not Cleopatra but a married woman as dryad, carving her husband's initials on a tree. What is astonishing is how little difference the differences make. In both cases, what compels and attracts is the appearance of the female body. And here, as in *Villette*, the object of art acts as a touchstone to reveal the men who look at it. Ned Van Alstyne's crude remark, "Deuced bold thing to show herself in that get-up" (p. 131), wakes "a moment of indignant contempt" in Selden—whose reading of Lily's tableau is distinguished chiefly by his superior knowledge of art. Unlike Van Alstyne, Selden is capable of putting Lily and her self-creation into an aesthetic framework which distances the purely sensual impact which the appearance of Lily makes. Selden refrains at first from speaking to Lily when he encounters her just afterwards; he remains standing alone when she leaves him. He prefers to remain in a reverie of contemplation of Lily as object of art.

Selden believes that he sees here "the real Lily Bart"—clearly an ironic suggestion, given that Lily is here impersonating a representation of a representation. She is disguised as a woman who disguises herself in the accoutrements of a dryad in order to be represented by conventions of art. Selden invokes this notion of the "real Lily" on two other key occasions which mirror this scene: in the opening chapter and at the very end. In the opening chapter, for example, the text informs us:

> He was aware that the qualities distinguishing her from the herd of her sex were chiefly external: as though a fine glaze of beauty and fastidiousness had been applied to vulgar clay. Yet the analogy left him unsatisfied, for a coarse texture will not take a high finish; and was it not possible that the material was fine, but that circumstance had fashioned it into a futile shape? (p. 7)

In a context stressing Lily's identification with objects of art, this passage suggests Selden's general opinion of women—or, more accurately, the terms in which Lily acts as representative woman for Selden, even though he sees her as distinguished from "the herd of her sex." The confusion in this little passage is not only over the unsatisfying analogy between Lily and a piece of pottery; it is implicitly over whether women generally are mere "vulgar clay," in which case Lily's "high finish" is what distinguishes her (and presumably what makes her herself); or whether the "material"—for which one must here read something like "femaleness" or "femininity"—is itself "fine," in which case the society that has created Lily is at fault for having given her a "futile shape" (and the "real Lily" is not the external glaze but the material itself). One question posed here is whether Woman, understood as some malleable material which might be given shape and finish, is itself fine or vulgar? The other is what Lily herself is—the "real Lily"—whether her "realness" exists in the first term, the raw material, or the second, its shape or finish. The passage creates a rhetoric of form and substance, distinguishing between the two, to suggest what is problematic in the very division. If Lily is aesthetically pleasing, is she fine material or a high finish? If not, is she a futile shape or a vulgar clay? And what is the relationship of the individual woman to Woman?

The tableau vivant scene appears to resolve this problem by disallowing the division. Lily Bart as Sir Joshua Reynolds's "Mrs. Lloyd" as a dryad is the "real Lily Bart" because as artistic representation she suggests why "substance" does not exist apart from the form in which it is cast; the division is merely rhetorical, a figure of speech only. The work of art does not encode something with a discrete, separable identity; rather, it decodes and gives existence to what otherwise has no existence at all. In suggesting that this tableau "is simply and undisguisedly the portrait of Miss Bart," the text suggests that there is no division between form and substance. But it is remarkable that the "real Lily Bart" can emerge only through recourse to a series of transformations. Playing herself, she constructs herself with reference to a constructed set of conventions. The "real Lily Bart" exists only as a representation of a representation, through a highly mediated set of romantic conventions appropriated from another artistic genre. If anything has priority in determining what is "real," it is, ironically, artifice.

Selden again invokes the rhetoric of "the real" in the novel's final scene, when he gazes on Lily Bart's body after she has taken her fatal overdose of chloral. In this revision of the scene of the woman-on-the-bed, Selden dissociates the reality of her dead body from the "reality" of his mental image of her:

> That it was her real self, every pulse in him ardently denied. Her real self had lain warm on his heart but a few hours earlier—what had he to do with this estranged and tranquil face which, for the first time, neither paled nor brightened at his coming? (p. 319)

He sees her face not as dead but as sleeping, lying "like a delicate impalpable mask over the living lineaments he had known." Nonetheless, he feels "that the real Lily was still there" (p. 321). Clearly, the fantasy of Selden's mental image of Lily is more "real" than her physical body, once that body is divested of the accessories which assign it to the realm of romance. (At the same time, for the novel's reader, the final scene is replete with such images; accordingly, as a textualized image, Lily's body here only more thoroughly inhabits that realm. If, then, the [woman as] reader [as spectator] must identify with Selden, she must also distance herself from him). What repeatedly drives Selden away from Lily are moments which break into his fantasy and disturb that "reality," where the conventions that frame his image of her are made discordant with what is exterior to the frame. When the "real Lily" as self-construction ceases to exist, she must be constructed retrospectively.[18] The problem is that Selden's "reading" of her is weak; it fails to account for the economic determinants that lead to her self-creation, for the production that has gone into her creation.

In other words, while Lily has shown "her artistic intelligence" in her self-creation, for Selden, that intelligence is always submerged to the representation. Suspicious of her power as artist (as his perceptions in the opening chapter suggest), Selden reduces her threat to himself by fetishizing her, turning her into an object. And in responding to her as art object, Selden's response is characteristic of an American culture which is steeped in materialism and monetary values, in that he makes an easy transition between the object of art and money. In *Villette*, the spectator of Vashti and the *Cleopatra* move to fetishize what is seen by reducing it to the familiar and the conventional; here the viewer translates Lily into money, which becomes the new fetish object. In the opening chapter, Selden has "a confused sense that she must have cost a great deal to make, that a great many dull and ugly people must, in some mysterious way, have been sacrificed to produce her" (p. 3); there, he reads her production from her appearance. By contrast, in the tableau scene, the "realness" of Lily as spectacle submerges whatever of "reality" went into her self-creation. And while the reader sees the machinations that contribute toward the production of the Bry's party, we see virtually nothing of the production of the tableaux themselves.

But the tableaux have not really been produced; rather, they themselves are signifiers of production, currency, like Lily herself when she acts as badge of entrance into society, in a relation between the nouveaux riches and the society into which they buy their way.[19] Lily's is an "art" with no redemptive value and little power to mask the money that buys it. The function of the tableaux in the narrative is as a medium of exchange; their purpose is to buy entrance into society for the Welly Brys. If the work of art which it reproduces possesses monetary value, the tableau not only represents value but also acts as negotiable commodity. Lily herself cashes it in, at first for the luxury of a few moments with Selden.

Selden is Lily's most expensive luxury, not only because for his company and ideas she pays so dearly, but also because he is so completely non-negotiable. By contrast, even her dresses and jewelry are capital expenses in her enterprise. Later, refused money by her aunt and unwilling to deliver to Trenor what he believes he has purchased—that is, her body, either sexually or socially—in effect she proposes to reconvert the tableau into romantic fantasy by making Selden's intervention in the "realistic" plot the heroic action of a rescuing knight, a suitable role that builds on the fantasy of her she believes he still carries. But Lily fails in her capitalistic venture as art speculator, just as she fails as stock market speculator, in spite of the money Gus Trenor makes for her, and for a similar reason: the unacknowledged stake in both transactions is her own body, which she is not permitted to withdraw at will. And as artist, she has insufficient control over her materials: Selden refuses to play the role to which her plot assigns him. Her artistry succeeds only at her death, where she once again, however unintentionally, creates herself as art object.

The tableau vivant scene, climax to Book I, is surrounded by an artfully arranged set of scenes which (uncannily) mirror one another, at the same time that they suggest how the tableau scene focuses the issues of sex, art, and money. For example, the scene where Gus Trenor's earlier demands on Lily reveal how thoroughly she has compromised herself socially (preceded by a short scene with Rosedale) is echoed by Trenor's attempted rape after the Bry's party, and then by Rosedale's first proposal to Lily as she awaits the arrival of Selden. This particular doubling of scenes suggests the issues at stake in Lily's repeated refusals, her impulse not to marry, which might also be read as merely evidence of Lily's self-destructiveness,[20] or of her fear of sex, or (in the case of Rosedale's proposal) of her anti-Semitism (and Wharton's, too). While all three readings may partially account for the psychological dynamics at work here, the paired scenes also formally argue for a different reading of what Lily's capitulation means: any match that Lily might make in effect becomes a kind of rape, because it would necessarily be dictated by constraint. The proximity of Rosedale's proposal to the tableau scene clarifies her status as art object for Rosedale, a "collector" like Selden, but with more money to build his collection, and the status of both herself and art as currency. For Lily, money has seductive power: "the clink of Mr. Rosedale's millions had a faintly seductive note" (p. 173). However, Lily resists easily by remembering the greater seductive power of Selden. If Rosedale represents a "realistic" perspective, the problem with realism is that it is not alluring enough. Lily's relationship with Selden, whatever his liabilities, is attractive in part because nothing dictates its advisability but Lily's free choice, which accordingly becomes linked with "romance"—but that is never a "real" choice for her because to make such a choice would imply that she, too, might become an owner. Rather, as an object of art, she can be held and tossed away at the will of the man who buys her. "Collecting" functions as metaphor for rape. However, as artist Lily is culpable because she has, by her artifice, her craftiness (which we recall from the first chapter, from Selden's perspective), "asked for it." In an aesthetic turn on the familiar double standard,[21] she is vulnerable and helpless because she is an art object; paradoxically, she is responsible for what happens to her because she is the artist. Her dual status both endangers her and makes her responsible for her own fate.

The misguided or incompletely destroyed letter is a stock item of Gothic fiction. In *The House of Mirth*, a series of love letters, or perversions of love letters, all incomplete or imperfectly realized, all for one reason or another failing to reach their intended destinations, echoes the function of the tableaux vivants. Thus the text suggests a series of transformations: the body of a woman becomes an art object which functions much like a written text. Like the tableaux, letters function as money. The significance of Bertha Dorset's letters as currency, the currency that Rosedale will later explain to Lily but that Lily will never use, is prefigured when Lily begins to compose a letter to Rosedale which will never be completed, with "the pen with which she had written to

Selden" (p. 176). Like Bertha Dorset's letters this one too proposes to be a "compromising" letter. While it is the existence of her letters to Selden that compromises Bertha, Lily would presumably write to Rosedale to compromise the refusal she has recently given him—and to compromise the "values" she so readily accepts from Selden. Like Bertha's letter, this one is also negotiable, representing money. The censoring of the letter (hence her silence) ironically signifies Lily's desire: she wants *not* to write to Rosedale. Even incomplete and unsent, this letter suggests a function in a signifying chain.

For like Poe's purloined letter in Lacan's reading, letters in *The House of Mirth*—Bertha's letters, Lily's letters—change in their signification depending on the signifying chain in which they become located.[22] What becomes readable is their placement rather than their content. After her night of triumph at the Wellington Brys's party, Lily dashes off a single line to Selden—"Tomorrow at four"—in response to his desire to see her in order to follow up his deluded appropriation of her. Unlike Bertha's letters, which too explicitly express a woman's desire for a man, Lily's note thoroughly hides the multidetermined desire that initiates it. And while Bertha's letters surely are read accurately by Selden but dismissed and partly destroyed by him, Lily's cynical note inspires fantasies: "Ah, he would take her beyond—beyond the ugliness, the pettiness...." (p. 151). At this moment his ardour annoys her, though she still wishes to enjoy their verbal erotic interplay (p. 136). But later, she oddly corroborates his (mis)reading of her note, cynically dashed off ("'I can easily put him off when tomorrow comes'" [p. 136], she murmurs), as she is seized with desire to see him. So much for authorial "intention" as a determining principle of "meaning," the text suggests, as Lily retrospectively revises what her own note "means." Both the tableaux vivants and letters function as discourses appropriable for specific purposes, depending on who acts as appropriating agent.

Like the narrative's "realistic" mode, which acts as a corrective to the romantic conventions which (as it suggests) both represent and fail to represent women, the failure and disruption of these letters indicate the limitations of romantic fantasy. These disruptions prefigure the final disruption of that "word" that fails to pass between Lily and Selden, though both imagine this word just before their final failed meeting. In the novel's final sentence, Selden kneels by Lily's deathbed, "draining their last moment to its lees; and in the silence there passed between them the word which made all clear" (p. 323). Is the word which Lily struggles toward in her final moments ("something she must tell Selden, some word she had found that should make life clear between them" [p. 317]) the same word that Selden finds the next morning? If so, romantic fantasy appears to be a kind of bridge which might be constructed to cover the inevitable gap in communication—a gap which opens up to the reader, in that we never learn what this "word" might be. Reading "romantically," assuming that for Selden, Lily, and the reader this word is the same, students often assume it to be "love." Here, the text appears to recant its previous indictment of such fantasies—that is, if we read this sentence as coming "straight," from a "reliable" narrative voice. A "realist" reading of the line, on the other hand, might read it ironically, as indicating Selden's final self-delusion and the cost of his previous idealization.[23]

I would suggest, however, that the inconclusiveness of this line invites us to double read the novel's conclusion. As in the ending of *Villette*, where we are given a choice as to whether or not to believe that Lucy Snowe is united with Paul Emmanuel, here we are implicitly (even if unintentionally) given a choice as to whether Lily and Selden are united by this final "word," or whether Selden ironically isolates himself in his romantic fantasy. In either case, signification can be read only through the woman's dead body. The corpse of Lily Bart serves as the tragic symbol of women's function—both *within* texts (as creative artists) and *as* text itself—to serve as the representative and bearer of the fantasy, the word, and the law of the spectator who appropriates her. Lily becomes a sacrifice, either to Selden's final rest in romance or to the reader's understanding of its limitations. As in *Daniel Deronda*, women are finally abjected—Lily is "thrown out into the rubbish heap" (p. 302)—as a mark of the law of the fathers.

Where, then, is the woman-as-artist in this final scene where all the spectator sees is a woman on a bed? True to its final tableau—a tableau mort, as it were—this novel leaves conspicuously vacant the space where a mother might be. But everywhere this absence of mothers is noted. Characters who are mothers become the absent authors of the plot. Although neither Lawrence Selden nor Lily Bart have mothers on the scene, their mothers' spirits guide them and motivate the action of the text: Selden in his aesthetic appreciation ("his views of womankind...were tinged by the remembrance of the one woman who had given him his sense of 'values'" [p. 149]) and Lily in her desire to avenge her family's loss of fortune by her looks (Lily's beauty is "some weapon [Mrs. Bart] had slowly fashioned for her vengeance...the last asset in their fortunes" [p. 32]). In her distress after Trenor's attempted rape, Lily goes to her cousin Gerty Farish to look for a mother's breast to lean on; but only on the day of her death does she find solace and temporary respite, in the maternal figure of Nettie Struther.

In her flight to her cousin's shabby apartment, Lily escapes those "Furies" who pursue her throughout the text. "'You know the noise of their wings—alone, at night, in the dark?'" she asks Gerty (p. 160). Who are these Furies, and why is Lily so afraid of them? Why might such dreadful mythological demigoddesses pursue a poor innocent dryad?

In the *Oresteia*, the Furies pursued Orestes for a specific crime: the murder of his mother. We have no evidence that Lily has murdered her mother (who has died "of a deep disgust" [p. 33]); but clearly Lily feels intensely guilty. Readers remark on Lily's sexual repression; but for Lily, sexual passion is only displaced by her desire for material luxury. In its chain of associations from the woman's body to art object to money to written text, this novel suggests a number of possible displacements, one for another. I would suggest that the guilt Lily suffers is not for anything she has done in the novel; rather, she suffers as a surrogate for her author (nicknamed "Lily"), and her "crime" is the text of the novel itself. Now, while Wharton criticism has noted Wharton's apparent identification with Lily Bart (for example, in giving her her own nickname), feminist critics have warned amply about reading fiction by women as transparently autobiographical. Here, where I am suggesting that a central issue in this text is the collapse of the distinction between writer and text, I feel a need to be especially careful on this point. But although I would resist any simple equivalence between Lily and her creator—the text's authorial voice always maintains a speculative distance from Lily—I would maintain a more complex, highly mediated way of seeing Lily as representative of the writer, in a symbolic sense. And in this connection, it is tempting to recall Wharton's own work habits: she did her writing each morning in her own bed—a tableau which comically revises the scene of the dead Lily.

Given the equivalents the text itself presents, Lily's desire for material luxury can be read as both sexual desire and desire to overreach her status as art object, to become artist herself. The text's linking of art, sex, and money suggests a double reason why Lily's need for money is guilty: not only is it sexual; it is artistic—and the role of artist is a guilty one for a woman to play.

Such an interpretation of course can be gleaned only in the novel's blank spaces, for Lily barely hints that a woman might hold the powerful position of artist. Lily can never reach resolution; she always oscillates, just as the text itself cannot rest in romantic fantasy or mockery of romance but rather wavers between the two. The terms under which a woman becomes an artist here can be read not through a single, determinate meaning but in the novel's very ambivalence. And in conjuring its absent "mother" texts, *The House of Mirth* points to the empty space of what might be the voice of the woman writer.

CHAPTER 8

Why Would a Textual Mother Haunt a House Like This?

The correspondence between George Eliot and Harriet Beecher Stowe is obsessed with the "other worldly."[1] Stowe introduces the subject, first in the discourse of spiritualism and later in terms of religion, both obsessions of her own that for her were certainly related.[2] She is especially interested in the possibility of the return of ghosts, in language that suggests the similar language of this convention in Gothic novels. As one might expect, George Eliot meets such remarks with polite skepticism.

But the letters suggest that Stowe's interest in such possibilities as spiritual presence clearly impelled her initiation of a correspondence with Eliot in the first place. From the beginning of the correspondence, spiritual presence is associated with a relationship that is characterized as "maternal"; and spiritual presence not only provides a central theme in the letters but also suggests a model for reading the correspondence itself—which in turn might be read as a model for reading relationships among women who write. Eliot, who surmounted her usual reserve in her warm first letter of reply to Stowe, at some level similarly understood the import of this concern as a matter of relevance to relationships between women who write. For as *Daniel Deronda* would later reveal, in spite of her expressed disdain, she herself was possessed by similar obsessions, with both the metaphors of the other worldly and the issues that lay behind such language.

In a letter dated July 11, 1869, Eliot wrote: "Your view as to the cause of that 'great wave of spiritualism' which is rushing over America, namely, that it is a sort of Rachel-cry of bereavement toward the invisible existence of the loved ones, is deeply affecting" (V, 48)—all the more affecting, one might infer, because Eliot may have known that the twelfth anniversary of

147

the death of Stowe's son Henry had just recently passed.[3] Perhaps Eliot also knew that almost immediately, Stowe had begun to attempt to communicate with Henry through mediums.

The idea that spiritualism was in vogue as a wish fulfillment, to reunify people with their husbands or brothers or sons lost in the Civil War, seems not so very remarkable. But to call this overdetermined expression of loss and wish fulfillment a "Rachel-cry of bereavement" is remarkable; for this phrase expresses the loss of the loved one specifically as a mother-loss: Rachel's cry was not for lost husbands or brothers but lost children. The phrase also explicitly associates spiritualism with both the language of the Bible and a theology of life after death, in a Judeo-Christian context.

But what is especially pertinent to my concerns here is the structural similarity between "spiritualism"—"by which," George Eliot notes parenthetically, "I mean, of course, spirit-communication, by rapping, guidance of the pencil, etc."—and the writing of letters, two activities particularly accessible to women. Both have as their objective the invocation of the presence of someone who is absent. And the phrase "a sort of Rachel-cry of bereavement" suggests that this invocation has particular implications for women. Eliot apparently read the Biblical passage in Jeremiah (31:15) (as it is generally read) to imply that Rachel's children are dead and that Rachel mourns their loss: "Thus saith the Lord; A voice was heard in Ramah, lamentation, and bitter weeping; Rachel weeping for her children refused to be comforted for her children, because they were not." If the passage is read this way, in the context of these letters, spiritualism becomes a way of invoking children who have died—and certainly it held this function for Stowe herself, as she consoled herself for the loss of her son and assured herself of his salvation. But the original Rachel in Genesis (30:1) mourned because she had no children of her own (though she later bore some). In light of the Genesis passage, spiritualism can be read as a way of mourning the absence not of children who have died but of those who have never been born, of replacing their absence with the presence of an imagined image, the child of one's imagination. And here writing, the analogue of spiritualism in its invocation of absent Others, clearly does have such a meaning for George Eliot.

Eliot remarks at the end of the July 1869 letter:

You have known so much of life, both in its more external tri-
als and in the peculiar struggles of a nature which is made
twofold in its demands by the yearnings of the author as well
as of the woman, that I can count on your indulgence and
power of understanding my present inability to correspond by
letter.[4]

In her earlier letters to Stowe, Eliot repeatedly recurs to this idea
that Stowe has experienced life more fully than she herself; and she
repeatedly remarks on Stowe's double experience, as a "woman"
and as a "writer." At this point, Stowe indeed had wide celebrity
as well as experience as a writer: *Uncle Tom's Cabin* had appeared
eighteen years earlier; she was in the middle of writing her seventh
major novel, in addition to the *Key to Uncle Tom's Cabin* and
other nonfiction. Although Eliot had actually produced a comparable volume, some of her best work was yet to be written; *Middlemarch* was three years in the future. In what sense, however,
could Stowe, who lived a most conventional life as wife to an aca-
demic, be said to be even the equal in experience to Eliot, who
bravely dared the censure of others in her legally unsanctioned
marriage? Was Eliot's reference to Stowe's "experience" no more
than a polite phrase?

Certainly not. For Eliot, here "woman" clearly means "mother"—a point evident in her use of similar phrasing earlier that year
(May) in her first letter to Stowe: "But I have little anxiety of that
kind in writing to you, dear friend and fellow-laborer, for you
have had longer experience than I as a writer, and fuller experience
as a woman, since you have borne children and known the
mother's history from the beginning" (V, 31). She reiterates the
idea in a later letter (June 24, 1872): "My experience has been narrow compared with yours." Evidently what Eliot is saying in relying on Stowe to understand her facial gestures and tone of voice in
spite of her absence is that Stowe has a certain power beyond that
of the writer. While Eliot invokes Stowe's experience as a "writer"
to understand her own written words that recount her similar
experience, she also invokes another power beyond words, a
power attributed to maternity. Eliot suggests that this power
enables Stowe to interpret a silent language of presence for which
the letter stands in, not as signifier but as an icon of Eliot herself,
and not an icon only as a representation but one that, like an icon

of the Holy Mother at a shrine, substitutes for the presence of the one being invoked.

The close association in these letters between the languages of spiritualism and maternity, and their presence in a correspondence between two women writers who never met, suggests how we might read this correspondence as a model for relationships among women who write, as a relationship radically different from the male Oedipal model often ascribed to relationships among writers.[5] The experience of writing itself becomes an attempt to invoke the woman who is absent—and who must remain absent if the writing is to continue, but whose presence is always desired.

Often expressing in these letters her wish for a visit, Stowe often expresses her dissatisfaction with the letter as substitute for physical presence. But the correspondents both finally accepted the severed quality of their relationship, contenting themselves with the written word. The relationship between Stowe and Eliot inverts a key scene from *Uncle Tom's Cabin*: Eliza, finally reunited with her mother Cassy, with a daughter of her own who uncannily resembles her and additionally supplements her prior loss in Cassy's eyes. But even Stowe, who explicitly glorifies the mother-child bond, depicts reunion with the mother as potentially terrifying. Correspondence, by contrast, enacts the negative fantasy of maintaining distance. Letters both invoke the presence of the absent writer and point to her absence.

Because both spiritualism and letters function to conjure as well as to express—not, as Eliot suggests, as a means to elicit spiritual *communication*, so much as to invoke spiritual *presence*—each also recapitulates the fantasy of the relationship between mother and child, with its nonverbal communication, the communication that precedes the child's inscription in language and the law of the father. Limited to the planchette and spirit-rappings, spiritualism has a merely communicative function; but in its ability actually to conjure up the absent Other, its function is greater. "Communication" under these circumstances means phantasmatic contact with the Other, not necessarily the reception of a verbal message. In the resemblance letter writing bears to spiritualism— its ability not only to communicate with an absent Other but also to act as surrogate for its author—it is both consoling (a stay against the threat the mother presents) and unsatisfactory (insofar as the presence of the mother is desired). And as Stowe would remark to Eliot in a later letter (May 1876), a serialized novel might be "as good as a letter," similarly evoking the presence and sympathy of its writer rather than mirroring its writer in its reader. Further, according to one line of feminist revision of psychoanalytic thinking (through the lens of object relations theory), the preverbal communication that a baby girl experiences with her own mother can be reexperienced when that child grows up to give birth to her own little girl, whom she experiences similarly as a double of herself.[6] In this sense, the same person experiences the same relationship with a daughter as with her mother. This emphasis on sameness and identification is what is most emphatically unlike the Oedipal model for father-son or even father-daughter relationships, where the emphasis is on difference and the goal is to usurp the father's place, to become him. The father must be annihilated in order to be replaced by the son. In the mother/daughter relationship, the daughter is multipositioned, in the place of the daughter and mother simultaneously.

Relationships between women generally have the potential to recapitulate mother-daughter relationships. Something of this recapitulation is evident in the relationship between Eliot and Stowe; but while Eliot tends to cast Stowe in a maternal role, the relationship is not stable. What is consistent is reliance on a kind of preverbal, mother-daughter "communication" established by writing, not primarily as the bearer of messages but as iconic representative of its author.

As linguistic structures, novels are always inscribed in paternal law; in one sense (a strictly psychoanalytic one), no text can really have a "mother" because inscription in language implies differentiation from the maternal. But as I have suggested, Gothic-marked narratives always point to the space where the absent mother might be. These texts seem specially conscious of the loss that occurs with that inscription. And while I am not claiming that these texts are marked only by women-authored predecessors (Lewis's *The Monk*, to choose what may be the best example, often provides another source), I believe they seize upon Gothic narrative's special potential to reinscribe what I am characterizing as "maternal" in their specular structure, which acts both to distance and to summon. Those moments when a woman-authored text reappears in such pages have special significance, not only as a model but as a presence, as in the correspondence between Eliot and Stowe.

In her letter of June 24, 1872, Eliot responds to Stowe's report of a spiritualistic encounter with Charlotte Brontë. She begins this letter by contrasting her own "country refuge" in Surrey with that of Stowe in Florida, which Stowe had urged her to visit "in spirit if not personally."[7] Eliot replies: "We shall never see it, I imagine, except in the mirror of your loving words; but thanks, many and warm, dear friend for saying that our presence would be welcome." She proceeds to send her thanks to "the Professor" (Calvin, Stowe's husband) for his letter and to comment on what Stowe has told her about his having been the model for the "visionary boy" (that is, the narrator, who has psychic experiences) in *Oldtown Folks*:

> Perhaps I am inclined, under the influence of the facts, physiological and psychological, which have been gathered of late years, to give larger place to the interpretation of vision-seeing as *subjective* [Eliot's emphasis] than the Professor would approve. It seems difficult to limit—at least to limit with any precision—the possibility of confounding sense by impressions, derived from inward conditions, with those which are directly dependent on external stimulus. In fact, the division between within and without in this sense seems to become every year a more subtle and bewildering problem. (V, 280)

Eliot's attempt at tact in debunking the Stowes's spiritualism (which she herself evidently thought to be nonsense), leads her here to a language suggestive of certain metaphysical questions: in what sense, for example, is the subjective "real"? And this question about the relationship between internal and external— between what is within the mind and what is actually visible outside it—is a specifically Gothic issue. Eliot's language here suggests her implicit appreciation, first of all, that though there may not be an "external" reality of visions or spirits, there is the possibility of a reality that does exist in a different dimension from that of the physical world (that is, a "subjective" reality) and that determines sense impressions and (perhaps) actions.

But if something characterized as "internal" has no independent existence, what sort of existence does it have? This question has as much relevance to our own modern-day controversy over the ethics of abortion as it had over the nineteenth-century issue of spiritualism. Eliot's description of this reality as "within" casts it in the terms of pregnancy and childbirth, where similarly the division between within and without is at issue. Margaret Homans has pointed out the "Gothic" character of childbirth in the fear produced by giving birth and thus projecting into the object world something that was once internal and that now takes on its own independent existence. As Homans suggests, "the gothic literalization of subjective states" resembles the process of childbirth, where something internal acquires its own objective reality. Further, in both situations, the woman in the center of the projection (the woman giving birth or the Gothic heroine) is in a position to become identified with the object on which her subjectivity is projected.[8] Eliot's letter seizes on precisely this "gothic literalization of subjective states," both to call it into question and (tactfully) to confine these subjective states to linguistic figuration—a remarkably easy and graceful move here—but in a context that associates subjectivity with a woman writer's identity as a mother.

Eliot's next sentence launches into skeptical commentary on what Stowe has told her about her "visit" with Charlotte Brontë:

> *Your* experience with the *planchette* is amazing; but that the words which you found it to have written were dictated by the spirit of Charlotte Brontë is to me (whether rightly or not) so enormously improbable, that I could only accept it if every condition were laid bare, and every other explanation demonstrated to be impossible. (V, 280)

In his book *Spiritual Manifestations*, Stowe's brother Charles Beecher reports the existence of a transcript of the conversation between Stowe and Brontë through the planchette operated by the mysterious amateur medium "Mrs. K."[9] But with this exception, Stowe makes her only written commentary on this experience in her correspondence with Eliot. Why? Stowe surely knew from Eliot's previous letters that her correspondent was not likely to be sympathetic with her psychic experiments. Perhaps she meant to convert Eliot, as she would later attempt to convert her to a Protestant theology which would be more orthodox than that to which Eliot evidently adhered. But also, Stowe's attempt to invoke the presence of Brontë through a medium bears analogy with her (even more successful) attempt to invoke the presence of Eliot through letters.[10] In both cases, Stowe summons the presence of an absent woman writer—through language, which acts less as a referential discourse than as a performative one; that is, it causes the action which it states actually to happen (as, for example in such a statement as, "I take you as my husband [or wife])." In the writing of the letters, the receiver of the letter becomes present to the writer. In both cases, what gets established is (at least the appearance of) a close *spiritual* relationship between women writers, bound less by the forms of the "communication," the letter or the séance, or the words that both employ, than by the fact that both correspondents *are* women and writers.

Eliot closes the letter by explicitly characterizing the correspondence between them in such a similar set of images and terms:

> Dear friend, how much you have lived through, both in the flesh and in the spirit! My experience has been narrow compared with yours. I assure you I feel this, so do not misinterpret anything I say to you as being written in a flippant or critical spirit. One always feels the want of the voice and eyes to accompany a letter and give it the right tone. [V, 281–282]

If "one always feels the want of the voice and eyes to accompany a letter," on the other hand it is precisely the "want of the voice and eyes" that always does accompany a written missive. This very lack of the presence of the letter's writer enables a letter to serve as a substitute for such physical presence. What is especially intriguing about Eliot's sentiment here is that her apology for her own skepticism appears in a context where "presence" and "absence" are always at issue. Here, where she speaks wistfully of what writing lacks—"One always feels the want of the voice and eyes to accompany a letter"—in a context stressing her own "narrow experience," she suggests that she understands her own relationship with her correspondent Stowe as a relationship structured in the same way as the communication Stowe describes with the spirit of Brontë.[11] Like Stowe's seance, the letters between them provide a (fantasy of a) sharing among women writers *as* women and writers that recapitulates a preverbal union between mothers and daughters, but that (again like the séance) confirms the distance between them. And here Eliot redeems her previous debunking of Calvin Stowe's visions. Whatever reservations she might have about their "subjective" character are held in check by the valorization of the subjective that she here confirms, when she wistfully speaks of the need for the voice and eyes to accompany a letter. And clearly, in both cases, what is "within"—governed by "internal" states—is characterized as maternal.

I have suggested that Eliot's own preoccupation with spiritist metaphors and Gothic conventions indicates a set of issues related to those suggested by similar language in the letters: recapitulated relationships between mothers and children in a literary context. In *Daniel Deronda*, a text in which art generally as a cultural entity (including music, visual art, and drama) so clearly implicates itself in the social structure, writing is specifically an important issue. Various characters serve to clarify the status of writing here. For example, Grandcourt is described as one who hates writing; he prefers to send a personal representative—his toady Lush, "who, to his mind, was as much an implement as pen and paper" (p. 657). For Grandcourt, that is, a human body replaces writing. In this case, hatred of writing (rather than, for example, the positioning of the gaze) is implicitly equated with sadistic control. For Daniel, who is described as unable to write as he awaits his mother's appearance, writing is the marker of an emotional state. But it is appropriate in this context that the imminent appearance of the mother precludes writing; for this novel establishes writing as a way not only of summoning a mother but also of banishing her. *Daniel Deronda* finally rewrites the story of the woman writer and her relationship to her craft as the story of the deliberate removal of the mother's presence and the establishment of writing in her place.

In rewriting the story this way, *Daniel Deronda* distances itself from other Gothic-marked texts by women—texts which, however, cast the issue in a similar set of terms. Like other Gothic-marked texts, it retrospectively excavates a "past" as if by way of discursive justification for a problematic "present"— but, as in a psychoanalytic narrative, this story must be retold for the express purpose of putting it finally to rest. Finally it con-

fines and holds off what it summons. Thematically and structurally, these novels are similar: they tend to recast an account of
women's creative power as a quest for a mother; a "dark" character ("racially" or ethnically) typically doubles the heroine, mirroring her relation to art. But the Gothic mode typically recreates
the story in terms of a double escape/confinement: while this
mother is finally subjected to the appropriating vision, she also
implicitly defies and eludes it. She is summoned by the same gaze
which holds her at a distance—but the specular relationship
never feels quite safe. *Daniel Deronda* makes clear not only that
her subjection is precisely what allows for her explicit abjection;
it also provides a case where, in more successfully assimilating
the Gothic mode to the conventions of realism, the novel more
explicitly casts the mother out. *The House of Mirth* rewrites the
metaphor of vision explicitly as a look that kills; its object is
frozen into an aestheticallly pleasing image where the woman's
ability to create is subordinated to the interpretive gaze of a man.
Invoking *Daniel Deronda*, Wharton builds a house from which
the mother has been banished; but her presence is still felt there.

In its double movement, what the Gothic mode provides is a
structure that not only (within the text) meditates on the problem of women writers' double status *as* women and writers; it
also redramatizes this relationship in its particular mode of
inscribing readers; it tends obsessively to repeat deliberately
staged scenes which additionally reconfigure this relationship;
and it consequently mirrors within itself the relationship it
invites between the text and its reader. Like the letters between
Stowe and Eliot, Gothic visions, with their implicit situating of
the artist-spectator, provide a model for recognizing our literary
mothers and also distancing ourselves from them.

NOTES

PREFACE

1. Ellen Moers was the first to use the term "Female Gothic" as the title of her essay on Mary Shelley's *Frankenstein*, Emily Bronte's *Wuthering Heights*, and Christina Rossetti's *Goblin Market*. This essay first appeared in the *New York Review of Books* and was later reprinted in *Literary Women: The Great Writers* (Garden City, N.Y.: Doubleday, 1977). Other essays which deal with a thematics of "women's issues" in Gothic narrative are Cynthia Griffin Wolff, "The Radcliffean Gothic Model: A Form for Feminine Sexuality," *Modern Language Studies 9*, No. 3 (1979), 98–113; and Claire Kahane, "The Gothic Mirror" in *The (M)other Tongue*, eds. Shirley Nelson Garner, Claire Kahane, and Madelon Springnether (Ithaca: Cornell University Press, 1985). In *The Contested Castle* (Urbana: University of Illinois Press, 1989), Kate Ellis designates a "masculine" (or Lewisite) and "feminine" (or Radcliffean) Gothic, the latter having much in common with the mode which other critics have linked with women's issues. Ellis's feminist project is historicist: to suggest how the establishment of the bourgeois home and the development of Gothic theme and conventions supported one another.

2. My understanding of "Gothic conventions" has been greatly influenced by Eve Sedgwick's *The Coherence of Gothic Conventions* (New York: Methuen, 1986).

3. See, for example, Coral Ann Howells, *Love, Mystery, and Misery: Feeling in Gothic Fiction* (London: The Athlone Press, 1978). Howells's discussion is especially pertinent because, unlike other critics who describe Gothic fiction as "visual" in the service of literary history which suggests how Gothic novels fed into a "mainstream" tradition, her emphasis is on the scene as a formal, structuring principle.

4. This mission is apparent in such classics of early Anglo-American feminist criticism as the studies of Ellen Moers, *Literary Women: The Great Writers*; and Elaine Showalter, *A Literature of Their Own* (Princeton: Princeton University Press, 1977). In spite of much criticism on the grounds of its reliance on a masculinist humanism as an implied

theoretical assumption, the study of texts by women remains a concern of North American feminist criticism; but some more recent texts, certainly made possible by these earlier studies, defy easy categorizing. For example, Margaret Homans's *Bearing the Word* (Chicago: University of Chicago Press, 1986) clearly shows the influence both of Anglo-American and psychoanalytic feminist thinking. Homans's book makes use of insights from recent theory to examine texts signed by women.

5. Feminist critics and theorists have established various taxonomies of feminist criticism. See, for example, Toril Moi, *Sexual/Textual Politics: Feminist Literary Theory* (London: Methuen, 1985). Other ways of classifying have been suggested by Linda Alcoff, "Cultural Feminism Versus Post-Structuralism: The Identity Crisis in Feminist Theory," *Signs: A Journal of Women in Culture and Society* 13, No. 3 (1988), 405–36; Michele Barrett, "Some Different Meanings of the Concept of 'Difference': Feminist Theory and the Concept of Ideology," *The Difference Within: Feminism and Critical Theory*," ed. Elizabeth Meese and Alice Parker (Amsterdam: John Benjamins, 1989), pp. 37–48. In "The Essence of the Triangle or, Taking the Risk of Essentialism Seriously: Feminist Theory in Italy, the U.S., and Britain" (*Differences* 1, No. 2 [1989]), Teresa de Lauretis critiques the whole business of taxonomies.

6. Clearly even the work of recent Anglo-American critics is continuous with much of the work it (justly) critiques. An interesting case in point, for example, is Toril Moi's *Sexual/Textual Politics*, which is rhetorically plotted as a kind of take-over: as she organizes her taxonomy, it appears that old, humanist-based Anglo-American feminism is replaced by the more radically subversive "French Feminist Theory." But even the title of her own book implicitly (even if ironically and correctively) acknowledges its debt to one of the earliest classics of Anglo-American theory.

7. The idea that "women writers" constitute a separable "tradition" in literary studies has been understood in these various ways by literary critics over the past century. De Lauretis speaks of symbolic exchange as a principle of women's relationships.

8. De Lauretis, "The Essence of the Triangle," p. 25.

CHAPTER 1

1. *Frankenstein*, ed. M. K. Joseph (London: Oxford University Press, 1969), p. 9. This edition uses the 1831 text of the novel. Further citations will be given parenthetically in the text.

2. Intro. to Harriet Beecher Stowe, *Uncle Tom's Cabin; or, Life Among the Lowly* (Boston: Houghton Mifflin and Co., 1882), p. xi. Stowe wrote the entire introduction in the third person. See also Annie Fields, ed., *Life and Letters of Harriet Beecher Stowe* (Boston: Houghton Mifflin and Co. [The Riverside Press], 1898), pp. 146–47. Fields cites at length Stowe's introduction.

3. Cited by E. F. Bleiler (Introduction to *The Castle of Otranto* in *Three Gothic Novels* [New York: Dover Publications 1966]), p. xi. The passage appears in a letter to Rev. William Cole, March 9, 1765.

4. A work of criticism suggesting how and why the position of artist is forbidden to women is Margaret Homans, *Bearing the Word*. I have found Homans's work especially helpful in structuring my own argument. But much feminist criticism has commented on the woman artist's negotiation of the territory of the writer, and on the relationship between identity as a woman and as an artist, especially the earlier wave of Anglo-American criticism. Among the best and best known of these studies are Sandra Gilbert and Susan Gubar's *The Madwoman in the Attic* (New Haven: Yale University Press, 1979) and Elaine Showalter, *A Literature of Their Own*.

5. Or, to extend the thought to what it logically implies, as Ezra Pound writes to H. D.: "You are a poem, though your poem's naught." Susan Gubar cites these instances and others in "'The Blank Page' and Female Creativity," *Writing and Sexual Difference*, ed. Elizabeth Abel (Chicago: University of Chicago Press, 1982). Gubar's essay considers a story by Isak Dinesen as the focus for the issue of women's authorship.

6. Howells, *Love, Mystery, and Misery*, p. 15–16. Howells is one critic who has avoided the problems associated with the vagueness of what "Gothic" means (as Sedgwick remarks, it has not been the most useful of rubrics), by using the term less descriptively than historically, confined to a specific genre written within a specific historical period (between 1790 and 1820 in England), dominated by women but not written exclusively by them, marked by an evident concern with repressed sex. Howells discusses Radcliffe, Lewis, and a group of popular novels published by the Minerva Press, and some novels written in reaction to these not actually "Gothic" themselves, such as *Northanger Abbey* and *Jane Eyre*. She suggests that "Gothic novels" appealed to a popular audience and were written by writers who understood their authorial roles as contributing to a revival of medievalism, however misconstrued.

7. While earlier critics have discussed Shakespeare as literary "influence" on Gothic novelists (such as Eino Railo, *The Haunted Cas-*

tle: *A Study of the Elements of English Romanticism* [New York: Humanities Press, 1964] and Devendra Varma, *The Gothic Flame* [1957; rpt. New York: Russell and Russell, 1964]), their emphasis is on the similar thematics of Shakespeare and Gothic novels. Howells emphasizes the writers's perceptions of Shakespeare and the stage as contributing a particular aesthetic effect, in terms of how the work aims at the reader's formal perception of it, related to that effect produced by a similar use of landscape painting.

8. Actually, to say "a man's gaze" or perhaps "masculine gaze" might seem more accurate than to say "male gaze," in keeping with the idea that "male" and "female" refer to biological sex; "masculine" and "feminine" to cultural gender coding. Obviously the gaze does not have sex. I wish to use the terms "male gaze" and "female gaze," however, in keeping with their use in film theory, as I will explain below.

9. This article appeared in *Screen* 16 (1975), 6–18. The film commentary informed by Mulvey's essay is extensive, but see especially Mary Ann Doane, *The Desire To Desire: The Woman's Film of the 1940's* (Bloomington: Indiana University Press, 1987); and Mary Ann Doane, Patricia Mellencamp, and Linda Williams, eds., "Revision: Essays in Feminist Film Criticism," The American Film Institute Monograph Series, Ann Martin, supervising ed. (Los Angeles: University Publications of America, 1984). In art criticism, a similar idea has been expressed by John Berger in *Ways of Seeing* (Hammondsworth: Penguin, 1972).

10. In a later essay, Mulvey counters the objection that sometimes the spectator is a woman. See "Afterthoughts on 'Visual Pleasure and Narrative Cinema' inspired by 'Duel in the Sun,'" *Framework*, Nos. 15, 16, 17 (1981), 12–15. See also Miriam Hansen, "Pleasure, Ambivalence, Identification: Valentino and Female Spectatorship," *Cinema Journal* 25, No. 4 (1986), 6–32.

11. "The 'Uncanny'" has generated considerable discussion. See especially Helene Cixous, "Fiction and Its Phantoms: A Reading of Freud's *Das Unheimliche* (The 'Uncanny')," *New Literary History*, 7 (1976), 525–48; Neil Hertz, "Freud and the Sandman," in *The End of the Line* (New York: Columbia University Press, 1985), pp. 97–121; Samuel Weber, "The Sideshow, or: Remarks on a Canny Moment," *Modern Language Notes*, 88 (1973), 1102–33; and Janet Todd, "The Veiled Woman in Freud's 'Das Unheimliche,'" *Signs* 11, No. 3 (1986), 519–28.

12. Cixous stresses this point, p. 543.

13. See Mary Ann Doane's related reading of Freud's essay (*The Desire to Desire*, pp. 18–19). Doane notes that the construction of a boy's masochistic fantasy is different from that of a girl; and she stresses the "aestheticizing" of sexuality for the girl.

14. As Doane suggests (p. 19), adding that the spectator's role and masochistic fantasy cost the girl "her very access to sexuality."

15. By comparison, it does operate similarly to one of the options Mulvey suggests: the girl-turned-asexual spectator here achieves her gratification in a manner similar to the male sadistic voyeur.

16. See Todd, who speaks of Freud averting his eyes from the woman in "The 'Uncanny.'"

17. For an example of literary criticism that suggests the relationship between contemporary horror narrative and Gothics, see Wolff, "The Radcliffean Gothic Model: A Form for Feminine Sexuality." Wolff discusses *Looking for Mr. Goodbar* as a Gothic. For film criticism that suggests the relationship between Gothic fiction and contemporary slasher films, see Carol J. Clover, "Her Body/Himself: Gender in the Slasher Film," *Representations*, 20 (1987), 187–228; see also Mary Ann Doane, *The Desire to Desire*, pp. 123–176; Linda Williams, "When the Woman Looks," in Doane et al., "Revision."

18. See especially the final chapter of Sedgwick's *The Coherence of Gothic Conventions*, "The Character in the Veil," pp. 140–75.

19. The "maternal" metaphor may itself feel oppressive to some readers. If this metaphor is invoked as a way of making women's authorship acceptable—it's okay for women to write because authorship is just one more manifestation of a woman's maternal role—such a metaphor is indeed repressive; and to understand writing as womb-related might simply rewrite nineteenth-century hysteria. I would like however to imagine this "absent maternal space" as a culturally constructed metaphor which offers a subversive cover, under which one might escape or at least challenge the paternal language in which one is always necessarily inscribed.

CHAPTER 2

1. Ann Radcliffe, *The Italian, or the Confessional of the Black Penitents*, ed. Frederick Garber (1797; rpt. Oxford: Oxford University Press, 1981), pp. 111; 165. Future citations refer to this edition and are cited in the text.

2. In one of the earliest modern considerations of Radcliffe, Clara McIntyre noted that *The Mysteries of Udolpho*, as well as *The Italian*, recalls *Macbeth*; McIntyre also perceived the influence of *Hamlet* on *The Italian*. McIntyre traces the influence of drama on the novel form itself to *The Castle of Otranto* and also suggests that servants in Radcliffe are modeled on similar servants in Shakespeare, not on Sancho Panza as others have suggested. See *Ann Radcliffe in Relation to Her Time* (New Haven: Archon Books [Yale Studies in English, vol. 63, 1920]; rpt. 1970), pp. 67–80.

3. David Punter also notes that the end of *The Italian* "reads as a modulation of a Shakespearean comic finale" (p. 63). Punter suggests that Radcliffe self-consciously attempted a synthesis of dramatic, narrative, and poetic modes. See *The Literature of Terror: A History of Gothic Fictions from 1765 to the Present Day* (London: Longman, 1980).

4. This of course is the thesis of Gilbert and Gubar, *The Madwoman in the Attic*.

5. The term was the title of an essay by Ellen Moers, first in an article prominently placed in *The New York Review of Books*, and then in that essay, revised as a chapter in *Literary Women*. That essay focused mainly on *Frankenstein* but also included *Wuthering Heights* and *Goblin Market*.

6. Gilbert and Gubar consider Milton as literary father, particularly to Mary Shelley.

7. James Boaden's adaptation *The Italian Monk* (*The Plays of James Boaden*, ed. Steven Cohan [New York: Garland Publishing, 1980]) emphasizes by contrast the privatized nature of Radcliffe's narrative "stagings." Although Boaden uses Gothic interior spaces as stage sets, he avoids closet scenes and enclosure. See also Cohan's introduction, p. lxi.

8. Sedgwick remarks that dreams reported in the narrative resemble post-Freudian dreams less than doubles of the narrative in which they are set (*The Coherence of Gothic Conventions*, pp. 27–29); but like dreams, such interiors establish privileged spaces, exempt from laws of the physical world. Speaking specifically of *The Italian* and noting the deliberately "anti-realist quality of the Gothic," David Punter writes: "The insistence on a poetic cogency of thematic oppositions at the expenses of narrative probability, the self-conscious references to the very processes of fictionalization; the refusal to distinguish decisively between character trait and environmental pressure: all these pro-

duce a literary mode which is 'bracketed' from reality from the very outset" (pp. 84–85). Gaston Bachelard discusses space as metaphor for human psychology, in *The Poetics of Space*, trans. Maria Jolas (New York: The Orion Press, 1964).

9. The phrase is suggested by Coral Ann Howells (p. 27).

10. Margaret Homans talks about the Gothic "literalization of subjective states" (*Bearing the Word*); Terry Castle, about the Gothic confusion of what is interior with what is exterior ("The Spectralization of the Other in *The Mysteries of Udolpho*," in *The New Eighteenth Century*, ed. Felicity Nussbaum and Laura Brown (New York and London: Methuen, 1987)—two ways of describing what I am reimagining as a textual matter, understandable in terms of the theater which this text deliberately invokes.

11. Janet Todd describes these to be the central concerns of Freud's essay in "The Veiled Woman in Freud's *Das Unheimliche*." One of the points Todd makes is that, as *heimlich* and *unheimlich* become indistinguishable from one another, so too do veiling and unveiling. In "The Character in the Veil" (the final chapter of *The Coherence of Gothic Conventions*) Sedgwick suggests that veiling simultaneously acts to cover and to reveal. Sedgwick's discussion of veils has been central to my understanding of how this metaphor works specular structures in this novel.

12. Todd suggests how Freud is a "veilmaker" ("Schleiermacher") in "The 'Uncanny.'"

13. Judith Fetterley has discussed at length this problem for the woman reader, though Fetterley concerns herself with male-authored American texts. I wish to stress that identification with a man's position is not limited to texts signed by biological males. See *The Resisting Reader: A Feminist Approach to American Fiction* (Bloomington: Indiana University Press, 1978). Of course Radcliffe does not always approach a scene through a masculine spectator; but this novel, written in response to a man's text (Lewis's *The Monk*) which was written in response to one of her own (*Udolpho*) offers a special opportunity for understanding the dynamics of the coding of the spectator.

14. This line of argument depends on Michel Foucault's discussion in *Discipline and Punish: The Birth of the Prison*, trans. Alan Sheridan, (New York: Vintage Books, 1979).

15. As we will see in other texts, the "Byronic" character at or near the center of virtually every Gothic novel is always explicitly a

male character but often implicitly "feminized"—that is, associated with women or with a structural position assigned to women.

16. John Allen Stevenson ("A Vampire in the Mirror: The Sexuality of *Dracula*," *PMLA* 103 [1988], 139–49) discusses Dracula as racially different.

17. On this point, see Cohan, pp. xlv–xlvi. Cohan stresses in particular that the proscenium was no guard against physical violence; an unhappy audience would not hesitate to express its disappointment by throwing apples or other objects at the actors, an action that occasionally inspired the actors to lecture the audience in return.

18. See *Gothic Conventions* (pp. 27–29), where Sedgwick makes this point about dreams.

19. In, for example, the model proposed by René Girard, *Deceit, Desire and the Novel*, trans. Yvonne Freccero (Baltimore: The Johns Hopkins University Press, 1980). Sedgwick exploits this idea in *Between Men: English Literature and Male Homosocial Desire* (New York: Columbia University Press, 1985). (See especially p. 24.)

20. As Sedgwick argues in *Between Men*.

21. In Boaden's adaptation, the family is even more clearly implicated. Even Spalatro is provided with a family, and his famly provides Paulo with a sweetheart. It's tempting to speculate that Paulo's devotion to his master may have smacked too heavily of homoerotic overtones for a public audience. Boaden finally unveils Olivia (that is, he takes her out of the convent), to install her as mother in a family, another sort of veil; Schedoni, merely an erring husband, is Ellena's true loving father; and the family is reunited.

22. See Sedgwick on the issues of the "unspeakable," both in *The Coherence of Gothic Conventions* and in her later book *Between Men*, where she ties this term specifically with male homosexuality. Here, the "ineffable" is a sign of female sexuality.

23. As Cohan points out; see his introduction, pp. li–lv. As Cohan remarks, the fantasies are often worse than the actual situation; contact with the villain permits some measure of control, and the heroine often, as here, finds some way of resisting him.

CHAPTER 3

1. George Levine, "The Ambiguous Heritage of *Frankenstein*," in

The Endurance of Frankenstein, ed. George Levine and U. C. Knoepflmacher (Berkeley: University of California Press, 1974), p. 9.

2. Since Fuseli painted *The Nightmare* more than once and the painting was also redone as engravings frequently, it is difficult to say *which* version was on Freud's wall. Max Eastman's description of "a horrid monster with a...laugh or leer squatting upon a sleeping maiden's naked breast" (in *Heroes I Have Known*; cited by Nicolas Powell, *Fuseli: The Nightmare* [New York: Viking Press, 1972]) suggests that Freud's version was *not* the First Version (1781?), now in the Detroit Institute of Arts, where the little monster is not so much leering as scowling and perched upon the dreamer's abdomen, not her breast. Closer to Eastman's description is the version in the Goethe Museum, Frankfurt-am-Main, which Powell dates cautiously between 1782 and 91 (p. 99). But Freud's copy may have been one of the many variant engravings of the subject—possibly even a copy of the lost original sketch (1781), which fits Eastman's description closely.

3. Anne K. Mellor has also connected Fuseli's painting with the scene of the dead Elizabeth Lavenza in Shelley's novel; Mellor suggests that Gerhard Joseph first noted this allusion, in "Frankenstein's Dream: The Child Is Father of the Monster," *Hartford Studies in Literature* 7 (1975), 97–115; but she notes that this association has been challenged (see Mellor's note 5, p. 231). But the connection can hardly be disputed when the film image is juxtaposed with narrative and painting. By making the novel's image visually explicit in terms of Fuseli's painting, this film frame demonstrates how close the two actually are and also how the specular dynamic works in both. See Mellor's essay "Possessing Nature: The Female in *Frankenstein*" in *Romanticism and Feminism,* ed. Anne K. Mellor (Bloomington: Indiana University Press, 1988), pp. 220–232.

4. H. W. Janson identified this portrait. See "Fuseli's *Nightmare,*" *Arts and Sciences* 2 (1963), 23–28.

5. Nicolas Powell draws a connection between the incubus in the painting and ancient phallic statuettes, many of whom, additionally, hold a phallus or play a flute. See *Fuseli: The Nightmare,* p. 75. (The incubus in the Frankfurt version of the painting also appears to me to be playing a pipe.) Powell argues persuasively that the painting depicts a rape. I am indebted to Powell for much of the factual information about Fuseli's painting.

6. At the same time, Mary Shelley's narrative appropriation of Fuseli's painting for her Introduction might be read as revenge for

Fuseli's rejection of her mother, who was in love with him. Given the popularity of *The Nightmare*, not only in prints but also in cartoons, Shelley must have known it well. In fact, one cartoon mocks explicitly the philosophies of Godwin and Wollstonecraft. Fuseli's ill-fated love affair with Mary Wollstonecraft may have given the painting additional fascination to Mary Shelley. In representing her "nightmare," she writes an episode of her own mother's life into the text of *Frankenstein*.

7. Powell, *Fuseli: The Nightmare*, p. 53.

8. Powell, *Fuseli: The Nightmare*, p. 54.

9. While "masculine hysteria" may seem more accurate, I am using the term "male hysteria" in keeping with its usage by Neil Hertz, in "Medusa's Head: Male Hysteria under Political Pressure," in his *The End of the Line: Essays on Psychoanalysis and the Sublime*.

10. Cited by Powell, *Fuseli: The Nightmare*, p. 60. Powell also points out that Fuseli and Darwin were friends and it is even possible that the poem influenced the painting itself (at least those versions that appeared after the early sketch, including the so-called "First Version" in the Detroit Institute).

11. Gert Schiff has suggested the powerful ambivalence expressed toward women in many of Fuseli's paintings, where often elaborate attention to hairstyles suggests their fetishistic use. See "Fuseli, Lucifer and the Medusa," in *Henry Fuseli, 1741–1825* (London: The Tate Gallery Publications Dept., 1975), p. 17. (This book, which also includes a chapter by Werner Hoffmann, was published for the Tate's Fuseli exhibition, February 19 to March 31, 1975.)

12. Kiely (*The Romantic Novel in England* [Cambridge: Harvard University Press, 1972]) notes that what makes the Gothic a revolutionary subgenre is that it pits fathers against sons, husbands against wives. The film, on the other hand, is particularly invested with reversing Shelley's novel as "revolutionary Gothic." In the film, father and son are joined in opposition to the Monster, whose role as the scientist's "child" is minimized.

13. See Mary Jacobus, "Is There a Woman in this Text?" in *Reading Woman* (New York: Columbia University Press, 1986), pp. 83–109, esp. 106–07.

14. I'd like to note further that even the iconography of the film is male, in what appears to be a landscape full of obvious symbols which almost parody images that, in a naively Freudian reading, might be

taken as phallic: for example, the dark rooms of Shelley's novel, such as Frankenstein's laboratory, here get replaced by erect stone towers.

15. Susan Brownmiller suggests the coercion implicit in the "protective" role that a spouse performs for a woman, a coercion reinforced by cultural reminders of the possibility of rape. See *Against Our Will: Men, Women, and Rape* (New York: Simon and Schuster, 1975).

16. U.C. Knoepflmacher similarly suggests that Mel Brooks is a particularly acute "reader" of Shelley's text: Knoepflmacher emphasizes the Monster's role as Elizabeth's double ("Thoughts on the Aggression of Daughters," in Levine and Knoepflmacher, p. 109).

17. Levine also links these two points in the text: "Obviously, the image [of Elizabeth on the bed] is profoundly phallic and profoundly violent, an unacceptable alternative to and consequence of the act of conception in the laboratory" (p. 9). I would stress that the two scenes are even more directly linked than that through the scene of Victor's nightmare, which directly follows the laboratory conception and which employs a specular structure similar to that of the scene of the dead Elizabeth.

18. Ken Russell makes a visual point of the resemblance of the scene that Mary Shelley describes in her preface to Fuseli's "The Nightmare" in his film *Gothic* (1986): the painting is on the wall right behind Mary Shelley's bed when she has her dream. *Gothic* might be read as yet another retelling of the *Frankenstein* story, one that, even more than James Whale's *The Bride of Frankenstein* (1932), makes use of the autobiographical frame and biographical doublings.

19. Andrew Griffin takes this approach:

> In Frankenstein's case (and in horror stories generally), it is clear that the taboo violated has as much to do with *seeing* as with *doing*, perhaps more.... In the novel it is not, strictly speaking, what Frankenstein has *done* that makes him shudder but rather what he has *seen*.

Griffin reads the central metaphors of the novel as suggesting a "primal scene." See "Fire and Ice in *Frankenstein*," in Levine and Knoepflmacher, p. 64.

20. *The Letters of Mary Wollstonecraft Shelley*, vol. 1, "A part of the elect," ed. Betty T. Bennett (Baltimore: The Johns Hopkins University Press, 1980), p. 378.

21. See Beth Newman's comments about the inner narratives of Elizabeth and Justine in "The Frame Structure of *Frankenstein*" (*ELH* 53,

No. 1 [1986], 141–63). The scene that the Monster later recounts, when he plants the locket on Justine, anticipates the later scene of the dead Elizabeth and (perhaps more directly) writes the "nightmare" scene, here (as Newman comments) clearly indicated as a seduction scene.

22. The two alternatives that, Laura Mulvey suggests, film offers its viewer. See "Visual Pleasure and Narrative Cinema."

23. See Mulvey, "Visual Pleasure and Narrative Cinema," p. 13.

24. For a pertinent discussion of this relationship see Ernest Jones, *On the Nightmare* (New York: Liveright Publishing Corporation, 1951), p. 255.

25. While Elizabeth and Justine briefly act as narrators, their narratives are failures. See Newman's discussion of Justine's narrative for an excellent discussion of women's incoherence in the novel.

26. Knoepflmacher's discussion of this point is especially interesting. Kate Ellis suggests that Shelley made significant use of her mother's writings, as well as what I'm calling her "phantasmal" presence. Also, Mellor maintains that the ideal of the De Lacey family is derived from *A Vindication of the Rights of Woman* and that the character Safie is "the incarnation of Mary Wollstonecraft in the novel" (p. 223). But even as described by Ellis and Mellor, Shelley's use of Wollstonecraft's feminism is more generalized than her use of specific turns of plots from Godwin.

27. See Gilbert and Gubar, *The Madwoman in the Attic.*

28. This is not to say that Mary Wollstonecraft is absent from the text, but only that a less specific maternal presence is also perceptible. In "My Monster/Myself"(*Diacritics* 12 [1982], 2–12), Barbara Johnson argues that Mary Shelley's struggle to "give birth" to herself as woman writer suggests a struggle with her mother; but here, too, "mother" is more a general category than a specific person. While Shelley may have had to deal with the additional complication that her mother was a writer, her struggle (as Johnson recounts it) was against a maternal image that threatened to devour her own ambition. For a discussion of *Frankenstein* as an allegory of childbirth, see Moers.

CHAPTER 4

1. As Coral Ann Howells describes the genre in *Love, Mystery, and Misery.* Howells sees *Jane Eyre* as a coda to the Gothic genre.

2. An exception to this vague association of Brontë and "Gothic" is Christina Crosby's "Charlotte Brontë's Haunted Text" [*Studies in English Literature* 24 (1984), 701–15]. Crosby suggests that *Villette* is "Gothic" in much the same sense that Sedgwick uses the term: that is, in its use of substitutions and slippage. My own reading differs from Crosby's Lacanian consideration of the novel's specular economy in my diffusion of Lacan through the medium of film theory, a perspective which concentrates my attention on the gendering of the individualized gaze and on its consequences for representation—*who* sees and the power relationships implicit in the narrative—as opposed to Crosby's more directly Lacanian reading, which emphasizes displacements of "identity" and the text's disruption of patriarchy's founding oppositions.

3. The contention of Robert B. Heilman in his influential essay "Charlotte Brontë's 'New' Gothic," in *From Austen to Conrad*, ed. R. C. Rathburn and M. Steinmann (Minneapolis: The University of Minnesota Press, 1958), pp. 118–32; rpt. *The Brontës: A Collection of Critical Essays [Twentieth Century Views]*, ed. Ian Gregor (Englewood Cliffs: Prentice Hall, 1970), pp. 96–109. Heilman argues that Brontë transforms the Gothic genre by using it in the service of psychological realism.

4. Charlotte Brontë, *Jane Eyre*, ed. Q. D. Leavis (1847; rpt. London: Penguin Books, 1966), pp. 138–39. Subsequent citations from the text of *Jane Eyre* refer to this edition and will be cited in my text.

5. See Heilman, for whom this scene paradigmatically suggests how Jane's reaction subordinates a Gothic moment to the ordinary. I see "Gothic" and "realistic" as more nearly balanced, less clearly establishing a hierarchy here.

6. A related way of considering the relationship between the two modes with feminist implications is suggested by Mary Jacobus, who considers the text's balancing of Reason and Imagination, Realism and Romance as a disjunction through which "the novelist is constituted as woman and writer." See "The Buried Letter: *Villette*" in *Reading Woman: Essays in Feminist Criticism*, pp. 41–61.

7. Letter to his sister, Mrs. Forster, April 1853. Cited by Inga-Stina Ewbank, *Their Proper Sphere: A Study of the Brontë Sisters as Early-Victorian Female Novelists* (Cambridge: Harvard University Press, 1966), p. 203.

8. *A Room of One's Own* (1929; rpt. New York: Harcourt, Brace, and World, 1957), p. 73.

9. Cf. Richard Chase's remark that Brontë's novels become "a series of set pieces, *tableaux*, or great scenes which periodically resolve themselves out of the interspersed areas of formless activity," in "The Brontës: A Centennial Observance," *The Kenyon Review* IX, No. 4 (1947), 487–506; rpt. Gregor, *The Brontës*.

10. Unlike Foucault's gaze, which internalizes such authority. For such a Foucauldian reading of *Villette*, see Sally Shuttleworth, "'The Surveillance of a Sleepless Eye': The Constitution of Neurosis in *Villette*," in *One Culture*, ed. George Levine (Madison, Wisconsin: The University of Wisconsin Press, 1987), pp. 313–335. This gaze is monolithic, unilaterally repressive in a specific way: feminine rebellion is directly subjected to it, even as it is internalized (by Lucy in *Villette*). My own readings (Freudian by way of film theory) are closer to Beth Newman's reading of *Wuthering Heights* (see "'The Situation of the Looker-On': Gender, Narration, and Gaze in *Wuthering Heights*," *PMLA* 105 [1990], 1029–41). She describes the gaze in that text as "gendered and intersubjective (involving specific, gendered subjects) rather than institutional (like Foucault's panoptic gaze)." While Newman's essay appeared too late to be of use to my general argument, I believe we are working from similar theoretical frameworks.

11. Charlotte Brontë, *Villette* (1853; rpt. New York: New American Library, 1987), p. 131. Subsequent citations from *Villette* refer to this edition and are cited in my text. As the title of Beth Newman's essay suggests ("'The Situation of the Looker-On'"), her essay examines Emily Brontë's use of the same awkward formulation, by another narrator, though this time a masculine one.

12. Kate Millett, *Sexual Politics* (New York: Avon Books, 1970), pp. 140–47.

13. Gilbert and Gubar (*The Madwoman in the Attic*) make the argument that Bertha is Jane's double—an argument that has become so familiar that it is almost difficult to understand why they push the point so hard, even defensively.

14. In a footnote to her essay on *Wuthering Heights*, Beth Newman notes that Jane's failure to recognize herself in the red-room scene is one of a series of such scenes of girls' lack of self-recognition in Victorian novels. She suggests that a similar scene in *Wuthering Heights* "overturns the misrecognition of Lacan's mirror stage, suggesting not the illusory control and wholeness provided by the mirror image but the lack of such self-mastery" (p. 1040).

Of course Bertha's face is not Jane's. But if we read her as Jane's double, we might make sense of Jane's dissociation from her through a Lacanian perspective similar to that provided by Crosby for *Villette*, where substitutions indicate a confinement to a Lacanian "Imaginary" which might be double-read.

15. In a recent essay, Laura E. Donaldson has also linked Jane's refusal of Rochester's gifts with her resistance to being turned into a female fetish via Rochester's specular appropriation of her. See "The Miranda Complex: Colonialism and the Question of Feminist Reading" in *Diacritics* 18, No. 3 (1988), 65–77. Donaldson suggests that Jane's resistance undercuts the role to which Gayatri Spivak's essay (noted below) casts her.

16. Alternatively, Gayatri Spivak reads Jean Rhys's *Wide Sargasso Sea* as an interpretation of *Jane Eyre* which critiques its imperialism. See "Three Women's Texts and a Critique of Imperialism," *Critical Inquiry* 12 (1985), 143–61. (The third novel she discusses is *Frankenstein*.) Read, however, as a "Gothic revision," Rhys's novel extends the sequence of texts I am discussing into the twentieth century—and stresses (rather than refutes) the subversiveness of Brontë's novel.

17. Compare, for example, Mary McCarthy's use of the psychoanalytic situation in her short story "Ghostly Father, I Confess." In this story, which thematizes among other issues the transition between theological and psychoanalytic discourses, a young woman "confesses" to her analyst.

18. Jacobus notes *Villette*'s use of the uncanny (Pp. 47–52), particularly in the service of challenging the text's use of "realistic" modes.

19. See Crosby on this point, who stresses that this series of displacements points to the text's refusal of determinate meaning.

20. I am reminded of the opening of Richard Strauss's opera *Der Rosenkavalier*, where the Marschallin and her young cavalier lover, a soprano played by a woman, are in bed together—a moment clearly meant to entice an audience presumed to be largely heterosexual with a peek at women's homoerotic lovemaking, especially until the audience adjusts to the fictiveness that the soprano represents a young man.

21. Elizabeth Gaskell cites Brontë's biographical notice of her sisters in an 1850 edition of *Wuthering Heights* and *Agnes Grey*. See *The Life of Charlotte Brontë*, ed. Alan Shelston (Middlesex, England: Penguin Books, 1975), p. 285.

22. René Girard's thesis in *Deceit, Desire and the Novel*.

23. See John Stokes, "Rachel's 'Terrible Beauty': An Actress among the Novelists," *ELH* 51 (1984), 771–93; also see Rachel M. Brownstein, "Representing the Self: Arnold and Brontë on Rachel," *Browning Institute Studies* 13 (1985), 1–24. Brownstein deals with ways of seeing and interpreting Rachel in the texts of Brontë and Arnold; her essay is illuminating, but I disagree with her conclusion that Brontë dismisses Rachel.

24. Both Jacobus and Crosby similarly suggest that much of the novel's power lies in its ambiguity.

25. In much the same sense as Judith Fetterley defines the term. See *The Resisting Reader*.

CHAPTER 5

1. Alexander Grinstein, M.D. (*"Uncle Tom's Cabin* and Harriet Beecher Stowe: Beating Fantasies and Thoughts of Dying," *American Imago* 40 [1983], pp. 115–44), deals with *Uncle Tom's Cabin* and "A Child Is Being Beaten." His point is biographical: his aim is to psychoanalyze Stowe's sibling rivalry and psychosexual problems.

2. For a reading of "A Child Is Being Beaten" that stresses this point, see Jean François Lyotard, "The Unconscious as *Mise en Scene*," in *Performance in Postmodern Culture*, ed. Michel Benamou and Charles Caramello (Madison, Wisconsin: Coda Press [Center for Twentieth Century Studies], 1977).

3. Probably Gilbert and Gubar were the first to suggest the Gothic affinities of *Uncle Tom's Cabin*, at least implicitly, in aligning the character Cassy with other "madwomen in the attic." Recently, Karen Halttunen has discussed this novel as Gothic. See "Gothic Imagination and Social Reform: The Haunted Houses of Lyman Beecher, Henry Ward Beecher, and Harriet Beecher Stowe," in *New Essays on "Uncle Tom's Cabin,"* ed. Eric J. Sundquist (Cambridge: Cambridge University Press, 1986), pp. 107–134. Halttunen's point is that Stowe, like her father and brother, used a "Gothic" frame to effect a moral end; she describes the "haunted house" features in all three writers.

4. As Ann Douglas's argument suggests in *The Feminization of American Culture* (New York: Knopf, 1977).

5. As Jane Tompkins implies, in "Sentimental Power: *Uncle Tom's Cabin* and the Politics of Literary History," in *Sensational Designs: The*

Cultural Work of American Fiction, 1790–1860 (New York: Oxford University Press, 1985).

6. "Everybody's Protest Novel" in *Critical Essays on Harriet Beecher Stowe*, ed. Elizabeth Ammons (Boston: G. K. Hall and Co., 1980), pp. 92–97.

7. In *Ain't I a Woman? Black Women and Feminism* (Boston: South End Press, 1981), Bell Hooks makes the point that abolitionism did not attack racism—and that white reformist women in general intended to perpetrate a hierarchy that allowed their own social status to be higher than that of black women and men.

8. For a discussion of the problem of the relationship between feminist concerns and abolitionist use of representations of slaves, see Karen Sanchez-Eppler, "Bodily Bonds: The Intersecting Rhetorics of Feminism and Abolition," *Representations* 24 (1988), pp. 28–59.

9. In addition to Tompkins, see, for example, Elizabeth Ammons's comment in her *Critical Essays on Harriet Beecher Stowe*: Douglas's work "is sometimes mislabeled feminist criticism" (p. xii).

10. "I have a respect for so-called 'toughness,' not as a good in itself, not isolated and reified as it so often is in male-dominated cultures, but as the necessary preservative for all virtues, even those of gentleness and generosity. My respect is deeply ingrained; my commitment to feminism requires that I explore it, not that I abjure it. Much more important, it does no good to shirk the fact that nineteenth-century American society tried to damage women like Harriet Beecher Stowe—and succeeded.... To view the victims of oppression simply as martyrs and heroes, however, undeniably heroic and martyred as they often were, is only to perpetuate the sentimental heresy I am attempting to study here" (*The Feminization of American Culture*, p. 11).

11. Baldwin, "Everybody's Protest Novel," in Ammons, *Critical Essays*, p. 93.

12. Baldwin, "Everybody's Protest Novel," p. 97.

13. My understanding of ideology has been influenced by Louis Althusser's essay "Ideology and Ideological State Apparatuses," in *Lenin and Philosophy and Other Essays*, trans. Ben Brewster (New York: Monthly Review Press, 1971). Baldwin's understanding of the novel as a "lived reality" seems to me in some respects congruent with Althusser's understanding of ideology.

14. Baldwin, "Everybody's Protest Novel," in Ammons, *Critical Essays*, p. 96.

15. "The Man That Was A Thing" was the novel's original subtitle, later replaced with "Life Among the Lowly." See Forrest Wilson's *Crusader in Crinoline: The Life of Harriet Beecher Stowe* (Phildelphia: J. B. Lippincott Co., 1941), p. 262.

16. Cited by Wilson, *Crusader in Crinoline*, p. 260.

17. Tompkins, *Sensational Designs*, p. 126.

18. Coral Ann Howells's point about Gothic is couched in similar terms: while Gothics have been criticized for being "sensational, theatrical and melodramatic," these words should not be negatively applied; they suggest a deliberate (not naive) effect. "Theatricality" is tied to the visual emphasis of Gothics. See *Love, Mystery, and Misery*.

19. Leslie Fiedler calls the novel a "gallery of homes" (p. 185) in *What Was Literature? Class Culture and Mass Society* (New York: Simon and Schuster, 1982).

20. Harriet Beecher Stowe, *Uncle Tom's Cabin*, ed. with an introduction by Ann Douglas (1852; rpt. New York: Penguin, 1981), p. 527. For the reader's convenience subsequent references to *Uncle Tom's Cabin* refer to this edition and will be cited parenthetically in the text.

21. *The Monk* (1796; rpt. New York: Grove Press, 1952), p. 396. Halttunen suggests that Henry Ward Beecher relied on Lewis's "horror romantic" conventions in describing a house of prostitution and that Stowe seems influenced by similar conventions.

22. In a note to her article, Tompkins mentions the similar structural positions of Eva and other interceding mothers in the novel: Mrs. Shelby, Mrs. Bird, Tom Loker's mother, Eliza Harris, and also Uncle Tom, who assumes a mother's role (p. 101).

23. While Stowe's "originary vision" of the death of Uncle Tom provides one account of both Stowe's conception of her task and its order of completion, E. Bruce Kirkham notes other alternative reports of when and how this scene occurred to Stowe—though I wish to stress that Stowe consistently described the "visions" that dictated the narrative to her. See *The Building of Uncle Tom's Cabin* (Knoxville: The University of Tennessee Press, 1977), pp. 72–75.

24. Tompkins cites other examples of the "dying child" image, such as in Lydia Sigourney.

25. Thomas De Quincey, *Confessions of an English Opium Eater and Kindred Papers* (Boston: Houghton, Osgood and Co., 1880), pp. 187–88.

26. De Quincey, *Confessions,* p. 168.

27. With thanks to my American literature class at Wells College, fall 1988, where we explored these implications, and especially to Rachel Welsh.

28. See Kirkham, *The Building of Uncle Tom's Cabin,* p. 130.

29. On Stowe's celebration of maternal power, in addition to Tompkins, see Dorothy Berkson, "Millenial Politics and the Feminine Fiction of Harriet Beecher Stowe" in Ammons, *Critical Essays on Harriet Beecher Stowe,* pp. 244–258; and Elizabeth Ammons, "Stowe's Dream of the Mother-Savior: *Uncle Tom's Cabin* and Women Writers Before the 1920's" in Eric Sundquist, ed., *New Essays on Uncle Tom's Cabin,* pp. 155–95.

30. Leslie Fiedler remarks that not only the story of Cassy and Emmeline but also the presence of the Quakers in the novel is less "memorable" because too "'novelistic'"—i.e., dependent for their credibility on psychological "realism" rather than hallucinatory vividness.

31. George L. Aiken, *Uncle Tom's Cabin,* in *Drama from the American Theatre, 1762–1909,* ed. Richard Moody (Cleveland: The World Publishing Co., 1966), p. 394. In the novel, the narrator's comment begins "Ah, Legree!" and continues with the same words as Cassy's in the play, with emphasis on the word *was* (p. 444).

32. James, *A Small Boy and Others* (New York: Charles Scribner's Sons, 1913), p. 159. Fiedler (p. 177) notes that James recollected *Uncle Tom's Cabin* "more vividly as theater than as printed text" and cites the "leaping fish" passage (which I discuss) as descriptive of "a quality which distinguishes all popular art from High Art, namely, its ability to move from one medium to another without loss of intensity or alteration of meaning, its independence, in short, of the form in which it is first rendered." Tompkins cites the same passage in a footnote as suggesting "a characteristic tendency of commentators on the most popular works of sentimental fiction to regard the success of these women as some sort of mysterious eruption, inexplicable by natural causes," along with Edmund Wilson's treatment of the novel in *Patriotic Gore*—James's point being "to deny Stowe any role in the process that produced such a wonder."

33. James, *A Small Boy,* p. 159–60.

34. See, for example, Knoepflmacher in Levine and Knoepflmacher, eds. (*The Endurance of Frankenstein*), as well as Ellen Moers in *Literary Women*. But "autobiographical" readings of *Frankenstein* have become part of the popular mythology associated with this text, as film has suggested, in both *The Bride of Frankenstein* (1932) and Ken Russell's *Gothic* (1986).

35. See Coral Ann Howells, *Love, Mystery, and Misery,* p. 10.

36. See John Stokes, "Rachel's 'Terrible Beauty': An Actress among the Novelists." The model for these two are different from those for Emily, however, because these two characters appear in the texts of novels as actresses; Sarah Siddons is a model only in terms of her appearance and in terms of the characters she played.

37. The relationship among various novels and their stage adaptations, and the suggestion that one woman (either real or fictional) substitutes for another, is especially evident in eighteenth-century Gothic novels in the choices of names. For example, in Boaden's adaptation of *The Italian*, Olivia's name as Schedoni's wife is revealed to be Matilda, the name of the demon in *The Monk*, clearly a deliberate reference, as Boaden's evocation of Lewis in his title ("The Italian Monk") suggests; but Boaden also adapted *The Monk* and changed the names. Stowe, whose religious convictions precluded the theater, was less likely to be directly influenced by stage conventions or names.

38. The criticism that is often leveled against American feminist criticism. In *On Deconstruction* (Ithaca: Cornell, 1982), Jonathan Culler describes feminist criticism of the "first moment," which assumes "continuity between women's experience of social and familial structures and their experience as readers," where "women readers identify with the concerns of woman characters."

39. Baldwin, "Everybody's Protest Novel," in Ammons, *Critical Essays,* p. 93.

40. Leslie Fiedler associates *Uncle Tom's Cabin* with these films in *What Was Literature?* Thomas P. Riggio makes a related analysis of novels generated by *Uncle Tom's Cabin*, including Thomas Dixon's *The Leopard's Spots*, the first novel in the trilogy that included *The Clansman*, the basis of Griffith's film. See "*Uncle Tom* Reconstructed: A Neglected Chapter in the History of a Book" in Ammons, orig. published in *The American Quarterly* 28 (Spring 1976), 65–70. Riggio notes that Stowe's "revisionists," countering Baldwin, "shifted the

responsibility of Uncle Tom's vulgar image to the popular Tom shows and Tom plays of the late nineteenth and twentieth centuries."

41. Riggio, in Ammons, *Critical Essays,* p. 143.

42. As Riggio points out, Dixon deliberately undoes Stowe's points by exploiting them ("*Uncle Tom* Reconstructed," pp. 144–48). He even deliberately echoes her. For example, in *The Leopard's Spots,* the first book of his trilogy, Legree tortures a poor white Southerner named Tom who lives in a cabin.

43. Baldwin, "Everybody's Protest Novel," p. 97.

44. Richard Wright, *Native Son* (New York: Harper and Row, 1940), p. 33.

45. Wright, *Native Son,* p. 35.

46. Wright, *Native Son,* p. 260.

CHAPTER 6

1. George Eliot, *Daniel Deronda,* ed. Barbara Hardy (1876; rpt. Great Britain: Penguin, 1967), p. 397. Page references are to this edition and are cited in parentheses in the text.

2. Jane Austen, *Pride and Prejudice,* ed. Donald J. Gray (1813; rpt. New York: W. W. Norton and Company, 1966), p. 1. This edition also includes, among its critical essays, a review of the novel by George Henry Lewes, originally published in *Blackwood's Magazine* (1859).

3. See John Stokes, "Rachel's 'Terrible Beauty': An Actress among the Novelists." Stokes connects Rachel in particular to Gwendolen's appearance as Hermione, where Rachel is specifically invoked in the dialogue, though he also comments on the Princess's "Rachelesque style." He sees the relationship between Eliot's text and *Villette* as a distancing: Eliot "estranges herself from her major predecessor by critically exposing the Rachelesque attitudes that Brontë had summoned up for Vashti" (p. 788). As Stokes notes, Eliot herself had seen Rachel perform; she also admired *Villette* (*The George Eliot Letters,* ed. Gordon S. Haight [New Haven: Yale University Press, 1955], 1:245–46 and 3:93).

4. Nancy Nystul studies visual perspective in the opening scene through a psychoanalytic perspective. She stresses the novel's emphasis on merging with the mother, whereas my own reading suggests more ambivalence toward the maternal. See "*Daniel Deronda*: A Family Romance," *Cinema Journal* 7, No. 1 (1983), 45–53.

5. One more point of contact, though less important to my own purpose of suggesting how *Daniel Deronda* meditates on the problem of writing as a woman, may be the accidental drownings which destroy the partners of Lucy Snowe and Gwendolen Harleth. Lucy of course is in love with Paul Emmanuel, and his death would appear to be tragic in most conventional readings of *Villette* (certainly Brontë's father felt that was the case). But in making this drowning a (possible) murder that liberates the protagonist, Eliot extracts a buried wish in *Villette*, for independence. Maybe she also expresses her feelings about such a lover as Paul Emmanuel, who surely has the potential to be a Grandcourt.

6. Gordon Haight, ed. *The George Eliot Letters*, V (New Haven: Yale University Press, 1955), p. 30. Subsequent citations from George Eliot's letters refer to this edition and are cited parenthetically in the text.

7. Stowe's brother Henry Ward Beecher had been publically accused of adultery by Victoria Woodhull, well-known spiritualist and feminist. Beecher was later brought to trial and eventually exonerated, though suspicion continued to hang over him. Eliot had written a supportive note to Stowe (*Letters*, VI, p. 77) on learning of the scandal. See Charles Edward Stowe, *Life of Harriet Beecher Stowe Compiled from Her Letters and Journals* (Boston: The Riverside Press, 1891), p. 481 (March 18, 1876).

8. Charles E. Stowe, *Life of Harriet Beecher Stowe*, p. 481.

9. Homans provides a different, more extended discussion of Eliot's use of maternity metaphors for writing, reading several of her earlier novels (especially *Middlemarch*) through such images. See *Bearing the Word*, pp. 179–88.

10. Alexander Welsh briefly comments that Stowe has had considerable influence on George Eliot (greater than Hawthorne's, he suggests) in *George Eliot and Blackmail* (Cambridge: Harvard University Press, 1985), p. 28.

11. See Lyn Pykett, "Typology and the End(s) of History in *Daniel Deronda*," *Literature and History* 9, No. 1 (1983), 52–75. Also see Mary Wilson Carpenter, "The Apocalypse of the Old Testament: *Daniel Deronda* and the Interpretation of Interpretation," *PMLA* 99 (1984), 56–71. Carpenter brilliantly elucidates the relationship between the novel and the Book of Daniel, while she also argues (rightly, I think) that there is finally no single "key" to the narrative. But I will end up describing the novel as "anti-apocalyptic" rather than "apoca-

lyptic." An emphasis on reading this text typologically, though illuminating and "right" in many ways, tends to overlook both the central position of the maternal presence in this novel and the text's undercutting of Mordecai—both textual moves that tend to critique the Biblical text on which this text relies.

12. As Carpenter proposes, in her suggestion that there is finally no "key" to interpretation here; interpretation is an ongoing process.

13. See Pykett, "Typology and the End(s) of History," p. 65.

14. It may be worth stressing that in the nineteenth century "the Jews" were perceived as a race. Leslie Fiedler has called Stowe's separatist vision at the end of *Uncle Tom's Cabin* "millenial black Zionism," a telling phrase that suggests how close Stowe's vision is to that of Eliot, who writes of Zionism itself in a context that suggests a similar millenial vision.

15. In *Essays of George Eliot*, ed. Thomas Pinney (New York: Columbia University Press, 1963), p. 288.

16. Devendra Varma, *The Gothic Flame*, p. 218.

17. See Homans's investigation of this myth and her explanation of why the absence of the mother makes the construction of culture possible, in *Bearing the Word*, pp. 2–39.

18. Neil Hertz presents a close reading of these scenes as a study in scapegoating. See the title essay ("Afterword: The End of the Line") in *The End of the Line*, pp. 224–33.

19. Against this ironic remark resounds Sir Hugo's bigoted warning to Daniel that he should not set "a dead Jew above a living Christian" (p. 786). However, the comment which Terry Castle applies to Radcliffe, that absence is preferable to presence, offers a way of reading both remarks: what makes both "a dead mother" and "a dead Jew" preferable is that both can be present in the mind. See "The Spectralization of the Other in *The Mysteries of Udolpho*" in *The New Eighteenth Century*, ed. Felicity Nussbaum and Laura Brown (New York and London: Methuen, 1987), pp. 231–53.

20. Hertz, *The End of the Line*, p. 224.

21. Hertz describes the Princess as being "sent packing" at the end of the novel.

22. A related image appears in Eliot's story "The Lifted Veil," whose details are appropriated from the legend of the Undine, popular

in the mid-nineteenth century in the romance published by Freidrich, Baron de la Motte Fouqué.

23. See Neil Hertz's "Medusa's Head: Male Hysteria Under Political Pressure," in *The End of the Line*, pp. 161–91. Mrs. Glasher's use of her body in this scene is remarkably close to those that Hertz cites, where women expose themselves as deliberate acts of defiance.

24. See Nystul, who maps the gaze in the opening scene of the novel.

25. Ernest Railo has devoted an entire chapter to the Wandering Jew, where he traces his lineage and suggests his significance. Particularly relevant to *Daniel Deronda* is Railo's description of him as symbol of the homeless and wandering yet indestructible Jewish nation, and the mouthpiece and pioneer of national and social liberty. Railo associates the Wandering Jew with the Faust legend but does not deal with his role as exorcist. See *The Haunted Castle*, pp. 191–217, esp. p. 216.

26. Is Klesmer Jewish? His name is; it refers to a kind of eastern European Jewish music. If so, anti-Semitism, and not just snobbery and anti-intellectualism, must form part of the grounds of the Arrowpoints's objection to their daughter's marriage. But the whole issue complicates Klesmer's role in a novel so centrally concerned with both Jewishness and art—for example, to (further) suggest that, while femininity here replaces the art *object*, Jewishness is a metaphor for "artist," both claiming a position of cultural marginality. Also, Eliot manages here to slip in an unacceptable (to her readers) "mixed marriage." But even if he is Jewish, Klesmer disclaims his identity as "Wandering Jew" when he marries. (Thanks to Judy Frank for more closely translating this name.)

27. See Erich Auerbach, *Scenes from the Drama of European Literature* (1959; rpt. Minneapolis: University of Minnesota Press [*Theory and History of Literature*, Vol. 9], 1984), p. 50. In an article concerned with authority in narrative read typologically ("Joseph's Bones and the Resurrection of the Text: Remembering in the Bible," *PMLA* 103 [1988], 114–24), Regina M. Schwartz notes these meanings (p. 115). Schwartz suggests that in the story of Joseph (as here), the authority of an antitype defers to ongoing interpretation.

28. Nystul sees the ending as a reunification with the mother; she suggests that the Hebrew language expresses a maternal valence. I think that the notion of this language as a "mother tongue" suggests precisely

what is at stake here in identifying women with language or with art as a language: they are put in place as the *bearers* of the word of the father (much as Homans uses the term), not as possible "namers" themselves.

29. See Nystul's discussion of this point, "*Daniel Deronda:* A Family Romance," p. 50.

30. A comparable effect is produced in recent horror films, of the "slasher" variety, where what produces terror and horror in the audience is the dead, often mutilated, body of a woman. The equivalence between monster and woman suggested by such earlier examples of horror as *Frankenstein* becomes literalized by the removal of the monster. See Linda Williams, "When the Woman Looks," in *"Re-vision: Essays in Feminist Film Criticism,"* ed. Doane, Mellencamp, and Williams, pp. 83–99; also see Carol J. Clover, "Gender in the Slasher Film," pp. 204–05.

31. John Stokes notes that this episode revises a real one between Helen Faucit and Macready, and that behind it lies a conventional belief about playing Shakespeare, "that the mutuality of art and nature revealed by Shakespeare can be demonstrated in performance when the intensity of the moment makes the actress playing Hermione forget her art and express her own nature" ("Rachel's 'Terrible Beauty,'" pp. 771–793).

32. In "The Decomposition of the Elephants: Double-Reading *Daniel Deronda*" (*PMLA* 93 [1978]: 215–27), Cynthia Chase notes that such discursive reconstruction marks the "Deronda" plot of the novel—which, as she suggests, discloses not the "effects of causes" but the "present causes of past effects." But I would maintain that a similar discursive reconstruction characterizes the "Gwendolen" plot: both characters are haunted by mysteries which are "explained" as the functions of bizarre (uncanny) coincidences. And I would say that such reconstructed "explanations" mark Gothic narrative generally.

33. See Catherine Gallagher, "George Eliot and *Daniel Deronda:* The Prostitute and the Jewish Question," in *Sex, Politics, and Science in the Nineteenth Century Novel* (ed. Ruth Yeazell [Baltimore: Johns Hopkins University Press, 1986]). Gallagher suggests that authors in the nineteenth century might be perceived either as fathers or as whores, two roles that Eliot needed to avoid.

34. See Carpenter, "The Apocalypse of the Old Testament," p. 56–67.

CHAPTER 7

1. On the subject of *The House of Mirth* as the novel which made Wharton a "professional" writer, see Cynthia Griffin Wolff, *A Feast of Words* (New York: Oxford University Press, 1977). The topic receives more detailed treatment in Amy Kaplan, *The Social Construction of American Realism* (Chicago: University of Chicago Press, 1988), pp. 65–87. Kaplan provides a literary and social context for understanding Wharton's entrance into the literary marketplace.

Constance Rooke has noted Wharton's dependence on Eliot. See "Beauty in Distress: *Daniel Deronda* and *The House of Mirth*," *Women and Literature* 4, No. 2 (1976), 18–39. While Rooke's concern is to establish influence and "to suggest that the parallels between the two novels reveal their common and essential concern with the perverse socialization of woman," I am interested in how the presence of *Daniel Deronda* in the *The House of Mirth* meditates on the problem of writing for and as a woman. In "'The Blank Page' and the Issues of Female Creativity" (in *Writing and Sexual Difference*, ed. Elizabeth Abel [Chicago: University of Chicago Press, 1982], pp. 73–93), Susan Gubar uses a story by Isak Dinesen to illustrate the problem of women's authorship. Gubar briefly discusses *Daniel Deronda* and *The House of Mirth* as suggesting the difficulty of writing for a woman, when one's own body is a text. That Wharton had read Eliot and been influenced by her work is well established. Cynthia Griffin Wolff, among others, discusses Wharton's review of Leslie Stephens's biography of Eliot. Also see Sandra M. Gilbert, "Life's Empty Pack: Notes toward a Literary Daughteronomy," *Critical Inquiry* 11 (1985), 355–84. Gilbert suggests Wharton's *Summer* is marked by *Silas Marner*'s assignment to the "Law of the Father," as described by Lacan. As Gilbert mentions, Henry James commented on the influence of Eliot on Wharton's writing (in a letter quoted by Millicent Bell, *Edith Wharton and Henry James: The Story of Their Friendship* [New York: George Braziller, 1965], p. 274).

2. Showalter particularly notes Wharton's use of Constance Cary Harrison's *The Anglomaniacs*, especially in her use of dryad imagery. But not only are realistic traditions rewritten in *The House of Mirth*; readers have traced Wharton's use of La Bruyere, for example, and Oscar Wilde also. See "The Death of the Lady (Novelist) Wharton's *House of Mirth*," *Representations* 9 (1985), 133–49.

3. See, for example, Elizabeth Ammons, *Edith Wharton's Argument with America* (Athens: University of Georgia Press, 1980); and

Joan Lidoff, "Another Sleeping Beauty: Narcissism in *The House of Mirth*," in *American Realism: New Essays*, ed. Eric J. Sundquist (Baltimore: Johns Hopkins University Press, 1982).

4. Lidoff's conclusion. Lidoff sees the novel as flawed by its confusion as to the meaning and function of such fantasies.

5. The publication of *Sister Carrie* preceded that of *The House of Mirth* by just five years.

6. In "Reflecting Vision in *The House of Mirth*" (*Twentieth Century Literature* 33 [1987], 211–22), Roslyn Dixon discusses Wharton's use of multiple points of view.

7. In her discussion of *The House of Mirth* as the "realistic" novel which professionalized Edith Wharton, Amy Kaplan comments on the balancing relationship between Selden and Rosedale: Rosedale is the "realistic" (in both a literary and non-literary sense) author of the "plot" to sell Bertha Dorset's letters back to her. Kaplan even thinks that Rosedale may have urged Mrs. Haffen to sell the letters to Lily. As Kaplan suggests, Rosedale is the suitor who knows about Lily in the same way that the working-class character Nettie Struther's husband knew about her. See Kaplan, pp. 102–03.

8. Edith Wharton, *The House of Mirth*, ed. with an introduction by R. W. B. Lewis (1905; rpt. New York: New York University Press, 1977), p. 247–254. All subsequent citations from *The House of Mirth* refer to this edition and will be cited in the text.

9. Wolff suggests: "The seventeen-year-old had been poised between the impulse to *make* beauty and the imperative to *be* beautiful; and as we have seen, for many years she had accepted the latter state as the only appropriate one for a nice young lady" (*A Feast of Words*, p. 100), a position from which she turned by committing herself to a career in writing. See also pp. 41–48 and her discussion of *The House of Mirth*, pp. 109–38.

10. Kaplan argues that the Chase thesis serves to blind readers to the historical nature of American fiction (pp. 2–4).

11. Wolff suggests that Wharton's boredom was a defense against the emotional directness of fairy tales; implicitly, her remark also denies the influence of this genre on her own work.

12. In my essay "Edith Wharton's Gibson Girl: The Virgin, the Undine and the Dynamo," (*American Literary Realism* 19 [1985], 48–65), I have suggested that in responding to Henry Adams's *Educa-*

tion, Wharton used the legend of the Undine as linking concepts suggested by Adams's two key metaphors. In *The Custom of the Country*, Wharton moves progressively toward the vantage point of pure satire; her use of romance is less ambivalent there.

13. While I have not located a specific source for Wharton's use of dryads, analogous to the *Undine* story for her later novel, the motif was a popular one in visual art, evidently classical in origin. With *The Custom of the Country*, Wharton may have been deliberately writing a companion text for the earlier *The House of Mirth*, the two constituting a diptych like that suggested by the related novels *Ethan Frome* and *Summer*.

14. Wolff makes this association. Showalter devotes considerable attention to the associations Lily's name bears: with art nouveau (and particularly with a Lily Dance performed by Loie Fuller), Amelia Bloomer's journal, and the heroines of Mary Wilkins Freeman.

15. In connection with woman-as-spectacle scenes in *Villette*, *Daniel Deronda*, and *The House of Mirth*, it may be worth remarking that the resemblance among these scenes is heightened when we realize that in all three, the woman is clothed in classical drapery. And the Greek attire of Vashti on stage, Gwendolen in her Hermione costume (the Princess is dressed in black lace when Daniel sees her), and Lily Bart in her tableau is in all of these cases a double displacement: they are imitations of imitations of classical art. Of course the original Greek models were themselves representations of "ideal" beauty rather than individualized portraits of specific people.

16. The phrase is Wolff's.

17. Frances Restuccia, reading *The House of Mirth* in terms of Roland Barthes's *Image Music Text*, discusses Lily's role as text rather than work, in Barthian terms. As Restuccia suggests, Selden often sees in her the fixity of a "work" rather than the oscillation of a "text." See "The Name of the Lily: Edith Wharton's Feminism(s)," *Contemporary Literature* 28, No. 2 (1987), 223–38. Restuccia's discussion agrees with mine at key points; she stresses Lily's refusal to be pinned down as evidence of a literary "feminism" the novel embraces; and she goes on to suggest how this "feminism" is in tension with a social feminism. I think a similar point about oscillation might be made of the novel's mode; and through this instability, the text reveals its special concern with women's authorship.

18. Read through this perspective, *The House of Mirth* becomes yet another illustration of Terry Castle's point that Gothic (and in this

instance, Gothic-marked) narrative tends to privilege a controllable mental image over what exists "outside." See "The Spectralization of the Other in *The Mysteries of Udolpho*," pp. 231–53.

19. Considered as object of exchange herself, Lily's emblematic function as signifier is different from her function as the one who pays, the function considered by Wai-chee Dimock in "Debasing Exchange: Edith Wharton's *The House of Mirth*" (*PMLA* 100, 5 [1985], 783–92). The economic terms in which I consider the novel shift the focus from those Dimock uses, from the inequity between contracting parties and the illogic of exchange to the signifying function (resembling money) occupied by Lily, art—and also, I will suggest, written letters.

20. Judith Fetterley's reading. See "'The Temptation to be a Beautiful Object': Double Standard and Double Bind in *The House of Mirth*," *Studies in American Fiction* 5 (1977), 199–211.

21. With a different emphasis, Fetterley discusses the novel's "double standard."

22. In *Felicitous Space* (Chapel Hill: University of North Carolina Press, 1986 [pp. 95–99]), Judith Fryer draws a different connection between Poe and Wharton, noting that Poe's concern with interiors matches Wharton's and that *The House of Mirth* ends with the death of a beautiful woman, the most poetical topic in the world, according to Poe.

23. Gubar ("'The Blank Page' and the Issues of Female Creativity") suggests that that "word" is Lily's body itself, which finally becomes a text for Selden to read (p. 81).

CHAPTER 8

1. The letters of Eliot to Stowe are accessible in *The George Eliot Letters*, ed. Gordon S. Haight. Further references to these letters are noted parenthetically in the text. Some of Stowe's letters to Eliot are available in Charles Edward Stowe, *Life of Harriet Beecher Stowe Compiled from her Letters and Journals*; these are heavily edited. For a description of the themes of the correspondence between the two writers, see Marlene Springer ("Stowe and Eliot: An Epistolary Friendship," *Biography* 9, No. 1 (1986), 59–81), who quotes some of Stowe's previously unpublished letters extensively. Springer reports in a footnote that Stowe's letters are currently being edited by E. Bruce Kirkman (she must mean "Kirkham"). The correspondence between the two writers,

who never met face to face although Stowe in particular expressed her desire for a meeting, began in 1869 and continued, with occasional interruptions, until the year of Eliot's death.

2. Joel Porte discusses the general relationship between theological concerns and Gothic fiction. See "In the Hands of an Angry God: Religious Terror in Gothic Fiction," in *The Gothic Imagination: Essays in Dark Romanticism*, ed. G. R. Thompson (Pullmann, Washington: Washington State University Press, 1974), pp. 42–64.

3. Forrest Wilson reports that Stowe learned of his death on the evening of Thursday, July 9, 1857. See *Crusader in Crinoline*, p. 434.

4. Three months later, Eliot's twenty-five–year-old stepson, "Thornie" Lewes would die; from January of that year, Eliot's letters are full of concern for him in his illness. She begins the letter to Stowe by excusing her failure to write earlier on the grounds of her preoccupation with him. Clearly here she shares a bond with Stowe in her understanding of maternal concern.

5. I am referring of course to Harold Bloom's idea of father-son Oedipal relationships among "strong writers" (who seem to be chiefly male for Bloom); Gilbert and Gubar have applied the model to women writers, but in particular to father-daughter (not mother-daughter) relationships.

6. See Nancy Chodorow, *The Reproduction of Mothering* (Berkeley and Los Angeles: University of California Press, 1978), pp. 109–10. See also Margaret Homans's use of Chodorow in *Bearing the Word*, especially pp. 1–29 and 68–100.

7. See Stowe's letter of May 11, 1872, in Charles Edward Stowe, *Life of Harriet Beecher Stowe* (pp. 468–70).

8. See Homans, *Bearing the Word*, pp. 86–89.

9. See Howard Kerr, "'The Blessed Dead': The Transformation of Occult Experience in Harriet Beecher Stowe's *Oldtown Folks*," (*Literature and the Occult: Essays in Comparative Literature*, Luanne Frank, ed. [Arlington: University of Texas at Arlington, 1977], pp. 174–87) for a report of Beecher's book and a discussion of how Stowe's second-hand psychic experiences, through her husband and through "Mrs. K.," were converted into her fiction in *Oldtown Folks*. The transcript Beecher reports is evidently no longer in existence.

10. It is also noteworthy in this context that the "Charlotte Brontë" that Stowe encountered through Mrs. K. was filtered through

another medium who was a woman writer, Mrs. Gaskell. Kerr describes the similarity in the language of Mrs. K. and Gaskell's *The Life of Charlotte Brontë* (Alan Shelston, ed. [Middlesex, U.K.: Penguin Books, 1975], p. 183); also see Springer, "Stowe and Eliot," p. 71: "Charlotte wrote through the Planchette in a conversational style typical of what Harriet knew of her through Mrs. Gaskell."

11. In this context, it hardly matters which correspondent is perceived as the mother, which the daughter, because, as I have suggested (following Homans and Chodorow), the essential feature of the relationship is identification, not generational difference (see *Bearing the Word*, p. 86). From the outset the relationship is more evenly balanced. This is the feature that most sharply, I think, distinguishes this model from the Oedipal model.

BIBLIOGRAPHY

Abel, Elizabeth, ed. *Writing and Sexual Difference*. Chicago: University of Chicago Press, 1982.

Aiken, George L. *Uncle Tom's Cabin*. In *Drama from the American Theatre, 1762–1909*. Ed. Richard Moody. Cleveland: The World Publishing Co., 1966, pp. 360–396.

Alcoff, Linda. "Cultural Feminism Versus Post-Structuralism: The Identity Crisis in Feminist Theory." *Signs: A Journal of Women in Culture and Society* 13, 3 (1988), 405–36.

Althusser, Louis. "Ideology and Ideological State Apparatuses." In *Lenin and Philosophy and Other Essays*. Trans. Ben Brewster. New York: Monthly Review Press, 1971.

Ammons, Elizabeth, ed. *Critical Essays on Harriet Beecher Stowe*. Boston: G.K. Hall and Co., 1980.

Auerbach, Erich. "Figura." In *Scenes from the Drama of European Literature*. 1959; rpt. Minneapolis: University of Minnesota Press, 1984, pp. 1–78.

Austen, Jane. *Pride and Prejudice*. Ed. Donald J. Gray. 1813; rpt. New York: W. W. Norton and Company, 1966.

Bachelard, Gaston. *The Poetics of Space*. Trans. Maria Jolas. New York: The Orion Press, 1964.

Barrett, Michèle. "Some Different Meanings of the Concept of 'Difference': Feminist Theory and the Concept of Ideology. In *The Difference Within: Feminism and Critical Theory*. Ed. Elizabeth Meese and Alice Parker. Amsterdam: John Benjamins, 1989, pp. 37–48.

Bennett, Betty T., ed. *The Letters of Mary Wollstonecraft Shelley*. Baltimore: The Johns Hopkins University Press, 1980. Vol. 1.

Berger, John. *Ways of Seeing*. Hammondsworth: Penguin, 1972.

Bleiler, E. F. *Three Gothic Novels*. New York: Dover Publications, 1966.

Boaden, James. *The Plays of James Boaden*. Ed. Steven Cohan. New York: Garland Publishing, 1980.

Brontë, Charlotte. *Jane Eyre*. Ed. Q. D. Leavis. 1847; rpt. London: Penguin Books, 1966.

———. *Villette*. 1853; rpt. New York: New American Library, 1987.

189

Brownmiller, Susan. *Against Our Will: Men, Women, and Rape.* New York: Simon and Schuster, 1975.

Brownstein, Rachel. "Representing the Self: Arnold and Brontë on Rachel." *Browning Institute Studies* 13 (1985), 1–24.

Carpenter, Mary Wilson. "The Apocalypse of the Old Testament: *Daniel Deronda* and the Interpretation of Interpretation." *PMLA* 99 (1984), 56–71.

Castle, Terry. "The Spectralization of the Other in *The Mysteries of Udolpho.*" In *The New Eighteenth Century.* Ed. Felicity Nussbaum and Laura Brown. New York and London: Methuen, 1987, pp. 231–53.

Chodorow, Nancy. *The Reproduction of Mothering.* Berkeley and Los Angeles: University of California Press, 1978.

Cixous, Helene. "Fiction and Its Phantoms: A Reading of Freud's *Das Unheimliche* (The 'uncanny')." *New Literary History* 7 (1976), 525–48.

Clover, Carol J. "Her Body/Himself: Gender in the Slasher Film." *Representations*, 20 (1987), 187–228.

Crosby, Christina. "Charlotte Brontë's Haunted Text." *Studies in English Literature* 24 (1984), 701–15.

Culler, Jonathan. *On Deconstruction.* Ithaca: Cornell University Press, 1982.

Day, William Patrick. *In the Circles of Fear and Desire.* Chicago: University of Chicago Press, 1985.

De Lauretis, Teresa. "The Essence of the Triangle or, Taking the Risk of Essentialism Seriously: Feminist Theory in Italy, the U.S., and Britain." *Differences* 1, No. 2 (1989), 3–37.

De Quincey, Thomas. *Confessions of an English Opium Eater and Kindred Papers.* Boston: Houghton, Osgood and Co., 1880.

Doane, Mary Ann. *The Desire to Desire: The Woman's Film of the 1940's.* Bloomington: Indiana University Press, 1987.

Doane, Mary Ann, Patricia Mellencamp, and Linda Williams, eds. "Revision: Essays in Feminist Film Criticism." *The American Film Institute Monograph Series.* Supervising ed. Ann Martin. Los Angeles: University Publications of America (The American Film Institute), 1984.

Donaldson, Laura E. "The Miranda Complex: Colonialism and the Question of Feminist Reading." *Diacritics* 18, No. 3 (1988), 65–77.

Douglas, Ann. *The Feminization of American Culture.* New York: Knopf, 1977.

Eliot, George. *Daniel Deronda.* Ed. Barbara Hardy. 1876; rpt. Great Britain: Penguin Books, 1967.

Ellis, Kate. *The Contested Castle*. Urbana: University of Illinois Press, 1989.

Ewbank, Inga-Stina. *Their Proper Sphere: A Study of the Brontë Sisters as Early Victorian Female Novelists*. Cambridge: Harvard University Press, 1966.

Fetterley, Judith. *The Resisting Reader: A Feminist Approach to American Fiction*. Bloomington: Indiana University Press, 1978.

————. "'The Temptation to be a Beautiful Object': Double Standard and Double Bind in *The House of Mirth*." *Studies in American Fiction* 5 (1977), 199–211.

Fiedler, Leslie. *What Was Literature? Class Culture and Mass Society*. New York: Simon and Schuster, 1982.

Fields, Annie, ed. *Life and Letters of Harriet Beecher Stowe*. Boston and New York: Houghton Mifflin and Co., 1898.

Flynn, Elizabeth A. and Patrocinio P. Schweickart. *Gender and Reading: Essays on Readers, Texts, and Contexts*. Baltimore: The Johns Hopkins University Press, 1986.

Foucault, Michel. *Discipline and Punish: The Birth of the Prison*. Trans. Alan Sheridan. New York: Vintage Books, 1979.

Freud, Sigmund. *The Standard Edition of the Complete Psychological Works of Sigmund Freud*. Ed. James Strachey. 24 vols. London: The Hogarth Press and the Institute of Psychoanalysis, 1953–74. Cited *SE*.

————. "'A Child Is Being Beaten', A Contribution to the Study of the Origin of Sexual Perversions" (1920), *SE* 17.

————. "The 'Uncanny'" (1919), *SE* 17.

————. "Medusa's Head" (1922), *SE* 18.

Fryer, Judith. *Felicitous Space*. Chapel Hill: University of North Carolina Press, 1986.

Garner, Shirley, Claire Kahane, and Madelon Springnether. *The (M)other Tongue*. Ithaca: Cornell University Press, 1985.

Gaskell, Elizabeth. *The Life of Charlotte Brontë*. Ed. Alan Shelston. Middlesex, U.K.: Penguin Books, 1975.

Gilbert, Sandra M. and Susan Gubar. *The Madwoman in the Attic: The Woman Writer and the Nineteenth-Century Imagination*. New Haven: Yale University Press, 1979.

Girard, René. *Deceit, Desire and the Novel*. Trans. Yvonne Freccero. Baltimore: The Johns Hopkins University Press, 1980.

Gregor, Ian. *The Brontës: A Collection of Critical Essays* (Twentieth Century Views). Englewood Cliffs, N.J.: Prentice Hall, 1970.

Grinstein, Alexander. "*Uncle Tom's Cabin* and Harriet Beecher Stowe: Beating Fantasies and Thoughts of Dying." *American Imago* 40, No. 2 (1983), 115–44.

Haight, Gordon. *The George Eliot Letters*. New Haven: Yale University Press, 1955, Vols. I, IV, VI, and VII.

Hansen, Miriam. "Pleasure, Ambivalence, Identification: Valentino and Female Spectatorship." *Cinema Journal* 25, No. 4 (1986), 6–32.

Hertz, Neil. *The End of the Line: Essays on Psychoanalysis and the Sublime*. New York: Columbia University Press, 1985.

Homans, Margaret. *Bearing the Word: Language and Female Experience in Nineteenth-Century Women's Writing*. Chicago: University of Chicago Press, 1986.

Howells, Coral Ann. *Love, Mystery, and Misery: Feeling in Gothic Fiction*. London: The Athlone Press, 1978.

Hume, Robert D. "Gothic versus Romantic: A Revaluation of the Gothic Novel." *PMLA* 84 (1969), 282–90.

Hume, Robert D. and Robert L. Platzner. "'Gothic versus Romantic': A Rejoinder." *PMLA* 86 (1971), 266–74.

Irigaray, Luce. *Speculum of the Other Woman*. Trans. Gillian C. Gill. Ithaca: Cornell University Press, 1985.

Jacobus, Mary. *Reading Woman: Essays in Feminist Criticism*. New York: Columbia University Press, 1986.

James, Henry. *A Small Boy and Others*. New York: Charles Scribner's Sons, 1913.

Johnson, Barbara. "My Monster/Myself." *Diacritics* 12 (1982), 2–12.

Jones, Ernest. *On the Nightmare*. 1931; rpt. New York: Liveright Publishing Co., 1951.

Joseph, Gerhard. "Frankenstein's Dream: The Child Is Father of the Monster." *Hartford Studies in Literature* 7 (1975), 97–115.

Kahane, Claire. "The Gothic Mirror." In *The (M)other Tongue*. Ed. Shirley Nelson Garner, Claire Kahane, and Madelon Springnether. Ithaca: Cornell University Press, 1985.

Kaplan, Amy. *The Social Construction of American Realism*. Chicago: University of Chicago Press, 1988.

Kerr, Howard. "'The Blessed Dead': The Transformation of Occult Experience in Harriet Beecher Stowe's *Oldtown Folks*." In *Literature and the Occult: Essays in Comparative Literature*. Ed. Luanne Frank. Arlington: University of Texas at Arlington, 1977, pp. 174–87.

Kiely, Robert. *The Romantic Novel in England*. Cambridge: Harvard University Press, 1972.

Kirkham, E. Bruce. *The Building of Uncle Tom's Cabin*. Knoxville: The University of Tennessee Press, 1977.

Lacan, Jacques. *Écrits: A Selection*. Trans. Alan Sheridan. London: Tavistock, 1977.

Levine, George and U. C. Knoepflmacher, eds. *The Endurance of Franken-*

stein: Essays on Mary Shelley's Novel. Berkeley: University of California Press, 1974.

Lewis, Matthew G. *The Monk.* Ed. Louis F. Peck. 1796; rpt. New York: Grove Press, 1952.

Lyotard, Jean François. "The Unconscious as *Mise en Scène.*" In *Performance in Postmodern Culture.* Ed. Michel Benamou and Charles Caramello. Madison, Wisconsin: Coda Press (Center for Twentieth Century Studies), 1977.

McIntyre, Clara. *Ann Radcliffe In Relation to Her Time. Yale Studies in English* 63. 1920; rpt. New Haven: Archon Books, 1970.

Mellor, Anne K., ed. *Romanticism and Feminism.* Bloomington: Indiana University Press, 1988.

Millett, Kate. *Sexual Politics.* New York: Avon Books, 1970.

Moers, Ellen. *Literary Women: The Great Writers.* Garden City, New York: Anchor Press/Doubleday, 1977.

Moi, Toril. *Sexual/Textual Politics: Feminist Literary Theory.* London: Methuen, 1985.

Mulvey, Laura. "Visual Pleasure and Narrative Cinema." *Screen* 16 (1975), 6–18.

——. "Afterthoughts on 'Visual Pleasure and Narrative Cinema' inspired by 'Duel in the Sun.'" *Framework,* Nos. 15, 16, 17 (1981), 12–15.

Newman, Beth. "Narratives of Seduction and the Seductions of Narrative: The Frame Structure of *Frankenstein.*" *ELH* 53, No. 1 (1986), 141–82.

——. "'The Situation of the Looker-On': Gender, Narration, and Gaze in *Wuthering Heights.*" *PMLA* 105 (1990), 1029–41.

Nystul, Nancy. "*Daniel Deronda*: A Family Romance." *Cinema Journal* 7, No. 1 (1983), 45–53.

Pinney, Thomas, ed. *Essays of George Eliot.* New York: Columbia University Press, 1963.

Poovey, Mary. "Ideology and *The Mysteries of Udolpho.*" *Criticism* 21 (1979), 307–30.

Powell, Nicolas. *Fuseli: The Nightmare.* New York: Viking Press, 1973.

Praz, Mario. *The Romantic Agony.* London: Oxford University Press, 1933.

Punter, David. *The Literature of Terror: A History of Gothic Fictions from 1765 to the Present Day.* London: Longman, 1980.

Pykett, Lyn. "Typology and the End(s) of History in *Daniel Deronda.*" *Literature and History* 9, No. 1 (1983), 52–75.

Radcliffe, Ann. *The Italian, or The Confessional of the Black Penitents.* Ed. Frederick Garber. 1797; rpt. Oxford: Oxford University Press, 1981.

Railo, Eino. *The Haunted Castle: A Study of the Elements of English Romanticism.* New York: Humanities Press, 1964.

Restuccia, Frances. "The Name of the Lily: Edith Wharton's Feminism(s)." *Contemporary Literature 28, No. 2 (1987), 223–38.*

Rooke, Constance. "Beauty in Distress: *Daniel Deronda* and *The House of Mirth.*" *Women and Literature* 4, No. 2 (1976), 18–39.

Sanchez-Eppler, Karen. "Bodily Bonds: The Intersecting Rhetorics of Feminism and Abolition." *Representations* 24 (1988), 28–59.

Schiff, Gert. "Fuseli, Lucifer and the Medusa." In *Henry Fuseli, 1741–1825.* London: The Tate Gallery Publications Department, 1975, pp. 9–20.

Sedgwick, Eve Kosofsky. *Between Men: English Literature and Male Homosocial Desire.* New York: Columbia University Press, 1985.

———. *The Coherence of Gothic Conventions.* 1980; rpt. New York: Methuen, 1986.

Shelley, Mary. *Frankenstein.* Ed. M. K. Joseph. 1818; rpt. Oxford: Oxford University Press, 1969.

Showalter, Elaine. *A Literature of Their Own.* Princeton: Princeton University Press, 1977.

———. "The Death of the Lady (Novelist): Wharton's *House of Mirth.*" *Representations* 9 (1985), 133–49.

Shuttleworth, Sally. "'The Surveillance of a Sleepless Eye': The Constitution of Neurosis in *Villette.*" In *One Culture.* Ed. George Levine. Madison, Wisconsin: University of Wisconsin Press, 1987.

Spivak, Gayatri. "Three Women's Texts and a Critique of Imperialism." *Critical Inquiry* 12 (1985), 143–61.

Springer, Marlene. "Stowe and Eliot: An Epistolary Friendship." *Biography* 9, No. 1 (1986), 59–81.

Stevenson, John Allen. "A Vampire in the Mirror: The Sexuality of *Dracula.*" *PMLA* 103 (1988), 139–49.

Stokes, John. "Rachel's 'Terrible Beauty': An Actress among the Novelists." *ELH* 51 (1984), 771–93.

Stowe, Charles Edward. *Life of Harriet Beecher Stowe Compiled from Her Letters and Journals.* Boston: The Riverside Press, 1891.

Stowe, Harriet Beecher. *Oldtown Folks.* Boston: Fields, Osgood, and Co., 1869.

———. *Uncle Tom's Cabin; or, Life Among the Lowly.* 1852; rpt. Boston: Houghton Mifflin and Company, 1882.

———. *Uncle Tom's Cabin; or, Life Among the Lowly.* Ed. with an introduction by Ann Douglas. New York: Penguin Books, 1981.

Sundquist, Eric, ed. *New Essays on Uncle Tom's Cabin.* Cambridge: Cambridge University Press, 1986.

————, ed. *American Realism: New Essays.* Baltimore: The Johns Hopkins University Press, 1982.

Thompson, G. R., ed. *The Gothic Imagination: Essays in Dark Romanticism.* Pullman, Washington: Washington State University Press, 1974.

Todd, Janet Marie. "The Veiled Woman in Freud's 'Das Unheimliche.'" *Signs* 11, No. 3 (1986), 519–28.

Tompkins, Jane. *Sensational Designs: The Cultural Work of American Fiction, 1790–1860.* New York: Oxford University Press, 1985.

Varma, Devendra. *The Gothic Flame.* 1957; rpt. New York: Russell and Russell, 1964.

Weber, Samuel. "The Sideshow, or: Remarks on a Canny Moment." *Modern Language Notes* 88 (1973), 1102–33.

Welsh, Alexander. *George Eliot and Blackmail.* Cambridge: Harvard University Press, 1985.

Wharton, Edith. *The House of Mirth.* Ed. with an introduction by R. W. B. Lewis. 1905; rpt. New York: New York Univeristy Press, 1977.

Wilson, Forrest. *Crusader in Crinoline: The Life of Harriet Beecher Stowe.* Philadelphia: J. B. Lippincott Co., 1941.

Wilt, Judith. *Ghosts of the Gothic: Austen, Eliot and Lawrence.* Princeton: Princeton University Press, 1980.

Wolff, Cynthia Griffin. *A Feast of Words.* New York: Oxford University Press, 1988.

————. "The Radcliffean Gothic Model: A Form for Feminine Sexuality." *Modern Language Studies* 9, No. 3 (1979), 98–113.

Wright, Richard. *Native Son.* New York: Harper and Row, 1940.

Yeazell, Ruth Bernard. *Sex, Politics, and Science in the Nineteenth-Century Novel.* Selected Papers from the English Institute, 1983–1984. Baltimore: Johns Hopkins University Press, 1986.

INDEX